Engines of Enterprise

.

Engines of Enterprise
An Economic History
of New England

EDITED BY

PETER TEMIN

HARVARD UNIVERSITY PRESS

Cambridge, Massachusetts

London, England

2000

Library of Congress Cataloging-in-Publication Data

Engines of enterprise : an economic history of New England / edited by Peter Temin.
p.   cm.
Includes bibliographical references and index.
ISBN 0-674-00099-4 (cloth : alk. paper)
1. New England—Economic conditions.   I. Title: Economic history of New England.
II. Temin, Peter.
HC107.A11 E53 2000
330.974—dc21   99-051691

Contents

6 REFLECTIONS ON THE ORIGINS, DEVELOPMENT, AND FUTURE OF THE NEW ENGLAND ECONOMY

Acknowledgments

This collection of essays is designed to serve as a useful one-volume survey of New England's economic history and to provide the intellectual foundation for a New England economic history museum being built by the Federal Reserve Bank of Boston. The Bank sponsored a museum conference, held at the Bank on October 2, 1998, and these essays are the results of that meeting.

I thank all of the authors, discussants, and advisors who contributed directly and indirectly to this volume. I also thank Nancy Gillespie for helping to arrange the conference, Robert Jabaily for selecting the illustrations for the volume, and Susan Rodburg for coordinating the publication process. Finally, I particularly thank Cathy E. Minehan, president and chief executive officer of the Federal Reserve Bank of Boston, for her sponsorship of the museum and the conference that produced this book, and Steven Sass of the Bank's Research Department and director of the museum project.

Introduction

THE ECONOMIC HISTORY OF NEW ENGLAND is as dramatic as the transformation of any region on earth. Starting from an unpromising situation of losing population in the eighteenth century, New England came to lead the United States in its progress from an agricultural to an industrial nation. Then, when the rest of the country caught up to this region in the middle of the twentieth century, New England reinvented itself as a leader in the complex economic scene that we call the "information economy."

A history of these developments is valuable for many reasons. History always is important to provide a sense of time and place. Where did we come from? How did we get to where we are now? What about our surroundings is new and what is old? We ask in this volume about the economic landscape, how the economy changed over time, how one activity developed out of another.

Economic history also is important because it illustrates the role of economic concepts that have been created to make the specific events described here part of more general developments. New England exploited its "comparative advantage" and "economies of scale" where applicable, as it invested in "human capital" and promoted "technical change" in New England and in the country at large with the aid of "financial intermediaries." These concepts, which appear and reappear in the following essays, will be explained briefly later in this Introduction.

In addition, this story helps us understand the choices to come. Economists are no better than weather forecasters at predicting the future. This history will not tell you how to make a fortune. But it will show you how decisions made in the past worked out for better or worse. The narratives show how our forefathers and foremothers responded to economic opportunities in the past; they suggest possibilities for the future.

The economic history of New England is distinct from its political history. The essays note the impact of political decisions throughout the history of New England, but economic changes take place over long periods of time. The essays consequently are organized around changes in the economy of New England rather than around political events. The time periods are not set by the timing of wars and revolutions, although the break at 1940 marks the beginning of World War II. The periods therefore correspond only roughly to the time periods in political or general histories.

The first essay, by Margaret Newell, covers the colonial period in New England. She discusses the organization of agriculture and the growth of trade over two centuries, far longer than the time period covered by any other essay. But she stops her narrative before the Revolution to show how the colonial economy developed in a period of relative unity. Her story shows how New Englanders transformed a deficiency, the absence of a staple export, into a stimulus for economic progress.

The second essay, by Winifred Rothenberg, includes the Revolutionary period in New England. She describes the economic revolution that took place at the same time as the more well-known political and military revolution. The economic changes were less visible and took somewhat longer, but were no less dramatic. The growth of markets within New England at the start of the nineteenth century transformed agricultural production and laid the foundation for even greater changes to come. The Revolution figures in her story, but as one among many developments impacting the economy. More important was the transition of people from largely self-sufficient jacks of all trades to participants and even specialists in a market economy.

The third essay starts and ends in peacetime at dates that have no political importance. Instead, this essay surveys the transformation of New England from an agricultural to an industrial region. As a result, New England changed also from a rural to an urban economy—and, starting just after the Revolution, from a relatively poor region of the new nation to a relatively rich one. This process of industrialization was as rapid as that of the new industrial countries of Asia in the last forty years and as fraught with implications for other regions as the more recent growth. The Civil War plays only a minor role in this economic transformation and consequently in the essay.

Joshua Rosenbloom continues the story through the Great Depression. New England in this period continued on the path set before while the rest of the country caught up to it. Although divergence was the focus of earlier essays, convergence is the theme of this one. As the rest of the country followed the economic path blazed by New England, this region appeared to be losing its distinctive role. The nation as a whole was becoming industrial and urban, and the quality of life in urban areas was improving due both to public works like sanitation and transportation and to private acquisition of better housing and goods.

The final narrative essay, by Lynn Browne and Steven Sass, carries the story from World War II to the present, that is, to the beginning of the twenty-first century. They show how New England reinvented itself in the postwar world to lead the economy once again toward what sometimes is called postindustrial society. Instead of producing products like cotton textiles and machine tools, New England increasingly produced and exported less tangible services, such as education and software. As it had done two centuries before, the region demonstrated great economic vitality and guided the nation into a new way of enhancing the lives of its residents.

These narratives are followed by a chapter posing questions stimulated by the narrations. Bernard Bailyn argues that slavery, while not prominent in colonial New England, was a critical part of that economy. Merritt Roe Smith contends that the federal government, also not a large factor in mid-nineteenth-century New England, played a crucial role in the development of New England industrial skills. Paul Krugman discusses the factors that make for regional growth in general and asks if residents of New

England can count on those attributes that contributed to the region's prosperity in the past to generate economic growth in the future. These brief essays by noted authorities in colonial history, the history of technology, and economic geography remind us that history is open-ended, that there always are living issues. They show how the narratives in this book provide a basis for further exploration of New England's economic history, a story that continues today.

Various economic concepts bring the narratives of these diverse periods together and unify this tale of economic growth. The first and oldest of these is comparative advantage. David Ricardo noted two centuries ago that there was scope for mutually beneficial trade between two countries or regions if their internal prices differed. His insight was that the relevant comparison was of prices within each country, not between them. It did not matter whether one country was larger or richer than the other, only how their internal prices differed.

Assume, for example, that iron was expensive in New England while cotton goods were cheap. Assume also that outside New England, in Pennsylvania or even farther afield, iron was cheap relative to other goods in those locales. Phrased differently, one hundred yards of cotton cloth would buy more iron outside New England than within it. Then it would make sense for people in New England to import iron, which they could get more cheaply in that way than by producing it. And it would make the same sense for residents of Pennsylvania and other states to import cotton cloth from New England instead of producing it themselves. Relative prices in the two regions would approach each other, and iron would not be so expensive in New England nor cotton cloth so expensive elsewhere. Both regions would benefit (although not necessarily to the same degree).

Comparative advantage of this sort promoted the centralization of cotton cloth production in New England for most of the nineteenth century. New England, which could produce cotton goods relatively cheaply, exported these goods to other regions in return for products made less expensively there. But this is only one example of how comparative advantage was used in New England, for this region has been active in trade throughout its history. Starting with the settlers trading with the Native Americans, often foreshadowing more recent events by trading goods for information, New England farmers exchanged their grain for a variety of goods and services, from furs to knowledge about growing food. New England merchants exploited the comparative advantages of New England and of the Caribbean Islands. Then New England industrialists took full advantage of the region's comparative advantage in cotton textile production (as noted in the example just discussed) and machine tools. More recently, entrepreneurs in New England have traded education and new ideas packaged as software for goods made in other regions. Economists speak of a region like New England as an "open economy" that lives by the shifting nature of its comparative advantage.

Comparative advantage changed largely because of technical change. New England Yankees always have been known for their inventive bent. They have found better ways to farm, to produce goods, to transport materials, to promote ideas. Technical change dominates the process of economic growth. Over the long run, over the time period considered in these essays, technical change was the prime mover of trade, economic growth, and other aspects of the economy. As some economists have said, technical change is so important that it is hard to concentrate on anything else.

We do not understand well the mechanisms that generate technical change, but we do know that certain conditions promote it. Stable governments and laws that encourage economic activity help. Being part of a huge free-trade area like the United States where comparative advantage can be exploited is an advantage. Education also is a powerful stimulus for technical change. All of these underlying conditions have been present in New England, as the following essays demonstrate, and New Englanders have rushed to build on these foundations.

Some productive activities are better done in groups or in one place than in scattered locations, due to what we call economies of scale or agglomeration economies. When an activity is done better (cheaper) on a large scale than a small scale, we speak of scale economies. So the location of cotton mills in Lowell in the early nineteenth century was stimulated by the economies of damming a river and selling power to individual mills.

More recently, the location of software and related companies around Route 128 near Boston was stimulated by the "agglomeration economies" of being near other companies, qualified labor, and venture capitalists. Route 128 in recent years has been what Alfred Marshall a century ago called an industrial district—a place where the presence of other, similar companies made production cheaper for all.

Farmers clustered together in the eighteenth century to share talents and information as the economic environment they lived in changed. The industrialists of the nineteenth century gathered in eastern Massachusetts and along the Connecticut River to form a similar and perhaps tighter community. Successful entrepreneurs and workers clustered together so that their talents could reinforce each other and communication could both smooth day-to-day fluctuations and help anticipate future developments. Entrepreneurs and workers moved between firms to pursue their own careers, bringing with them information about how to build machines and how to produce cotton cloth. And the region just north and west of Boston, as just noted, has been a Marshallian industrial district in recent years. The concentration of these clusters of economic activity in southern rather than northern New England has generated diversity even within the region.

Venture capitalists engage in what economists call financial intermediation. They match companies that want to utilize resources with people who have money to lend or invest. Partly this intermediation consists of informing borrowers and lenders about each other. Partly it entails repackaging financial assets to allow people to loan in one form and companies to borrow in another. Banks were the primary financial intermediary throughout the history of New England, and early banks functioned more like venture capitalists than do modern banks. They played a central role in the innovation process during early industrialization, much as venture capitalists today encourage innovation in New England software and biotechnology.

The economy was intertwined with the government throughout the region's history. Governments often tried to ameliorate the human cost of change, but that was only one of their many functions. From the very start of New England, governments created a framework for economic activity by providing stability and ways to adjudicate disputes. The importance of this underlying framework for economic activity, and particularly for technical change, cannot be overestimated. Who would invest in the long process of designing a better mousetrap without the potential for reward? The patent system and the rule of contracts provided this incentive; educated New England Yankees responded spectacularly to it. Government also affected the economy in other ways, from the encouragement of wartime profits to the training of machinists to the construction of roads. The government is in the background of all these stories; it moves often into the foreground.

The vitality that has sustained and propelled New England through all these changes comes from the New England culture. As with the economy, the culture of New England has changed greatly over the years. New Englanders educated their young in adherence with the strict Puritan culture, but education proved useful for economic activities as well, and it became central to the overall culture of the region. Puritanism is now a thing of the past, but the New England commitment to education is as vital today as it was in the seventeenth century.

Education can be thought of as an investment that makes people more productive and inventive. Investment in buildings and machines produces physical capital. By analogy, education produces human capital. It may not be too strong to say that the New England focus on education and the production (and export) of human capital have sustained the region through the changes described in these essays. It may well be the key to New England's future prosperity.

The theme of these essays is change, albeit change that has familiar characteristics over time. It has become fashionable to assert that the pace of change has increased in recent years. These essays suggest the opposite. New England farmers at the beginning of the nineteenth century were adapting to a sharp increase in the size of the world that affected their day-to-day living, even as we are adapting to an increase in the size of the world that affects our lives today. They traveled by foot and wagon to sell their goods while we "travel" over the Internet, but the expansion and strain on their consciousness was just as great.

In all of this ferment and growth, there were winners and losers. The winners tend to be the subject of these pages; after all, we are their beneficiaries. But we should not forget that some were unable to adapt easily to change. Farmers who clung to the old ways found that they were in trouble economically. Industrial workers a century later likewise found the opportunity to work in the traditional New England towns disappearing, and those who would not or could not move were at an economic disadvantage. As large groups of people were left behind in this account of progress, their communities could suffer and even fragment. The owners of capital should not be forgotten in this list, for the industries of New England in the nineteenth century required capital to be sunk into machines and buildings. Many of these buildings—particularly the mills that line many New England rivers—had no alternate use for many years, and their owners suffered when demand for mill space declined.

The people who have suffered as New England's economy has evolved appear and reappear in these essays, but they do not surface equally at all times. They are noticed more as we come to more recent times, and they are noticed more when economic problems turn into social problems. But there were similar people in earlier years, even if we do not know as much about them. We do not want to deny the undoubted progress that has taken place in New England over the past several centuries; we simply want to remember that there have been human costs to bear along the way.

One way to understand the process of economic growth described in these essays is through the tripartite division of the economy introduced by Simon Kuznets in the 1930s. He divided all economies into A, M, and S sectors. The A sector is composed of agriculture, joined by fishing and other minor activities. The M sector is composed of manufacturing and mining, with construction. The S sector includes services of all sorts, ranging from personal to financial. New England started out, like almost all other economies in the colonial years, with most of its workers employed in A. Then workers moved from A to M, from the countryside to the city.

And finally, in the last half of the twentieth century, New England workers moved again from M to S. As described in these essays, these changes were good for most, although not all, residents of the region. Many other countries and regions have made these transitions. New England has managed to remain a special place by keeping a step or two in front of other regions in the United States, which in turn has stayed in front of other countries.

CHAPTER I

The Birth of New England in the Atlantic Economy: From Its Beginning to 1770

MARGARET ELLEN NEWELL

FOR MUCH OF THIS CENTURY the United States has represented the global archetype of successful economic development. America's prosperity seems all the more striking in comparison with the struggles of so-called developing nations to diversify their economies, industrialize, and deliver a high standard of living to their citizens. Yet for nearly two centuries, mainland British America was an underdeveloped, dependent outpost of one of the most powerful commercial empires in Europe. In the seventeenth century, most English men and women (when they thought of America at all) viewed the colonies as objects of exploitation. America represented a staging ground for economic experiments; a source of cheap land, raw materials, and exotic staple crops such as sugar and tobacco; and an outlet for such "surplus" members of the populace as younger sons, political cronies, underemployed workers, religious dissidents, and criminals.

By the eighteenth century, the North American colonies had assumed new prominence in a global British mercantile system that cast the southern colonies in the role of staple producers, the northern settlements in the role of provisioner to more valuable but less self-sufficient colonies in the Caribbean, and both regions in the role of market for British exports. Many colonists prospered from these arrangements. Still, even this more reciprocal vision of imperial relations presumed the subordination of colonial interests to the superior claims of the mother country. English regulatory policy between 1660 and 1774 explicitly aimed to limit colonial economic development in order to secure for the mother country a monopoly of key industries, trades, and financial services.

Aside from economic and political dependency, the American colonies grappled with other pressures familiar to modern developing nations. Even had English authorities not attempted to restrict colonial manufacturing, would-be entrepreneurs faced huge obstacles, including low population density and correspondingly high prices for labor, lack of capital, and an absence of infrastructure and managerial know-how. Any new manufacturing venture had to compete with imported goods, which tended to be cheaper and of better quality. The high material expectations of settlers who emigrated from an industrializing society to a colonial periphery created another set of problems familiar to the Third World today. Consumer demand could only be satisfied by imports, yet how were the colonists to pay for desired foreign goods? Moreover, many of the colonists viewed some of the consequences of economic change—such as mobility, competition, and the open pursuit of self-interest—as potential threats to the moral, political, and social order.

Thinking about colonial America as an underdeveloped nation restores an appropriate sense of contingency to the story of its postindependence economic success. This is especially true in the case of New England. There was nothing inevitable about seventeenth-century New England's development. During the first decades of settlement, the colonists struggled to construct a viable economy. They depended upon imports from Europe to supply their most basic necessities, and upon Indian trade and the money carried by new immigrants to pay for their foreign exchange. Once the stream of immigration slowed around 1640, the region plunged into an economic depression. New England lacked a readily marketable export crop to fill the role that sugar or tobacco played in Barbados and Virginia, and its agricultural lands were inferior to those of the middle colonies. As a result, the New England settlements had little to recommend them in the eyes of potential immigrants or English officials. Sir Francis Brewster dismissed New England in 1654 as "that unprofitable Plantation, which now brings nothing to this Nation, but to the contrary buries

Numbers of industrious People in a Wilderness, that produceth nothing but Provisions to feed them." Another influential English writer, William Petty, gloomily recommended in 1691 that New Englanders be relocated to more promising colonies in the Caribbean or Ireland.[1] Yet a little more than a century later, New England had become the catalyst for America's industrial revolution. How did this transformation occur?

This essay attempts to explain the problem of New England's economic development by focusing on five central themes. The first is that although New England was lacking in many of the building blocks of economic success, the region and its people had qualities that gave them comparative advantages in certain trades and services. One of the most important qualities was the colonists' culture. We take it for granted that Third World nations' political and legal institutions and their social values affect their economic performance—sometimes even more profoundly than the presence or absence of natural resources. The same was true in the colonial period. After all, development is about more than physical change; it is also "a cultural expression and a social process, a . . . manifestation of the values of a people."[2] Certainly, one reason for New England's unique pathway was the physical environment the settlers encountered, which closed off some options even as it opened others. But material circumstances were only one factor in this equation. The colonists' English background, their religious beliefs, their ideas about community, and especially their ability to create effective public institutions also shaped the outcome. To put it bluntly, the culture of New England helped the colonists excel at producing exportable goods and services.

As English immigrants, the first settlers came from a society already undergoing a capitalist transformation. They were able to take advantage of new commercial organizations, such as the joint-stock company, and they benefited from English credit and investment. Many New England settlers had firsthand experience with commercial agriculture, trade, or manufacturing. As Puritans, they were committed to a religion that valued hard work and to a civic culture that favored strong government action in the name of the common good. After several decades of trial and error, New England's town and provincial governments played a central role in economic development. Small in size and resource-poor, local governments still managed to support economic diversification and aid entrepreneurs in ways that facilitated the growth of markets and the colonists' economic productivity. They distributed land, offered tax incentives to new projects, invested in roads and bridges, and provided inspection services that enhanced the value of New England exports. Within sixteen years of its founding, Massachusetts Bay Colony boasted a printing press, a university, the rudiments of a public school system, a written legal code, and a court system capable of enforcing contracts.

Second, the colonists encountered not a virgin environment but one that had already been shaped and cultivated by Native Americans. Settlers in Plymouth, Massachusetts Bay, Rhode Island, and Connecticut were able to live in shelters built by Indians, to farm fields already cleared by the Indians, to plant seed obtained from the native inhabitants, and to trade for meat. These early appropriations and exchanges made all the difference between starvation and survival in the difficult early years of settlement. Later, the Indian fur trade provided the colonists with their only real export commodity with which to pay for needed imports from home.

The fur trade and some early experiments in local industry helped tide the settlers over, but it was not until the middle of the seventeenth century that New England began to prove its critics wrong. The third theme of this essay stresses the creative way in which the colonists managed to make the most of the region's limited natural assets after 1640. Although there were few direct markets in England for New England produce, by the mid-seventeenth century New Englanders found that they had a comparative advantage in the production of nonstaple goods and provisions aimed at nearer markets. Farmers and traders discovered that they could prosper by supplying surplus meat, horses, and grain to other colonies where specialization in tobacco, sugar, or fishing had replaced production of foodstuffs. At the same time, the rapid deforestation of the booming Caribbean created demand for shingles, barrels, and house frames. The rich fishing banks off New England provided another export "crop," codfish; virulent anti-Catholicism did not prevent Puritan New Englanders from shipping fish to Spain and Portugal, where meatless Fridays and Lenten season meant high demand.

Through these exchanges, New England merchants acquired cash and desirable products such as sugar, wine, and tobacco for consumption at home and re-export to England, which in turn enabled them to pay for the cloth and iron that the colonists so desperately needed. New England merchants also discovered something that their English counterparts already knew: the business of conducting trade is itself an exportable service. In other words, carrying cargoes for other colonies and nations netted ship owners extra profits. Processing foreign goods for re-export created yet more value, and New Englanders became expert at turning waste products such as molasses into cash commodities like rum. In this way, New England's very lack of a staple proved to be a long-term economic advantage. Although extremely lucrative, tobacco and sugar cultivation required fairly simple fixed investments, mostly in slave labor. In contrast, the goods that New Englanders traded required investment in many "linkages" or subsidiary enterprises.

The fourth theme of this essay is that by the late seventeenth century New England had begun to emulate the mother country's path to economic success. Ironically, since English policy focused upon monopolizing the trade in plantation products such as tobacco, imperial economic regulation during this period largely helped rather than hindered the activities of New Englanders. They could trade most of the goods they produced— fish, timber, farm products—directly with customers in the West Indies and Europe free from duties or prohibitions, even as English restrictions on foreign ships gave New England captains a competitive edge in colonial markets. By 1700 New Englanders had settled into an economy where they shipped, processed, and marketed the staples of their fellow North American and Caribbean colonists, supplied them with provisions, and participated in a complex transatlantic exchange network—becoming simultaneously both key customers and competitors of English merchants and manufacturers.

The basic contours of this Atlantic trading economy remained the same through the rest of the colonial period, but New Englanders faced some new challenges in the eighteenth century. Rapid population growth put pressure on local resources, and the average farm size declined. Per capita wealth lagged behind levels in the southern and middle colonies. A series of imperial wars created opportunities for some merchants, but also led to serious economic dislocation at times. By the mid-eighteenth century, New York City had begun to siphon off some of Boston's trade; in fact, Boston's population stagnated after 1750 even as New York and Philadelphia grew. Poverty, which had been practically nonexistent in the seventeenth century, became a problem in Boston. Currency and capital to fund economic expansion were chronically short.

The result might have been a regional Malthusian crisis, but once again New Englanders responded creatively. The fifth theme of this essay is that well before the Revolution New England's internal economy had begun to change. Under pressure from shrinking farms, individuals, towns, and even entire regions began to specialize in certain agricultural commodities. Moreover, provincial New England's domestic economy consisted of much more than the exchange of farm goods and raw materials for foreign "trifles." Following a pattern set by England a century earlier, the colonists supplemented farm income by engaging in crafts and household manufactures. Merchants found new trades and exports; some even began to put capital into simple manufacturing. Local government helped once again, most notably by issuing paper money and operating public mortgage loan banks that pumped huge sums of cash and credit into the regional economy.

Together, such efforts helped supply local markets with earthenware, iron and metal goods, cloth, hats, furniture, ships, and shoes. Even as imports from England peaked around 1760, import-substitution industries and agricultural productivity were on the rise in New England; in addition, outbound cargoes destined for other colonial markets and for England itself included an ever-larger proportion of goods made in New England. This meant that as the colonial period came to a close, the region had some of the building blocks of an independent economy—and industrial capitalism—already in place.

THE ENGLISH BACKGROUND TO COLONIZATION

Any history of New England's early economic development must begin with the background of the first immigrants. The exploration and colonization of America occurred at a time of dramatic social, political, and economic change in Europe, which influenced the colonists' plans for settlement and the institutions they adopted in the New World. In the century before the founding of Massachusetts, England experienced a population boom. This unprecedented growth placed great pressure on England's capacity to house, employ, and sustain its citizens.[3] High demand for land, food, and other necessities drove up rents and prices, which in turn encouraged landlords to enclose or privatize former common lands and forests. Enclosure allowed market-savvy landowners to experiment with more efficient techniques and new crops, but it also displaced many cottagers and laborers, creating a pool of unemployed and virtually homeless men and women who teetered on the edge of starvation. Some migrated to cities such as London, whose population skyrocketed from 60,000 in 1500 to about 450,000 by 1640; some found work in new cottage industries that sprang up across England in the first half of the seventeenth century. In the late 1600s, the English joined the Dutch as leading producers of inexpensive, mass-produced consumer items, including linen, stockings, pins, and ribbons. By pricing their goods within the limited means of lower- and middle-class buyers, the new industries set the stage for a consumer revolution.

Would-be entrepreneurs also found attractive investments in areas other than land and manufacturing. Beginning in the late sixteenth century, a financial innovation called the joint-stock company—a forerunner of the modern corporation—allowed investors to pool their funds and obtain a government charter that gave them exclusive commercial privileges and protection from competition. Because joint-stock companies permitted the accumulation of unprecedented amounts of capital, they made possible ambitious overseas ventures—including the initiation of colonies. Joint-stock companies also offered cash-strapped English monarchs from Queen Elizabeth on a way of achieving national goals through private spending. English joint-stock companies organized trade with the Middle East (the Levant Company), Russia (the Muscovy Company), and South Asia (the East India Company). Such ventures generated huge profits and brought new goods like silks, light cotton fabrics, tea, and currants to the attention of European consumers. The structure of joint-stock companies also meant that these quasi-private English overseas settlements operated under far less direct government control than did most other European colonies.

English merchants were not alone in their aggressive entrepreneurialism during the early seventeenth century, a time when European nations viewed international trade as a new battlefield for power and wealth. England vied with Spain, the Netherlands, Portugal, and France over markets, resources, and commodities. Colonies and overseas trading companies gave a country an edge in this contest; they reduced the mother country's dependence on its rivals, provided exciting new products for re-export, and served as a captive market. English policymakers in particular also hoped that overseas trading posts and colonies might drain some of the "masterless" men and women who thronged the nation's cities and poor rolls. Spain and Portugal had a head start on the rest of Europe— both had been in the business of colonization since the late 1400s—and England scrambled to catch up. Seeing an opportunity to enhance England's competitive advantage and to enrich the royal treasury through fees and loans, the Crown actively encouraged commercial expansion by chartering enterprises and giving entrepreneurs bounties, monopolies, patents, and other forms of government assistance.

Adam Smith coined the term "mercantilism" to describe this official policy of fostering a nation's economic development, but it is easy to exaggerate the consistency and effectiveness of early English mercantilism. First, because policymakers focused almost exclusively upon foreign trade, they ignored many of the more innovative new domestic industries. Second, all sorts of noneconomic factors shaped policy decisions. Often, official privileges and protections rewarded entrepreneurs not for the efficiency and quality of their proposed enterprises but because they paid bribes or performed some service for the Crown. And whatever his intentions, by the 1620s the English king, Charles I, was headed into a confrontation with his own Parliament that would result in his execution and outright civil war—political crises that prevented the Crown from micromanaging overseas expansion.

Moreover, English policymakers sometimes used the law to restrict economic activity in the name of social peace. Classical economic theory has so penetrated our own culture that we assume the naturalness of the economic person: rational, striving, improving, and best left alone by the government. But market-oriented behavior seemed highly unnatural— and sometimes threatening—to many seventeenth- and eighteenth-century Europeans, for whom the pursuit of wealth unleashed a cornucopia of sins and dangerous social crimes. England's capitalist transformation took well over a century, and its effects—and benefits—were distributed unevenly. Classical liberalism assumes an infinitely expanding economy: even though the pie is divided unequally, everyone's slices can grow larger over time. But most early modern English men and women conceived of wealth and markets as fixed or even declining in the face of increased competition for resources and jobs. On the eve of his departure to New England in 1629, future Massachusetts governor John Winthrop worried that "the whole land of the kingdome [England] it is reckoned is scarce sufficient to give employment to one half of the people."[4] Famine and plague remained very real threats through the 1660s. As a result, both rich and poor assumed that the state would regulate wages and prices, prosecute people for dressing too finely for their social rank, take some responsibility for the poor, and limit interest rates—especially in times of want. There were a few voices in seventeenth-century England who argued in favor of fewer restrictions and freer trade, but it was not until the mid-eighteenth century that such thinking began to dominate English policy circles.

England's market revolution provided a general backdrop for the colonization of America, but other forces helped shape the settlement of New England. One was Puritanism. Puritans believed that England's Protestant Reformation had not gone far enough. They wished to further "purify" the Church of England by stripping the liturgy of any remnants of Catholicism. Like other predestinarian Calvinists, Puritans thought that most humans were depraved sinners destined for hell, and that only a few would be saved by God's grace. Dedicated Puritans withdrew from their traditional parish churches and formed new, unofficial congregations of fellow "saints." Yet Puritanism also had a strong humanistic core. The movement vested power in the laity and stressed the independence of the local congregation, as opposed to church hierarchy. Literacy was highly valued in this text-centered religion, and many Puritans embraced the new science of the Enlightenment.

Puritanism acquired most of its followers in English universities, law courts, and gentry households, as well as among craftsmen, farmers, clothiers, and merchants. As a group, Puritans tended to be in those occupations and professions most affected by the economic changes sweeping England. Much has been written about the so-called Protestant work ethic, which posits a link between Puritanism and economic success. True, the Puritans, like other Calvinists, believed that work was a vocation; one could glorify God through any kind of disciplined, steady labor. A duty of stewardship—that is, a duty to improve one's holdings for the common good—accompanied the particular calling to work. Contemporaries used the word "industry" to describe these desirable personal qualities of hard work, productivity, and honesty.

These beliefs certainly helped create a group of highly motivated, hardworking individuals. Yet hardworking entrepreneurs were to be found in many non-Puritan societies in the seventeenth century, from colonial Peru to Genoa to Goa. And Puritan doctrine also put a damper on some kinds of economic activity. Puritan preachers constantly warned of the dangers of worldliness and greed. One had to work, but not be seduced by profits; frugality was as important as industry. If taken to an extreme, such emphasis could have resulted in a rather ascetic community of nonconsumers—hardly the ideal citizens of a capitalist society. So if the work ethic did not exactly make Puritans into proto-capitalists, did their religion pose any economic advantages? Once the Puritans had arrived in New England, the answer to this question would become clearer, but there were some hints even in Old England. English Puritans' determination to use the power of the state, combined with a belief that economic growth and employment could solve social problems, made for a potent mix.

The Puritans' reformist zeal led many to take an active role in English political and social life. Despite their rather exclusive views on salvation, they acknowledged an obligation to foster the common good of society. Since work, discipline, and stewardship were so central to the Puritans' social vision, many of the reforms they supported meshed with the demands of a market society. Puritan county officials and members of Parliament pushed for legislation to reduce drunkenness and to force the poor to work. They supported enclosure of land. They strongly opposed the granting of monopolies to a few merchants and pushed for greater access to royal trading privileges. In addition, they favored the development of colonies. In part this was because of the attractive prospect of carrying on a holy war against Spanish and French Catholicism in the New World. But economic opportunity also attracted many. In the sixteenth century, a number of powerful English Puritan entrepreneurs—such as Robert Rich, the earl of Warwick, and Sir Humphrey Gilbert—invested in colonial ventures in Ireland, Roanoke, and Virginia.

English Puritans might have remained content to push their agenda in their communities and in Parliament, but during the early 1600s relations with the Crown took a turn for the worse. First James I, and then his son Charles I, viewed Puritanism as a challenge to royal power and took action to suppress the movement. One group of Puritans became so discouraged by repressive royal tactics that they decided to withdraw first from the Church of England and eventually from England itself. The group initially emigrated to Holland, but thirty-five of these "Separatists," led by a weaver named William Bradford, formed a joint-stock company with English merchants and founded the colony of Plymouth, Massachusetts, in 1620. By the late 1620s, even those Puritans who were reluctant to abandon the English church had begun to consider continuing their reform efforts from a safer distance across the Atlantic.

THE SETTLEMENT OF NEW ENGLAND

New England had attracted the interest of entrepreneurs since 1602. In that year two English adventurers, Bartholomew Gosnold and Bartholomew Gilbert, explored the New England coast as far north as Maine and spent a summer in Martha's Vineyard. One member of the company, John Brereton, published a glowing account of the region's resources (complete with current English market prices). Brereton's *Briefe and true Relation* detailed the ready availability of iron and copper ore, fish, sassafras (a supposed cure for syphilis), "Whale and Seale oiles, Soape ashes and Soape, Tarre and Pitch, . . . boords of Cedars, . . . Hempe, Flaxe, Cables and Ropes, Saile-clothes, Grapes, and Raisens and Wines, Corne, Rape-seeds [for canola oil] & oiles, Hides, Skinnes, Furres, [clothing] Dies and Colour."[5] Some Englishmen knew about the rich fishing banks off New England long before Brereton wrote. European and West English fishermen had been fishing those waters, drying their catch ashore, and trading with the Indians for decades, possibly even before Columbus's voyage. In fact, Brereton was shocked when Indians dressed in bits of European clothing and, shouting Basque words, approached his ship by canoe to trade.

Like their counterparts in Virginia, founded in 1607, the first investors who turned to New England had in mind the model that France, Holland, Portugal, and England's own East India Company had followed: the establishment of small outposts or "factories," staffed mostly by male employees who would trade with indigenous peoples and engage in fishing, lumbering, and perhaps mining or other extractive industries. They did not initially plan to settle large numbers of English immigrants there, or to farm much. But the first attempt to establish such an outpost in Sagadahoc, Maine, in 1607 proved a dismal failure. Poorly prepared, unequipped even to feed themselves, and finding none of the precious metals they had expected, the few men who survived the first year returned to England. They were particularly shocked at the extremely cold winter—after all, New England is on the same latitude as Spain. For decades English visitors were confounded by New England's hot summers and cruel winters.

Luckily, the collapse of Sagadahoc never made it into print; meanwhile, more literature praising New England continued to pour from English presses. By the 1620s, patrons of English town libraries could read as many as twelve published accounts of New England's possibilities, and still more information circulated in unpublished form among merchant circles.[6] Most notable was the account of Captain John Smith, a former mercenary and one-time leader of Virginia, who published in 1616 an enthusiastic eyewitness description of the north's economic potential. It was Smith who coined the term "New England," whose maps gave the land English place-names, and who suggested that (the winters notwithstanding) New England's healthful water, air, and climate made it suitable for English habitation—in contrast to Virginia, where nearly 80 percent of the immigrants who arrived between 1607 and 1699 died within a few years. Smith recommended full-scale colonization, not just trading posts; he warned that the French and Spanish might beat England to the region. In fact, the French had tried to establish an outpost in Massachusetts in 1606, only to be driven off by the Indians.

The successful settlement of Plymouth by Bradford and his company increased both interest and the flow of information about New England. Several other joint-stock company ventures formed: the Council for New England (1620), the Dorchester Company (1623), and the New England Company (1628). None of the three enjoyed much success, however, and all were planned as trading-post–style settlements staffed by operatives. The Dorchester Company, brainchild of the Reverend John White, hoped to develop fisheries near modern-day Gloucester. Even Plymouth's merchant backers expected that the inhabitants would pay their debt through fishing or the Indian fur trade. Of the 102 initial settlers, only thirty-five were actually religious exiles; the rest were servants and employees whose values in fact clashed mightily with the pious Separatists. Plymouth's early history also proved that achieving self-sufficiency in food alone was more difficult than many anticipated; half of the inhabitants died during the first year. Improving the New England landscape, some of the more honest promotional tracts admitted, would require unremitting work. "[I]t is a country," warned Christopher Levett in 1623, "where none can live except he either labor himself, or be able to keep others to labor for him."[7] By now, too, recruiters for New England companies were competing with the already booming colonies of the Chesapeake and Caribbean, which promised rich profits from the cultivation of tobacco and sugar.

In 1629, however, representatives from the New England Company, which had founded a settlement near present-day Salem, Massachusetts, joined forces with another set of investors and formed the Massachusetts Bay Company. They received a very advantageous charter of incorporation from Charles I. In addition to an infusion of capital, the new partners brought to the deal the assets of a religious mission and a highly motivated group of potential immigrants. A portion of this group, under their newly elected company governor, the lawyer-landowner John Winthrop, set sail for Massachusetts aboard the *Arbella* and founded the town of Boston in the summer of 1630. Over the next twelve years, approximately 21,000 immigrants followed in what became known as the "Great Migration."

Scholars have devoted considerable effort to determining which was the stronger influence upon Puritans' decisions to migrate—piety or profit. But the colonists and investors themselves seldom drew such distinctions, nor did they view these goals as mutually exclusive. While they intended to establish a "plantation in religion"—churches in the congregational model and a state informed by religious ideals—the group's leaders made ambitious economic plans as well. After all, the company was ostensibly a for-profit venture. Pious shareholders might be willing to sacrifice their investment to the greater glory of the Lord, but not without trying first to turn a profit. Aside from extractable resources like fish and timber, company leaders envisioned the creation of a diverse colonial economy based upon farming, manufacturing, and industry—an economy, in other words, as developed as England's. Along with shoes, arms, clothing, and common English seeds like wheat, peas, and barley, the company outfitted its earliest vessels to the New World with madder seed (a clothing dye), "hoproote," cherry and apple cuttings, and other new market crops. In addition to godly Puritans, John Winthrop recruited skilled craftsmen such as carpenters, miners, tanners, millers, sawyers, and blacksmiths. The Reverend Francis Higginson, member of a sortie sent to survey the company's land, mentioned several ongoing and potential enterprises near Salem: a

"Bricke-Kill[n] on work to Make Brickes and Tyles," the cutting of cedar shingles, potash making, leather tanning, the manufacture of ships' stores, and dye making for English clothiers.[8]

Economic concerns also motivated individual immigrants. Many were not Puritans, after all. Those who were stressed that economic competency aided one's ability to exercise "freedome of Religion." Economic opportunity provided a chance to exercise the self-discipline of the calling, and ensured the perpetuation of the family. Among the compelling reasons behind the Pilgrims' decision to abandon their temporary refuge in Holland for the New World, William Bradford emphasized the fact that "necessitie was a taskmaster over them."[9] In other words, economic want had discouraged the Separatists'—and especially their children's—religious enthusiasm. True, immigration itself was costly, and in the short run some settlers made financial sacrifices. But for many, the prospect of personal material improvement and land ownership in the New World offered an incentive to migrate that complemented religious goals.

WHO WERE THE FIRST IMMIGRANTS?

After 1630, New England received a very different immigrant stream from other English colonies. Instead of the young, mostly male indentured servants that made up nearly three-fourths of all migrants to the rest of colonial America, families headed by middle-aged parents of average social class predominated in the Great Migration. The settlers of Massachusetts Bay generally were a more prosperous group than the Pilgrims, but overall neither the very rich nor the very poor chose to emigrate. Only about a third came from an agricultural background; more than half of the men were craftsmen, traders, or clothiers, and a small fraction were merchants, professionals, or gentry landowners. The roughly equal ratio of men to women and the range of ages present—from infants to the elderly—meant that Massachusetts society resembled Old England much more than did Barbados and Virginia; in the latter, for example, men still outnumbered women 3:2 in 1700, and the numbers were even more skewed before 1650. Records are incomplete, but historians speculate that anywhere from one-seventh to one-fourth of the immigrants were servants—young people of both sexes either hired by the Massachusetts Bay Company or contracted to work for an individual family for a set period. Still, single persons who came to New England could reasonably expect to marry and start their own families in turn, unlike their southern counterparts.[10] This normalcy —the presence of women, families, and elders—probably helped New England avoid some of the disorder and violence that afflicted other English colonial outposts in the early decades, notably Jamestown.

If they made it through the "starving times," the tough winters before crops had been planted and harvested, and avoided accident or Indian attack, the first generation of immigrants to New England often enjoyed long and healthy lives. The median age at death for men was astounding for a nonindustrial country even by today's standards: seventy-one. For women, who ran a high risk of death during childbirth, it was sixty-seven. Many of the diseases that plagued Europe—measles, smallpox, chickenpox, mumps, influenza—were unknown in America until the settlers and their livestock introduced them. Even though the settlers carried microbes to the New World, the climate still was much more disease-free than the one they had left; major epidemics did not rock white New England settlements until the 1700s. Good diet and a low population density also helped prevent the spread of disease. Fertility in seventeenth-century New England was extremely high—higher even than in the England the settlers had left. Marriage was a universal state for healthy adults, and people married younger in America because the availability of land permitted couples to set up household sooner. Since women could expect to bear a child approximately every two and a half years until menopause, earlier marriage meant more children—an average of six to eight live births per woman.

Families were central to more than just New England's social stability; they underpinned its growth and economic productivity. As discussed later, immigration to New England slowed to a trickle after 1640; in fact, more people left New England than immigrated there between 1650 and 1700. Thereafter, white population growth depended on family fertility. The household came to be the key unit of economic activity in New England. Children also supplied the main source of farm labor. Within a few

The "Onion Maidens" of Wethersfield, Connecticut. *(Courtesy of Wethersfield Historical Society.)*

Most people in New England during the seventeenth and eighteenth centuries—men, women, and children—worked in agriculture. The main crops were wheat and corn, which were eaten by people and animals. As the New England colonies prospered, other crops, like onions, became important to some regions. Success in farming allowed New England's population to rise, without much immigration, from about 30,000 at the end of the Great Migration in 1640 to one million at the end of the Revolution.

years of their arrival, servants had become proprietors in their own right. Unlike England, where an established rural labor market made it possible to hire female servants and long-term male farmworkers, and where farm laborers made up 8 to 14 percent of the population in some locales, New Englanders wishing to obtain extra workers had to recruit servants in England, purchase such servants from others, or hire their friends and neighbors by the day or week.[11]

Complaints about the lack of domestic and field help resounded in New Englanders' correspondence as early as the 1630s. Some New England farmers and employers turned to ethnic outsiders. William Pynchon of Springfield bought the contracts of Scottish and Irish prisoners of war who had been sold by English officials. Others hired, or forcibly commandeered, the labor of Indians. Some, especially in Rhode Island and Plymouth, invested in African and Indian slaves. But most heads of household relied heavily upon the labor of their teenaged and adult children.

NATIVE AMERICANS AND THE
NEW ENGLAND ECONOMY

At first, the new arrivals in Plymouth and Massachusetts struggled simply to survive. They probably would not have succeeded—or at least the economic history of New England would have been quite different—if they indeed had settled in a virgin wilderness. The exact number of Indians in sixteenth-century New England is a matter of some dispute, but one estimate puts the precontact population at approximately 120,000. Different tribes had different economies; the more sedentary Narragansetts and Pequots obtained over half of their food supply through planting, while the Pennacooks of northern New England relied more heavily on the hunt, occasionally trading furs for grain with their southern neighbors. Overall, however, the Indians' previous use of the land and their continued presence made possible the early economic development of New England.

William Bradford referred to the Americas as "devoid of all civil inhabitants, where there are only savage and brutish men which range up and down, little otherwise than the wild beasts of the same," but he knew better.[12] Indians manipulated their surroundings in a variety of ways. They cut networks of trails for trade and communication. They set fire to bushy undergrowth on a seasonal basis both to replenish the soil and to create attractive grazing habitats for large game. They burned timber for fuel and to clear fields for the planting of corn, squash, and beans.[13] When their fields became less fertile, they simply moved on to new land. At least one English observer admitted that the Indians' per acre output equaled that of fertilized English fields. They built fishing weirs (wooden sieves) in rivers to trap the spring runs; recently, archaeologists in the Back Bay area of Boston uncovered the remains of a four-hundred-year-old weir that was nearly two miles long.

As a result of the native inhabitants' efforts, colonists in southern New England encountered not impenetrable forests but rather park-like stands of trees, cultivated fields, and meadows where they could cut fodder for their livestock. Describing Salem in 1629, Francis Higginson noted that "there is much ground cleared by the Indians, and especially about the plantation . . . a man might stand on a little hilly place and see divers thousands of acres of ground as good as need be, and not a tree to the same."[14] In choosing sites for their own settlements and cornfields, Europeans showed a decided preference for these so-called champion or open lands. The first Plymouth settlers actually lived in an abandoned Indian village and farmed Indian fields.

But why had that village been abandoned? By the time the Pilgrims arrived, many Indian settlements throughout New England had been decimated by disease. The very absence of microbes that made early New England so healthful for Europeans meant that the native inhabitants had built up little or no immunity against many pathogens current in Europe. In Europe, humans and livestock had passed diseases back and forth for millennia, a process that had engendered antibodies in the human population. By contrast, the ancient migrations that took the ancestors of the American Indians out of Europe and Asia had insulated them from many Old World diseases, as had the absence of domesticated animals; but this isolation left them extremely vulnerable to sickness brought by traders, settlers, and their livestock. Measles, influenza, bubonic plague, and smallpox began to rip through northern New England Indian communities in the sixteenth century—soon after European fishermen had initiated casual contact with the coast. In 1617, a pandemic hit southern New England, killing an estimated 90 percent of the dense coastal Indian population over several years. Other epidemics followed. Even childhood diseases like mumps and chickenpox proved lethal. Not all of the deaths were from disease; sickness so disrupted the native inhabitants' ability to plant and gather food that even those who survived illness died of starvation later or were vulnerable to the next infection. The Pilgrims had heard about the 1617 epidemic before they arrived; John Winthrop later described it as a "miraculous plague" sent by God to clear the way for European settlement.

Despite these disasters, Native Americans remained a formidable presence in New England for decades, and continued to play an economic role. The first settlers' ability to purchase—or take—corn and game from the Indians made the difference between starvation and survival. The *Mayflower*'s passengers obtained the seed corn and beans they planted for their first harvest from a Nauset Indian cache on Cape Cod; purchases of venison and grain from Native Americans fed Massachusetts Bay in 1630 and 1634, and Connecticut in 1637–1638. Once the colonists had harvested a few crops, this type of dependency declined, but even then the Indians' continued willingness to trade provided Plymouth and Massachusetts with their most valuable export commodity of the 1620s and 1630s: furs.

Colonial leaders justified their expropriation of Indian land on a number of grounds, but foremost was an economic argument: the labor theory of value. Winthrop, Bradford, and others claimed that the Indians' common land ownership, their wasteful practices, and the lack of fences, livestock, and other "improvements" made the native inhabitants unworthy proprietors. As the century wore on, New England courts generally only recognized Indian ownership of tilled agricultural lands, which represented a small fraction of the territories that the eastern woodland tribes of southern New England actually used in their annual subsistence cycles. The irony was that Plymouth and Puritan Massachusetts resembled nothing so much as Indian villages, at least initially. In Plymouth, family units and singles were grouped by authorities into twelve artificial families. They lived in what one colonist, Edward Johnson, disparagingly referred to as "English Wigwams"; they fished, hunted, gathered, clammed, and farmed common fields already cleared by Indians, traded with the Indians, and borrowed the native inhabitants' seed and techniques. They girdled trees in the "lazy" Indian style—killing them by cutting off a wide strip of bark rather than cutting them down — and burned the woods to clear fields. As among the Indians, Pilgrim women and children provided much of the daily agricultural labor at first. Well into the eighteenth century, localities in Plymouth, Massachusetts, and Connecticut continued to reserve some lands in common, and to administer collective rights to woodlots, clam banks, and fishing weirs in ways not so foreign from Indian practice.

Not all Euro-Indian relations were hostile. Indians and settlers traded, parleyed, and formed strategic alliances; Indians sometimes voluntarily transferred land ownership to whites; Indians returned lost Englishmen to their settlements; and well-meaning ministers tried to evangelize the Native Americans, with some success on Martha's Vineyard. Some groups, such as the Mohegans of southern Connecticut, became permanent client-allies of English colonies. Quickly, though, the settlers moved from "wigwams" into nailed, framed, clapboard houses and fenced, fertilized fields. Without the Indians' fires, forest undergrowth reappeared; but Puritan "improvements," such as the clear-cutting of timber and the damming of streams for industry, left their own marks on the landscape. And when New England settlers put up fences and introduced livestock that damaged Indian crops, clam banks, and game habitats, serious conflict ensued.

In 1637, the New England colonists and the Narragansett Indians formed an alliance against the Pequot tribe, all but destroying them. At war's end, Massachusetts, Plymouth, and Connecticut enslaved several hundred Pequot captives, sending some to Bermuda and the Caribbean, and keeping others—especially women and children—as household workers. In 1675, it was the Narragansetts' turn. That year, the bloodiest war in New England's history pitted the colonists against the Narragansetts and Wampanoags. By 1676, at the end of "King Philip's War," the Indians had destroyed one out of six English towns and killed 5 percent of the adult white population. But the war sealed European domination of southern New England. Four thousand Indians (25 percent of the already decimated population) died, and hundreds more were sold as slaves by the victors.

Some of those who survived kept their land, maintained a tribal identity, and continued to live in a kind of reservation system on the margins of English society or in Christian "praying towns" such as Natick, Massachusetts. Other Indians lived among the colonists and worked as farm laborers, broom makers, servants, and seamen, forming a kind of rural proletariat. Even after King Philip's War, though, tribes from New York and northern New England still represented a threat to the settlers' security. Raiders, often allied with the French, attacked settlements in Maine, New Hampshire, and central and western Massachusetts many times in the eighteenth century, destroying the town of Deerfield in 1704 and generally limiting the ability of those regions to develop fully until after the French and Indian War.

WORKING IT OUT

For all their condemnation of Indian land-use practices, the settlers themselves brought a mixed economic legacy from England. Members of the Great Migration came from a society in transition from the manor to the marketplace, where capitalist and precapitalist behaviors coexisted. In addition, the reality of the land and resources they encountered rendered many of their careful plans and expectations useless. Over time, practical experience led the settlers to reject some tactics and to adopt new ones.

The Massachusetts settlers moved quickly to create a set of political and social institutions from which to order their economic and spiritual experiments. On board the ship *Arbella*, anchored off the Massachusetts coast, Governor John Winthrop gave a speech to his fellow emigrants in which he outlined the importance of collective goals and a communal ethos: "The care of the public must oversway all private respects, . . . for it is a true rule that particular estates cannot subsist in the ruin of the public."[15] The company's shareholders had made a bold move: they had transferred their royal charter of incorporation to the immigrants themselves, to be used as a template for government. The head of the company became the governor of the colony, while the Assistants—a kind of board of directors—advised the governor. Under the company charter, all stockholders or "freemen" had the right to help choose the governor and Assistants. The Bay company extended the right of freemanship—in other words, the right to vote in elections—to all resident adult male Puritan churchmembers, whether they actually owned shares or not. Four years later, the freemen demanded yet another privilege: the right to elect representatives from each of the towns to sit with the governor and Assistants. This new body, the Deputies, formed a kind of lower house. Together, both sets of "magistrates" and the governor constituted the "General Court."

The Massachusetts General Court was simultaneously a court that heard legal disputes and appeals and a representative legislative body that passed laws, levied taxes, created towns, and oversaw the colony's development. At the town level, even non-churchmembers could participate in political life, and after 1691 the religious requirements for voting were dropped. The other New England colonies created similar institutions, with some regional variations. Rhode Island, for example, had a weaker central administration but stronger town governments. While by no means modern democracies, colonial New England governments were effective bodies that enjoyed widespread support. They were certainly more participatory than their English counterparts.

One of the first issues taken up by the new governments—and the one that required their first adjustment—involved land. Puritan gentry in England had supported the enclosure or privatization of public land as a positive economic reform. Their company charters freed the New England colonists of many feudal restrictions that limited how an owner could use his land in England. Still, experience with the social impact of enclosure in England—vagrancy, homelessness, rural agitation—gave some New Englanders pause. Moreover, some immigrants came from English regions where farmers collectively owned land—the so-called common-field system—and thus were inclined to recreate this type of land organization in towns such as Rowley and Andover in Massachusetts and Milford in Connecticut.[16] The founders' religious ideals further reinforced this commitment to communalism. Both William Bradford and John Winthrop hoped that shared ownership of property and other resources would reinforce the covenants that bound their respective communities together and prevent the scattering of the tiny initial settlements, a process that they viewed as detrimental to church and community cohesion.

These intentions were soon overturned by human nature and the resources of New England. The Puritans' own ethic of improvement, the uncontrollable urge of settlers to move away from the first centers, and the sheer availability of land in New England ensured that New Englanders quickly moved toward private ownership. In Plymouth, settlers complained that instead of community the collectivist system bred discontent and laziness and retarded production. After two years of food shortages, the Pilgrims abandoned their experiment in communal farming and agreed to adopt individual plots. Once Governor Bradford had surrendered to the distribution of land, he admitted that Plymouth "had very good success, for it made all hands very industrious, so as much more corn was planted than otherwise."[17] Massachusetts Bay endorsed land distribution almost immediately. Its first legal code of 1641, the Body of Liberties, defined land as an alienable commodity and granted private owners freedom from feudal or other restrictions.

Massachusetts leaders also hit upon a cost-effective way of distributing land that bowed to expansion yet protected some of their social and religious values: town founding.[18] The process of starting a town harnessed the energy of interested investors to the achievement of a public goal in much the same way that joint-stock companies did. A group of speculators would approach the General Court and ask for a grant of land for a town. These new proprietors in turn would assume responsibility for cutting roads, surveying the land, and making basic improvements. Sometimes they would actually settle in the towns themselves, or they might sell their land rights to another group of interested inhabitants at a profit. A few individuals in early New England specialized in this speculative kind of town founding, including John Winthrop Jr., future governor of Connecticut.

Laws prevented speculators from gouging potential settlers or leaving land unimproved for too long.

Once a group of settlers who planned to live in the town had acquired proprietary rights, they distributed a portion of the town land to each inhabitant in unequal shares, each according to his social station. In Windsor, Connecticut, for example, the upper tenth of society received 40 percent of the land allotments. Undistributed land was reserved for future grants to children and desirable new settlers, or for common grazing and firewood cutting. Government officials also required that resident proprietors establish and support communal institutions: a congregational church, a regular town meeting to administer local affairs, and, after 1647, a school. Towns were thus simultaneously minicorporations that facilitated entrepreneurship and centers of civic life. Sometimes the settlers chose to live in tightly nucleated villages and travel to their fields, as in Wethersfield, Connecticut; inhabitants in other towns, such as Sudbury, Massachusetts, spaced their homesteads widely in search of good grazing for their cattle.

Privatization of land had important economic consequences, some of them contradictory. On the one hand, because allotments generally went to heads of households, these mechanisms tended to reinforce patriarchy and to affirm the importance of the family farm as the main productive unit in the New England economy. The possibility of owning land seduced many former artisans, fishermen, and other townsmen away from their crafts, thus reversing the English trend toward greater specialization, population density, and division of labor—all necessary building blocks for capitalist development. Aside from Boston, there were few central places; settlers quickly scattered, and by 1636 groups from Massachusetts had moved into Connecticut, New Hampshire, and Rhode Island. On the other hand, New Englanders turned the family farm into a remarkably productive unit capable of adjusting to a wide variety of conditions and tasks, from agriculture to dairying to piecework under the putting-out system. And the clearing and planting of land represented an important kind of development. Indeed, the creation of farms and speculation in land be-

Adams Houses, Braintree, Massachusetts. *(Courtesy U.S. Dept. of the Interior, National Park Service, Adams National Historical Park.)*

Although a few merchants and sea captains lived in the mansions we still see in Salem and Cambridge, most colonial New Englanders lived in modest houses with few rooms. They cooked over open fires and during the long winters lived in their kitchens to stay warm. They educated their children for religious reasons, and this education helped New Englanders connect to other people as well as to the deity.

came key capital-creating activities for inhabitants in the colonial period. People who could not have imagined owning land in England had access to property.

Even as New Englanders moved toward privatization of land in the 1620s and 1630s, another shift from communal, centralized control to a greater degree of liberalization took place, this time in the realm of trade. For both practical and ideological reasons, Puritan leaders had expected to oversee the inhabitants' economic behavior. According to Puritan belief, the pious businessman deserved a profit, but he could not cheat his neighbor, charge usurious rates, or take advantage in times of short supply; laborers owed employers good work at reasonable rates. In England, government regulated wages, prices, and interest rates, and New England leaders immediately did the same. On a more pragmatic note, previous joint-stock ventures like Virginia and the New England Company had all attempted to monopolize commerce. It was by controlling the trade in furs and imported goods that the New England colonies' backers and leaders expected to reap the bulk of their profits. To this end, the General Court passed laws in 1632 and 1635 that licensed nine merchants to handle imports and to vend them in a central clearinghouse in Boston under the magistrates' jurisdiction.

Fully enforced, these measures would have restricted the inhabitants' economic behavior and adversely affected development. Instead, one after another of the controls collapsed. The restrictions on trade were the first to fall. In Massachusetts Bay, settlers simply rowed directly out to ships in the harbor to purchase their wares, and sailors and ships' captains sold goods right on the quays. The scenes that attended this unrestricted commerce horrified John Winthrop, who condemned the "loss of time, and drunkenness, which sometimes happened, by people's running to the ships, and the excessive prices of commodities"; but he acknowledged that the merchants' monopoly "took no good effect; for most of the people would not buy, except they might buy for themselves." Wage and price controls proved equally ineffective because, as Winthrop groused, "being restrained, they [the artisans] would either move to other places where they might have more, or else being able to live by planting and other employments of their own, they would not be hired at all."[19] Artisans and even day laborers quickly commanded wages two to four times greater than their English equivalents, although, as workers pointed out to authorities, the cost of living was higher in America. The Massachusetts General Court turned the whole problem of both wages and commodity prices over to the towns in 1636, and Connecticut repealed its wage controls in 1650.

Puritan leaders noted another problem in the 1630s. Within the first two decades, the list of necessaries that families needed to survive, such as ironware, cloth, and salt, began to expand. New Englanders were purchasing goods that were relative luxuries in England: "gay cloathing," "sack [sherry], sugar and plums, . . . all of which are but ordinary among those that were not able to bring their own persons over at first coming."[20] Such behavior not only suggested excessive worldliness; it also blurred class distinctions, making it difficult to discern servants from masters. The Massachusetts General Court and other New England governments tried to define the boundaries of proper consumption with sumptuary laws—statutes that regulated the purchase of clothing, alcohol, and some foods. But despite the magistrates' "utter detestation & dislike that men or women of meane condition, education, & callinges should take upon them the garbe of gentlemen, by the wearinge of gold or silver lace, or buttons, or . . . great bootes," the court had to give up on these laws as well.[21] Even laws against usury, which remained on the books, were difficult to enforce.

This does not mean that New Englanders abandoned all of their ambivalence about the market, or their commitment to moral economic relations. Merchants came under suspicion and censure in sermons and public opinion. The Massachusetts General Court gave up the practice but not the principle of such regulation, and as late as 1670 reasserted its right to set wage policy through statute. Calls for controls occasionally were sparked by hard times, most notably during the American Revolution. Especially in urban areas, local officials continued to regulate markets and set prices for bread. Yet although this transformation was not neat and linear, the general trend in New England after the 1640s was away from traditional forms of socioeconomic regulation.

Instead, New Englanders shifted the emphasis of government involvement to the promotion of trade. New England's climate and soil supported many European-style crops and livestock as well as impressive stands of timber, but shipping such bulky items across the Atlantic to England cost more than the cargoes were worth. What Europeans wanted from the colonies were relatively exotic new products such as sugar and tobacco, rice and indigo—the kinds of goods that came from England's more "profitable" plantations: Virginia, Barbados, and later, South Carolina. Insatiable markets for these exports brought profit to colonial producers and English merchants as well as tax revenue to the English Crown; but New England lacked any such staple. At the same time, the inhabitants' demands for an English standard of living placed enormous pressure on their undeveloped colonial economy. Aside from food, almost everything required for a comfortable existence—clothing, tools and hardware for the construction of homes, firearms, pots and pans, dishes, liquor, salt, and sugar—had to be imported from Europe or the Caribbean. Without any established industries or trades, how were New England colonists to pay for these desired goods?

The fur trade represented the single most important source of foreign exchange before 1640, and New Englanders avidly pursued their modest comparative advantage in this industry. Plymouth maintained fur trading posts in Maine near the Penobscot and Kennebec rivers, at Windsor on the Connecticut River, at Narragansett Bay, and on Long Island Sound. Those residents of Salem, Boston, and Cambridge who were licensed by the Massachusetts General Court—and some who were not—trucked with the Mohegans, Pequots, Narragansetts, Shinnecocks, and other southern New England and Long Island tribes, exchanging for beaver the necessities of corn, knives, kettles, and cloth (and despite legislation to the contrary, liquor, firearms, and powder). First the Pilgrims and then the Puritans began to experiment with the commercial production of wampum with which to buy beaver, with impressive results. Both wampum and beaver actually functioned as legal money in Massachusetts through the 1640s. Entrepreneurs from Connecticut and Massachusetts Bay expanded their trading operations on the Connecticut River. In the 1650s, William

Pynchon of Springfield and his son John shipped cargoes of beaver worth nearly £5,600 to England. Such profits enabled men like the Pynchons to purchase land and invest in agriculture, cattle, mills, and shop goods for European customers, paving the way for a more diversified local economy later. Rivers that had once contained beaver could be exploited for their falls and dams as potential mill sites.

Already by the mid-1630s, however, the fur trade had suffered some setbacks. None of the rivers within easy reach, with the exception of the Connecticut, proved to be a major source of furs. Indian trappers had all but extinguished the coastal beaver population within a few years. Further west, the Dutch blocked New Englanders' access to the richest artery of the fur trade—the Hudson River—and to the north the French harassed their Maine outposts.

Moreover, the fur trade was the provenance of adventurers and individuals with political connections and capital. Most New Englanders were neither, and so relied upon sales of food, cattle, and seed to incoming settlers to secure their necessaries. "To sell every year a Cow or two," noted Edward Johnson, "cloath'd their backs, fil'd their bellies with more varieties than the Country of it self afforded, and put gold and silver in their purses beside."[22] Credit, coin, and manufactured goods obtained from newcomers generally flowed immediately back into the hands of importing merchants. The erratic nature of this commerce disturbed many Bay Colony leaders, and not just because it was difficult to regulate. First, it depended upon the immigrants bringing goods or coin with them to trade. Second, upon disembarking their human and animal cargoes, English and Dutch captains did not fill up their holds with New England products, nor did they expect to; in other words, many ships serviced New England because they brought passengers, not because they were drawn to local markets. Thus New Englanders exercised little control over the comings and goings of ships, prices, or the contents of their cargoes, and any decline in the constant supply of new immigrants could spell disaster.

Disaster is exactly what happened. Events in England had changed dramatically since the beginning of the Great Migration. By 1639, revolution was imminent—a civil war between the Puritan Parliament and royal forces that the Parliament would win. Now, good Puritans stayed at home rather than fleeing to the colonies; some New Englanders even felt duty-bound to return. Immigration levels plateaued in 1639–1641 and then declined precipitously, plunging the region into a depression. Prices for all local goods plummeted. Corn, which like furs had served as a money substitute, dropped so low in value that it threw contracts into disarray. English merchants stopped extending credit, and the supply of money and imported goods dwindled further. Foreclosures, suits, and bankruptcies mounted. New Englanders faced a situation characterized by what economic historian Gavin Wright calls "creative tension." The colonists could follow two possible paths: they could exploit their comparative advantage in the production of provisions and trade for what they needed to consume—that is, if they could find adequate markets; or they could develop industries to supply themselves with iron, clothing, and other goods. Ultimately, leaders and entrepreneurs tried to do both.

Beginning in the late 1630s and especially after 1640, New England town and provincial governments used all of the tools within their power to foster economic growth. They gave out bounties and special concessions to desired projects, relying, as they had in the past, on "mixed enterprise," in which government provided a variety of incentives to private individuals who engaged in commercial activities deemed in the public interest: sawmills, gristmills, iron slitting mills that produced nails, or fulling mills that treated cloth, saltworks, and glassworks. They built or supported the building of roads, bridges, inns, and ferries. They issued patents and monopoly grants to inventors. And the General Court of Massachusetts (soon copied by the other colonies) tried to create a legal framework conducive to commerce—one that would resolve disputes, enforce contracts, and protect property rights. England was the model they deliberately emulated; yet ironically, in seeking to satisfy consumer demand through domestic development, New England governments violated the mercantilist assumptions of English authorities concerning the proper subordinate role of colonies in an imperial system. In fact, with the mother country embroiled in its own domestic problems, the colonies themselves began to behave like mercantilist states.

Some of the most generous support went to the extremely ambitious Saugus Ironworks that John Winthrop Jr. and his circle founded near Lynn, Massachusetts.[23] Using the most advanced technology available in Europe, the Walloon or indirect process, and capitalized at over £12,000, Saugus had a staff of more than 100 part- and full-time workers. Ore entered the bloomery; finished pots, nails, and bar iron came out of the forge. The "Company of Undertakers," composed of Winthrop, Robert Child, and other investors in Boston and London, received thousands of acres of land, tax abatements, a twenty-one-year monopoly, and employee exemption from militia service. The General Court even helped sell company shares to local inhabitants, appealing to investors who "intend their own benefit, with the common good." Government aid came at a price, however: Saugus had to sell at least a portion of its iron locally rather than exporting it, and accept farm products in payment. In the end, the works met neither the investors' nor the colony's expectations.

Like Saugus, many of the more ambitious mixed-enterprise schemes of the 1640s also fell short of their goals. The output of iron, cloth, and other finished goods remained small, although not because of a lack of government support. High start-up costs, shortages of labor and capital, poor management, and the logistical challenges posed by the frontier situation hampered efforts at establishing a large-scale manufacturing sector, at least in the seventeenth century.

Yet considering that barely thirty years had passed since the settlement of Plymouth, these early industrial efforts were impressive. They produced some products to satisfy local demand, introduced skilled workers from Europe, and disseminated new technologies throughout the region. Saugus workers, investors, and their descendants turned up at more modest, locally run ironworks in Taunton, Rowley, Pawtucket, Concord, Raynham, and New Haven. By 1770 American forges were producing more iron each year than those in England and Wales combined. And the Saugus project had established an important principle: although New England assemblies backed fewer blue-ribbon projects after the 1650s, they continued to offer tax breaks and land grants to smaller entrepreneurial efforts, and to view manufactures as a public goal worth pursuing.

Economic activity and mixed enterprise did generate profound tensions within Puritan society, and in the 1640s social and religious goals conflicted with the interests of development on several fronts. For example, some New Englanders remained uneasy with the idea of a free labor market despite the desperate need for skilled workers. In forming their settlement plan, John Winthrop and other leaders urged selective admission to New England on the grounds that too many "unmeete tools" would undermine the colony's religious goals. Indeed, workers at the Saugus Ironworks and the Essex fisheries made frequent appearances in colonial criminal courts for such offenses as slander, blasphemy, drunkenness, and assault. Religious intolerance led colonial officials to jail, banish, and even kill theological dissenters, which scared off potential immigrants and expelled economically useful inhabitants from the Massachusetts community. The Antinomian crisis of 1636 forced the departure of the Hutchinsons, an important Boston merchant family, to schismatic Rhode Island; another group of Anne Hutchinson's followers, under minister John Wheelwright, chose exile on the New Hampshire frontier.

Yet while these conflicts clearly robbed the Bay Colony of some of its most enterprising citizenry, dissenting men and women invigorated the economic life of other New England colonies, and their talents were not lost to the region at large. Roger Williams founded Providence Plantations. Edward Hutchinson, William Coddington, and Thomas Savage formed the nucleus of future merchant communities in Portsmouth, New Hampshire, and Newport, Rhode Island. Wheelwright and his followers established the towns of Exeter and Hampton in New Hampshire and Wells in Maine, building gristmills and sawmills as well as churches in the new communities. Massachusetts also rescinded some of its banishment orders in the 1650s, permitting former merchant exiles once again to live and do business within the bounds of the colony.

THE BEGINNINGS OF ATLANTIC COMMERCE

If the results of its experiments in manufacturing were mixed initially, New England had better success with its efforts to find an export commerce.

The possibility of commercial fishing had inspired promoters since the early 1600s, but efforts by Plymouth and Massachusetts in the early years had foundered in the face of serious competition from England and the lack of skilled labor. Beginning in 1642, however, the English Civil War diverted or disabled much of the home fishing fleet, raising the price of fish in Europe and creating opportunities for interlopers. Meanwhile, strong local recruiting efforts in Salem, Boston, and Marblehead (including free house lots for fishermen) offered added inducement. Initially, merchants in Boston, Charlestown, and Salem—often drawing on English credit—capitalized the voyages, extending loans to fishermen in exchange for a share of the catch, which the traders then shipped to Spain, Portugal, and Madeira. Fishermen worked from small boats near shore.

After 1675, merchants such as Salem's George Corwin more often sent out their own larger ships to the deepwater banks farther from the coast, hiring crews on a free-labor basis—that is, with few legal constraints. They also found new markets in the West Indies, especially for poorer quality "refuse fish." Unsaleable in Europe, New England refuse fish became a major part of the diet of enslaved Africans who worked on sugar and tobacco plantations. Thus in 1675, a New England fishing industry employing about 1,300 men shipped 6,600 tons of fish abroad; a century later, about 4,500 workers produced 42,000 tons.[24] Whaling, a subsidiary enterprise of the fishing trade early in the seventeenth century, played an increasingly valuable role in New England's export trade in the eighteenth century.

Once established, the fishing trade helped merchants set up credit relationships abroad and stimulated the exchange of other commodities within the same markets. During the first two decades of settlement, Massachusetts and Connecticut had attempted to establish trade with the Caribbean in cotton, dyes, enslaved Indians, and provisions, with mixed success. After 1647, this commerce between New England and the West Indies grew steadily and soon included more than fish. New England travelers noted that Barbadian settlers "are so intent upon planting sugar that they had rather buy foode at very deare rates than produce it by labour, soe infinite is the profitt of sugar workes after once accomplished."[25] The trend toward monoculture in the Caribbean, and to a lesser extent in the Chesapeake, created a market for the flour, preserved meats, dairy goods, and other provisions produced on Massachusetts and Connecticut farms. Cane-crushing machinery in the sugar islands used horse power, so Rhode Island landowners such as William Withington raised horses and other livestock for export to this growing market after 1649. Thus the prosperity of colonial New England became intimately intertwined with the emerging slave economies of the Caribbean and the southeast.

That same decade, Massachusetts Bay Colony dispatched quasimilitary expeditions that virtually annexed those towns and territories in northern and western New England that had been under the jurisdiction of two other English trading companies. By the mid-1640s, sawmills in Cape Ann, the Connecticut River valley, New Hampshire, and Maine—a region now claimed by Massachusetts—turned out clapboards, shingles, and barrel staves for domestic use and export. One of Governor John Winthrop's sons, Adam, initiated the export of New England timber, and others soon followed, sending out cargoes of shingles, ready-made house frames, and barrels to the nearly deforested Wine Islands (Madeira, the Canaries, and the Azores), Spain, and the Caribbean.

After 1650, conflict with the Dutch threatened England's access to its traditional Baltic sources of timber, which made colonial wood products—especially masts, turpentine and pitch, and potash—more competitive. Making potash and pearl ash, the fine ashes used in glassmaking and cloth processing, gave capital-poor farmers a chance to make some quick money as they cleared fields for planting. It became such an important commodity that by the 1760s potash and whale products together made up 85 percent of Massachusetts merchants' direct exports to England.

Fishing and shipbuilding also were intertwined. By 1675, according to one English observer, there were thirty master shipwrights working in Massachusetts and New Hampshire ports, where "Good ships are built for foure pounds the tun." The intense demand for ships that accompanied the Anglo-Dutch wars helped New England shipwrights to break into the English market in the last quarter of the seventeenth century. Along with producing a valuable export commodity, the expansion of the regional shipbuilding industry allowed New Englanders to exercise greater control over the region's commerce. Of the 1,118 vessels constructed in Massachusetts between 1696 and 1713, 59 percent went to Boston owners. By 1700, 300 Bostonians either owned and operated a ship outright, or had joined with other investors to purchase shares in a vessel, with Salem residents boasting nearly this many. Rhode Island and Connecticut developed their fleets more slowly, although the former experienced a rapid commercial expansion in the early 1700s. By 1708 both colonies' ports boasted thirty and twenty oceangoing vessels, respectively.

Historians John J. McCusker and Russell R. Menard have stressed the importance of the backward and forward "linkages" associated with the production and marketing of an export staple commodity, and the impact of these connections on economic development in the British colonies. In the case of New England, the region's very economic backwardness and lack of immediate promise promoted the creation of linkages. Unlike the plantation colonies, which shipped products that required either minimal processing or only one type of specialized processing, the types of goods that New Englanders produced and shipped stimulated the growth of a wide range of related enterprises and financial services: the processing and milling of grain, timber, and turpentine; the building of special casks for provisions; the construction and capitalization of ships and equipment for the fisheries; and finally, the storage, financing, and transportation facilities needed to gather cargoes and ship them abroad.

This commerce also required that merchants develop the means of marketing and distributing the consumer goods they secured in return—that is, "forward" or "consumption" linkages. Crucially, again in contrast with the plantation colonies, New England established its own infrastructure to meet these needs. In 1690, Governor Edmund Andros explained this phenomenon to the English bureaucrats who oversaw colonial commerce, the Board of Trade. Massachusetts, he noted, "though considerable for number of towns and inhabitants and well situated for trade, is one of the smallest and poorest tracts of land, and produces least of any of the other colonies for exportation." Yet, he continued, "by reason of the great number of artificers particularly in Boston, shipwrights, smiths, etc., they build many ships and other vessels, some whereof they employ in trading with all sorts of provisions and lumber to other colonies and plantations, who bring home their produce and make Boston the store of all the plantation commodities."[26]

In fact, New England furnished transportation, processing, and distribution services not only for itself but for other colonies as well. New England merchants imported partly processed materials like molasses and raw sugar from the Indies, then turned out rum and white sugar for colonial, Caribbean, and African markets. Massachusetts, Rhode Island, and Connecticut soon boasted more rum distilleries and sugar refineries than the rest of the North American colonies put together, a position of dominance they retained through the 1770s. New Yorkers complained that Boston merchants purchased their wheat, milled it in New England, then sold the finished flour back to them at a profit.

Not content with managing the fishing trade off Cape Cod, Boston and Salem merchants exercised a near monopoly on trade with fisheries near the new English colony of Newfoundland as well, where they aggressively competed with merchants from England for commercial control. New England traders supplied the fishermen with tobacco, sugar, pitch, rum, and other provisions on credit at huge markups in exchange for their future catches, then vended the fish to British and European ships that came directly to the banks in exchange for cloth, iron, and wine. The Newfoundland trade became extremely important in the eighteenth century, and it made the fortunes of Thomas Hancock and Peter Faneuil. Merchants on the New England coast picked up tobacco and provisions in Maryland and Virginia, and hides and turpentine off Cape Fear in North Carolina. One recent estimate suggests that the coastal trade was worth £304,000 sterling by the decade before the Revolution; others put it at over £400,000, or nearly equal to the annual value of New England's foreign trade.[27]

English merchants found it easier to deal with a single distribution center and thus extended credit more readily to Boston merchants, guaranteeing that colonists from Canada to Virginia received their imported consumer goods via Boston as well. These included "brandy, Canary, Spanish and French wines, bullion, salt, fruits, oyles, silkes, laces, linnen of all sorts, cloath, serges, bayes, kersies, stockings, and many other commodities, which they distribute into all parts . . . so that there is little left for merchants residing in England to import into any of the plantations," complained an English observer.[28] Profitable in itself, the trade in consumer items had important consequences for New England manufacturing many decades later. Through retailing imports, New England merchants gained valuable market information that made later efforts at import substitution possible. They learned about the capacities of domestic markets; which items sold well in various markets; and the tastes of local consumers. Also, by conducting this commerce themselves, in locally made and locally owned ships, New Englanders profited not only from the sale of goods, but also from the sale of services—freight costs, insurance, interest charges on credit—that would otherwise have accrued to English shippers. These earnings from shipping, or so-called invisible exports, the value of which even the colonists themselves consistently underestimated, constituted the region's single most valuable export commodity.

Although competition from New York, Philadelphia, and local ports undermined its primacy in the 1700s, Boston dominated the coastal and regional colonial trades through most of the seventeenth century. By 1660, its population numbered 3,000. Its aspect reminded one admiring visitor of a bustling English port city, with fine public buildings, wharves, warehouses, and handsome homes "close together on each side the streets as in London, and furnished with many fair shops . . . Their streets are many and large . . . On the North-west and North-east two constant Fairs [markets] are kept for daily Traffick thereunto. On the South there is a small but pleasant Common where the Gallants a little before Sun-set walk with their Marmalet-Madams."[29] Boston's public and private schools were so well reputed that some Barbados planters sent their sons and daughters to be educated there. At the imposing new Town House in the central market square, merchants and shipmasters could mingle, exchange news, and do business, much like the Royal Exchange in London.

By 1720, a fine new brick Town House had replaced the former wooden structure. Now, merchants could stroll to one of the city's four coffee

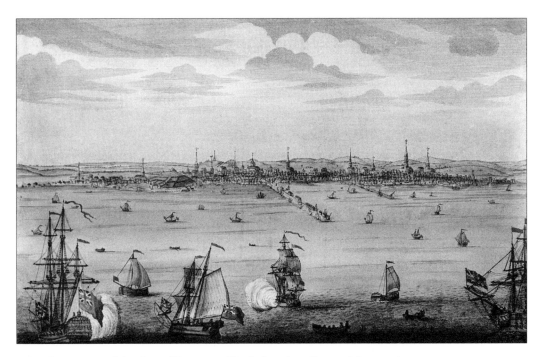

A Southeast View of the City of Boston in North America. *(Boston Athenæum.)*

This view of the Boston waterfront shows a small town clustered around an active port. New England ships sailed to Europe with fish, iron, and wood products, and provided the slave colonies to the south and in the Caribbean with provisions, shipping, and mercantile services. The merchants and captains involved in this trade earned large profits and kept New England in touch with developments in the wider world.

houses and eighty-one taverns to share information or sit and read one of the two newspapers published weekly (the first in the colonies). Or traders could visit their warehouses near the fifty-eight public and private wharves that jutted into Boston Harbor, including the massive Long Wharf, constructed in 1713, which alone accommodated thirty ships.

Maritime trade brought enormous wealth to some in the city. Successful merchants such as Samuel Shrimpton, who owned Beacon Hill, built imposing, many-roomed mansions furnished with richly carved chests and bedsteads, high-backed wooden chairs, silk and velvet hangings and cushions, and silver plate. In the eighteenth century the North End and South End became fashionable, and grandee merchants rushed to build themselves three-story brick houses with large windows and hand-painted wallpaper. They traveled in elegant coaches, attended soirees at hostelries such as the Green Dragon, or crossed over to Charlestown to dance at public balls.[30] All the while, though, they kept their ships busy. During a seven-month period in 1671–1672, Boston trader and goldsmith John Hull commissioned or shared in voyages to and from Virginia, Jamaica, Honduras, Curaçao, Bristol, London, Ireland, Nevis, and Antigua.

By the late 1600s, however, other New England ports had begun to give Boston some healthy competition. Salem's success in shipbuilding and its proximity to the fisheries made it a vibrant port by 1700, with fleets that plied both Caribbean and European markets. In 1683, New Hampshire merchants attempted to wrest some control over the timber trade from Massachusetts merchants Charles Lidget and William Vaughan. After a slow start, traders in Newport and Providence rapidly penetrated the Caribbean trade, particularly with Dutch Surinam and Curaçao, where they obtained cash—as much as £20,000 annually—with which to purchase manufactures from Boston. Rhode Island's dependence on Boston was short-lived in the eighteenth century, as the colony's merchants aggressively pursued the export of horses and provisions, the slave trade, distilling, and other activities related to West Indian trade. In contrast, Connecticut continued to rely on Massachusetts ports to manage its international trade in provisions, grain, and dairy products; as late as 1708, only two ships departed from Connecticut ports for England. But small boats from Wethersfield used the Connecticut River to tap suppliers and markets in the hinterland, and seaports such as New London began to develop viable merchant communities in the 1700s.

New England's success in the carrying trade drew complaints from English merchants as early as the 1640s, but the mother country was surprisingly slow to respond. With the exception of regulations in the 1650s that restricted trade between the colonists and the Dutch, New Englanders pursued their economic affairs with remarkably little interference. After 1660, a restored English monarchy under Charles II adopted policies designed to impose greater royal control on trade in the English empire. Regulatory legislation in 1661, 1662, and 1663 aimed to increase the economic benefits that the mother country derived from colonial trade, principally by eliminating Dutch, French, and Spanish competition. Modifications of this system, part of England's commercial revolution of the late seventeenth century, continued through 1696, by which time a full-blown imperial economic administration was in place.

These so-called Navigation Acts restricted the carrying of colonial goods to English ships manned by English crews. Certain "enumerated goods" (mostly valuable plantation commodities), which the government identified on an official list, had to be shipped directly to England before re-export to other markets. To ensure English manufacturers and exporters a steady colonial market, regulations required that European finished goods intended for the colonies had to pass through England first as well. Enforcement of these regulations and collection of the accompanying taxes and duties fell to a newly created transatlantic bureaucracy centered in a few port cities.

Although the new rules hurt many colonies, notably Virginia, New England largely benefited from England's imperial policy. The Navigation Acts created a huge imperial free-trade zone linking the Caribbean with North America. Since New England ships and sailors qualified as "English" under the acts, the elimination of the Dutch and other competitors allowed New England carriers to penetrate new markets and to take advantage of an increased volume of trade. The restrictions on exports of "enumerated goods" affected the staple-producing colonies adversely, but most of the commodities that New England exported were exempt, so its merchants continued to engage in direct trade with Europe. Within a single week in June of 1676, for example, an irate Edward Randolph, the agent who had been sent by the Crown to check on the colonists' adherence to the Navigation Acts, observed no fewer than five ships (all but one owned by "Bostoners") unloading cargoes from France, Spain, the Canaries, and the Azores; at other times he recorded voyages to Holland, the

Hanse Towns, Madagascar, Guinea, and Honduras. Even worse, in his eyes, the New England governments actively encouraged smuggling in violation of the Navigation Acts.[31]

It is important to note that colonial protests and evasions did not signal a desire to escape from English trade and credit networks. Indeed, the more complex and multisided these exchanges became, the more such relationships became crucial. Many New England merchants sought close ties with merchant houses and officials in the mother country during this period. Participation in the Atlantic trade required a great deal of capital, and ironically, it was the willingness of English merchants to advance New Englanders goods on credit that helped the colonials enter this commerce. Huge transactions took place with no more security than a written IOU; personal trust and a relationship based on honest trading were crucial. Merchant communities simultaneously became more inbred and more international. Families intermarried; they sent their sons to work as ship captains or clerks in ports throughout England, Spain, and the Caribbean.[32] And even though more people left New England than migrated there in the late seventeenth century, the period brought a small wave of newcomers from England, France, and the Channel Islands who arrived with capital and mercantile business connections: men like Philippe D'Anglois, who, as Philip English, became a leading merchant in Salem; and Andrew Faneuil, a French Protestant refugee whose son Peter funded the building of Boston's Faneuil Hall.

Subsequent additions to the network of commercial regulations did attempt to discourage the trade in sugar and molasses from the non-English West Indies, but enforcement was spotty. Meanwhile, New England's early iron industry and its trade in salt and dyes with Spanish America received outright English protection and encouragement. Overall, according to one historian, the New England economy enjoyed more exemptions and privileges than did Scotland.[33] Much more effective were the colonies' efforts to manage trade for their own benefit. Beginning in the 1640s, and more confidently in the 1650s and 1660s, Massachusetts gradually established an inspection and quality-control system to enforce comprehensive grades and standards for export goods like fish, preserved meat, timber, and other lumber products. On the whole, merchants welcomed the grading system, since it inspired more confidence from their overseas buyers; and traders used it to determine appropriate markets and prices for their exports.

The fact that New England's commercial economy placed the colonists in direct competition with the metropolis did not go unnoticed at home. Edward Randolph's investigation prompted English officials to annul the Massachusetts charter in 1684. This act, and a short-lived effort to consolidate the New England governments in 1686 under a royal appointee, Edmund Andros, in part reflected English unease over the implications of the region's economic development. After 1691, England succeeded in forcing religious toleration upon Puritan New Englanders and an appointed royal governor upon Massachusetts Bay. Henry Martin, inspector general of Customs, informed the Board of Trade in 1717 that Britain was, in effect, importing from the colonies when it permitted them to control so much shipping.

Yet other voices, both in New England and within English officialdom, contended that the northern colonies played a crucial economic role in the imperial system. Barbados, Virginia, and other valuable staple colonies depended upon the supplies and commercial services of northern merchants. Backed by the Navigation Acts, New England merchants had helped England to displace the French and Dutch from much of the southern carrying trade, and to penetrate Latin American markets. New England's importance as a market also attracted notice. Most profits that New England merchants made returned to the mother country to pay for manufactures. Annual English exports to the northern colonies amounted to approximately £235,000 by 1715; these figures helped to prevent the tightening of commercial regulations affecting New England, except laws regarding manufactures, until the 1760s.

THE DOMESTIC ECONOMY

Although oriented outward to the Atlantic, New England commerce had a profound effect on the development of the domestic economy. At the most basic level, population growth and opportunities for trade fostered a physical expansion of the New England colonies. Between 1660 and 1710, New Englanders settled 209 new townships from the New York border to Maine. Nearer the coast, the New England economy was beginning to mature. After all, barrel staves, salt cod, provisions, iron, and other products did not appear magically aboard merchants' ships. New England's mixed agricultural, fishing, and commercial economy drew upon the efforts and services of many inhabitants living in the port cities and beyond. Nor did the retail linkages of the market begin and end with the great Atlantic merchants. Just as the success of New England's export industries required the mobilization of producers, so the success of its import commerce depended on the efforts of peddlers and country storekeepers, who distributed goods to consumers and collected the cargoes that merchants shipped abroad.

Penetration of the market was uneven. Inhabitants of towns near the coast and along the Connecticut River were most commercially active. Distance from market centers and the effects of Indian warfare meant that those in the western part of Connecticut and Massachusetts and the "near frontier" of Worcester County had fewer opportunities to participate. Even the most distant, marginal farms still could not have been self-sufficient, however, so that some involvement in market exchange was part of life for these regions.

In a few areas, economies of scale and new types of labor arrangements began to emerge, as exporting merchants sought direct control of farms, mills, potash works, or other enterprises in order to ensure steady supplies. For example, the Hutchinson family of Boston purchased nineteen sawmills on the Great Works River in New Hampshire, which provided lumber products for their West Indian trade. Some of these wood and turpentine mills were quite extensive and factory-like. The Gibbons mill in Portsmouth, Maine, employed thirty people on site, twenty-two of them women, in sawing and potash making. Other merchants speculated in huge tracts of land—sometimes literally millions of acres—in the Narragansett area of Rhode Island, the Merrimac River region of Massachusetts, and Maine. Economies of scale also appeared in farming. Landowners in parts of Massachusetts, and especially in Rhode Island, operated plantation-style commercial farms for stock- and grain-raising on a large scale, with results not too distinct from similar enterprises in Virginia and South Carolina. These "Narragansett planters" employed large numbers of enslaved Indians and Africans; in South Kingstown, Rhode Island, alone, there were 223 enslaved Indians and 333 enslaved Africans by 1730. Merchants such as John Hull hired families to oversee their commercial farms, signaling a shift away from ownership to tenancy for some New Englanders.

Still, the bulk of production—and consumption—was carried on by individual farm families who owned their own land. Alongside the reciprocal local exchange of everyday goods and services (like cider, meat, grain, and harvest labor) that were a part of life for New England families, a more market-oriented traffic took place. Nowhere does this become clearer than in the account books of farmers, traders, and storekeepers. Merchants Robert Gibbs of Boston and Jonathan Corwin of Salem acted as both wholesalers and retailers, operating their own general stores where they exchanged earthenware, cloth, sugar, ironware, and other imported goods for beef, pork, and corn. Inland shopkeepers such as Jonathan Trumbull in Lebanon, Connecticut, organized huge cattle drives, gathering livestock from many individual farmers for sale in coastal cities.

Farm families engaged in more than agriculture and grazing. Newbury farmer Thomas Bartlet lent livestock to neighbors at plowing time and engaged in other neighborly acts, but Bartlet also hired out himself, his sons, and his horses by the day or week. He performed such tasks as shoemaking, plastering, chimneymaking, carting, shingle cutting, flax breaking, and cloth dying, and traded in goods like indigo, hardware, and clothing on a small scale. Another anonymous farmer/trader near Marblehead made shoes as well, including a pair "with heals" for his wife and other customers. This enterprising individual and his spouse rented pasturage; made and sold cider and beer; mowed flax; and exchanged provisions and skins purchased from their neighbors to urban traders for silks, hats, gloves, "fine cloth," and nails for their own use and for resale.[34]

Some storekeepers, including Robert Gibbs, began to organize cottage industries in the last quarter of the seventeenth century and the beginning of the eighteenth. Women supplied the lion's share of the labor. Tasks formerly performed solely for the family—spinning thread, weaving linen cloth, growing vegetables, making cheese, starching shirts, even baking cakes—became marketable commodities that women could exchange for clothing and thread, as well as extras such as pins, ribbons, and spices. Gibbs provided female customers with wool in exchange for half of the yarn they spun. In Marblehead between 1703 and 1705, an anonymous trader hired a number of women, including one Goody Quarles, to spin flax and cotton thread, and to manufacture a variety of wool, worsted, and linen cloth in quantities of thirty or forty yards. Women also worked as midwives and nurses for wages or credit with merchants.[35] Stores and petty traders extended financial services to country areas, loaning money and transferring goods and credits from one locality to another. Atlantic merchants had various sources of credit: English contacts, government contracts, relatives, and associates in the business world. In addition, merchants had adopted paper financial instruments, such as the bill of exchange. But small farmers wishing to invest in new equipment or property, tools, or even consumer goods, turned to local shopkeepers. Given the scarcity of cash outside of ports like Boston and Newport, traders generally kept running accounts of their customers' debits or credits, extending credit until buyers cleared their "book debt" with payment in produce or work. In turn, carpenters, blacksmiths, and other craftsmen, as well as many farmers, also kept their own account books and recorded their transactions.

In part, these ordinary New Englanders engaged in their multifarious occupations so they could buy consumer goods. Judging from estate inventories, former luxuries such as forks, chairs, and looking glasses were purchased at a rapid rate by households near the coast. By 1700, 31 percent of homes in Essex County boasted mirrors; the number of chairs per household had quadrupled since 1675, and the presence of table linens had doubled.[36] The letterbooks of John Hull and other merchants indicate that New England consumers demanded—and often received—goods of the same quality and fashionableness as those available in London. Fine wines and brandy, rather than just rum; olives, capers and anchovies; cutlery and

A Prospect of the Colledges in Cambridge in New England. *(Boston Athenæum.)*

The colonists took an active interest in education and established Harvard University in 1636. The emphasis on education has been a hallmark of New England ever since. Two of the buildings pictured above are still in use by Harvard University.

glasses, silks and satins—all these decorated the homes, tables, and persons of wealthier port residents. Even in more middling urban and rural households, material lives changed. In central Connecticut during the 1730s, 1740s, and 1750s, country storekeeper Jonathan Trumbull did a land-office business in looking glasses, butter dishes, china tea sets, earthenware plates, buttons, and even a "green silk gown." One study of consumer behavior in the eighteenth century estimates that in a given year nearly a quarter of household expenditures for a typical Massachusetts family went toward buying goods brought in from outside the province.[37] British exports to North America increased nearly eightfold between 1700 and 1783, and since New Englanders produced some "necessities" themselves by the eighteenth century, or secured them from other plantations, consumer demand grew even more rapidly than import levels from Great Britain might suggest.

CHALLENGES AT MIDCENTURY

The flexibility and industry shown by these farm households proved to be an asset as the colonial period waned. Between 1730 and 1770, New England faced a number of new social, political, and economic challenges. First, despite the lack of much in-migration, high fertility had led to a rapidly growing white population: from about 22,400 in 1650, to 91,000 in 1700, to 566,000 in 1770; the African-American population was approximately 15,400. Because New Englanders, unlike most Europeans, split up the inheritance among all children rather than leaving it to the eldest son, this growth put pressure on families in the older towns to provide farmland for the next generation. Children could migrate to other places, especially Boston, and sometimes parents speculated in land in new towns to help their kin get a start. Still, the average farm size dropped from 242 acres to 81 acres between 1730 and 1791 in Connecticut, and from between 200–300 acres to 100 acres by 1750 in southeastern Massachusetts.[38]

Second, New England farmers and merchants faced competition from new colonial sources. Overall, the middle colonies, with their superior resources and agricultural lands, had the economic edge over New England in commercial farming and industries such as ironworks. After 1740, merchants in Philadelphia and New York succeeded in establishing an independent commerce in grain to England and Europe, and eventually to the Caribbean as well. As a result, they also depended less on Boston for their manufactured goods. Philadelphia's trade was the greater, but New York's proximity added to the threat, since former Boston customers on Long Island and Connecticut sometimes found it easier to work with New York merchants. In addition, between 1689 and 1763 a nearly continual series of Anglo-American wars against the French, Native Americans, and Spanish further battered the region's, and especially Boston's, economy. Supplying provincial and English troops with food and equipment brought lucrative contracts to some Massachusetts and Connecticut merchants, but the five wars also drained colonial treasuries, disrupted foreign trade, siphoned off precious manpower, and left destitute widows and families. Many of the impoverished joined the stream of migration to Boston. Despite these additions, Boston's population, unlike that of any other major American city, remained stagnant; it leveled off at around 16,000 in 1750 and did not change for several decades. Meanwhile, the proportion of the city's population that collected poor relief grew to 20 percent.

Third, although New England had finessed many of the disadvantages of its colonial dependency, one area remained rather intractable: money, capital, and credit. English policymakers made no provision for a colonial currency. Massachusetts briefly operated a mint in the seventeenth century, but English authorities shut it down in 1686. Some foreign coin from the Caribbean and Latin American trades (and from pirates) made its way into the regional economy, but merchants tended to snap up all available gold and silver at high premiums in order to settle their commercial contracts abroad. The lack of cash made even the most basic transactions difficult. People paid their taxes in corn and timber, and reluctantly engaged in barter. For merchants trying to raise capital, or even farmers and artisans desirous of investing in property or tools to increase their productivity, the credit situation was equally dire. Only international merchants had regular access to large amounts of liquid credit, and even they borrowed mostly from family, friends, and business associates. In England during this period, regular mortgage markets, private banks, and the public Bank of England met the needs of a growing capitalist economy. But beyond the occasional private mortgage agreement, New Englanders had far less recourse.

Because of all these circumstances, some historians see the mid-eighteenth century as a time of "Europeanization" for New England, marked by the erosion of the high quality of life they had enjoyed in the seventeenth century. The average age at marriage (and premarital conceptions) rose, and more epidemics attacked the now denser population. Per capita wealth among the white population in New England in 1774 (£33) was lower than in either the middle colonies (£51) or the southern colonies (£132); the wealth of West Indian planters was almost forty times greater.[39] Was New England facing an economic crisis? A closer look at the figures for wealth and income suggests that the situation was not quite so bleak.

These figures count African-Americans as possessions, not as owners of wealth. In the case of the south and the Caribbean, and even the middle colonies, anywhere from three-quarters to one-quarter of all wealth took the form of enslaved humans (the number for New England was more like 3 percent). New England had one-third of America's "wealth-owners," even though it had less than one-third of the total colonial population. Although economic maturity had brought increasing inequality to the region, wealth and income were far more equitably distributed in New England than in slave-based societies. If we include both blacks and whites, and look at income per capita, the figures for New England (£10.4–£12.1) are identical to those for the south, and only slightly lower than the middle colonies. Alice Hanson Jones, the historian who compiled these data, notes that the colonial New England annual per capita income figures compare to about $580 in 1978 dollars—not bad for a developing nation in the twentieth century, and not much below the standard of eighteenth-century England and Wales.[40] (It should be noted that all of these calculations of wealth and well-being exclude Native Americans; scholars are currently compiling new inclusive figures for colonial America. Given that many of the settlers' gains during the first century of colonization came at the expense of the indigenous inhabitants, either directly or indirectly, inclusion of New England's Native American population would almost certainly push the figures on per capita wealth downward, although the same is true for other regions of North America.)

Declining farm size and Boston's woes need to be viewed with similar caution. The inhabitants of New England responded creatively to the stresses of increased population and limited landed resources. Their tactics were threefold. First, some households, towns, and even subregions began to specialize in particular crops or processes in response to changing markets. Wethersfield, Connecticut, became known as the "onion town"; others shifted to flax, tobacco, or sheep raising. Farmers in Massachusetts, Rhode Island, and parts of Connecticut found that dairying and grazing livestock garnered much higher profits than grain cultivation, and that such activities took better advantage of smaller plots. Specialization came at a price, however; unless the citizens of Wethersfield wished to dine exclusively on onions, they had to enter the marketplace more than ever before.

Second, there is evidence that households began to increase agricultural productivity, especially after 1750. This issue is explored at much greater length in the following essay on the Revolutionary economy, but the roots of the increase in productivity lay in the colonial period. Farmers began to follow the advice of Connecticut minister Jared Eliot, whose *Essays on Field Husbandry* (1748) recommended English-style agricultural improvements: the cultivation of European clover grasses for better hay and the fertilizing and draining of marginal land. Provincial governments gave an added boost to agricultural productivity by building roads and bridges at an unprecedented rate between 1730 and 1760 to aid farmers' access to markets.

Third, the New England colonists devoted more energy to the kinds of crafts, household manufacturing, and small-scale industry that had supplemented farm household income since the late seventeenth century—spinning, weaving, cheesemaking, flax breaking, shoemaking—as well as some newer home crafts, such as cloth dyeing and processing for other home weavers and the making of straw brooms and hats. Productivity in these activities, and the cumulative effect of small-scale industry for the colonial period, is extremely hard to quantify. Nor was this type of activity unique to New England. Farmers in Pennsylvania, Maryland, and Virginia were beginning to engage in the same types of activities. We do know, however, that New England imported more capital goods—the tools of industry—than did other areas of early America. These included large equipment, such as millstones and forge bellows, as well as small items like spinning wheels, the hand-held wire-toothed wool cards used to comb wool before spinning, and the chemical alum used to fix cloth dyes. We also know that nearly one-fourth of adult males in Connecticut on the eve of the Revolution participated in some artisanal activity. Farmer-cobblers spent the winter on the road, boarding at homes while making shoes for the occupants. Goodwives and their daughters, servants, and daughters-in-law produced cheese, butter, and linen cloth. Entire towns devoted themselves to manufactures. Benning Wentworth, governor of New Hampshire, described Londonderry (near Manchester and Amoskeag Falls, later centers of industry) as a town where "every family employs all the leisure hours they can spare from tending their farms, in making Linen cloth," wool-felt hats, and "mittens."[41] And rural patriarchs found other ways to provide for their children. They invested in education, sending farm boys from Braintree, Andover, Dedham, and Newtown to Harvard and Yale (future president John Adams was one), or to be trained in crafts as apprentices. Connecticut had a grand total of 13 silversmiths before 1750, but 125 more opened shop between 1750 and 1790.

This cottage industry proved to be tenacious in the face of economic change. It could adjust flexibly to the demands of changing markets and the entry of more aggressive merchant-capitalists. These sorts of partnerships, in which merchants supplied materials to household workers, became more common after the Revolution, as later essays will show, but they were present at the end of the colonial period. In Lynn, Massachusetts, a center of the shoemaking trade in the nineteenth century, households and "manufactories" (workshops where production involved no input of mechanical technology, but where labor was divided among specialized workers) were turning out 80,000 pairs of shoes a year by 1768, and 170,000 by the 1780s.

Specialization and cottage industry helped New England families maintain and even improve their material standard of living. The fact that farm families enjoyed greater purchasing power after 1740 also helped. Although technology in America did not change much, colonial consumers were able to benefit from improvements in English manufacturing technology in the form of lower prices for imported goods. The demands of rival armies in the French and Indian War (1755–1763) helped boost the price of farm products. In Connecticut, one historian estimates that live-stock and dairy products enjoyed a fivefold increase in price; 100 bushels of Massachusetts grain bought 150 yards of imported woolen cloth in 1740 but purchased 250 yards in the early 1760s.[42]

Finally, prospects for New England traders and craftsmen in general were not as bleak as the late-colonial condition of Boston might suggest. Eighteenth-century Boston's loss of trade and stagnant population was the region's gain. Its merchants lost some ground to their counterparts in New York and Philadelphia, true, but they also lost ground to aggressive merchant communities in Providence, Salem, and Newport, and to enterprising inland traders such as Jonathan Trumbull who were in a better position to tap the resources of the hinterland and who independently pursued foreign trade. Crafts, tanneries, distilleries, ironworks, and shipbuilding followed a similar pattern of dispersal to other towns within the region. On the eve of the Revolution, nine of the thirteen colonies' fifteen most rapidly growing "secondary cities" (those with a population of over 3,000) were located in New England. When the Boston Town Meeting complained that its shipbuilding industry had declined in the 1740s and 1750s, they knew where to place the blame: on competition from Newbury, Massachusetts; Portsmouth, New Hampshire; and Newport and Bristol, Rhode Island.

Signs of new, more intensive industries that seeded later advances appeared outside of Massachusetts as the colonial period came to a close. One example is the Connecticut tool and die industry, so crucial to New England's nineteenth-century economy. In the 1730s, Philip Livingston and Jared Eliot founded an ironworks on the Saugus model in Salisbury, Connecticut. By the 1770s the furnace consisted of a series of forges that employed seventy-five men and a refining plant that manufactured capital goods essential to other industries: potash kettles, sawmill hardware, carriage parts, ships' anchors, blacksmiths' tools, specialized castings, and equipment for clothiers and hatters. Among the biggest customers for their bar iron, however, were the colony's own large number of secondary iron manufacturers. Already in 1748, Connecticut had more metal shops than did the rest of British America combined. They turned sheet metal into nails, barrel hoops, hardware, tin plate (using copper from the nearby Simsbury mines), and forge bellows. This kind of synergy took place across the colonial economy. Tanners welcomed the opening of new ironworks, because ironworks used charcoal; colliers who made charcoal discarded tree bark, which produced an acid used in the tanning of leather hides.

There is also some evidence that merchants and even small traders were beginning to invest capital in manufactures and small industry. As in the case of agricultural productivity, the most dramatic shifts in this direction took place after our period, in the 1780s and 1790s, but we can identify some trends in the late colonial era. Jonathan Trumbull had shares in the Simsbury mine, as well as in several cloth fulling mills. The Brown family of Providence, Rhode Island, made their initial fortune in the Caribbean provisions and slave trades. In the 1760s, however, the Browns moved heavily into the manufacture of whale oil candles and started an ironworks, Hope Furnace, on the Pawtuxet River. This led to a kind of vertical integration of the Brown family's overseas trade and domestic interests. Over the next decade, nonagricultural products took up more and more space on their outbound ships. The invoice of their brig *George*, bound for Surinam in 1768, listed 200 boxes of Rhode Island candles, 500 bricks from Taunton, Massachusetts, and 379 locally made axes.[43] The iron barrel hoops and wooden staves that held pickled beef and pork came from Brown-owned enterprises. Even the shackles on the wrists of enslaved Africans imported aboard their ships came from Providence. Iron and candles were also the commodities that finally helped the Browns break into the direct export trade with England and France.

This kind of trade could subvert a merchant's priorities. By the 1770s the Browns had conducted some overseas trading voyages to obtain the materials for manufacturing rather than vice versa. Other merchants contented themselves with exporting, but even they provided craftsmen and manufacturers with new markets. New England shoes, furniture, iron goods, and hats turned up in Charleston, Virginia, and Jamaica.

The active intervention of New England governments helped make all of these changes possible. Beginning in 1691, Massachusetts issued the first paper money in colonial America. Initially, the paper was intended to be a short-term emergency measure, a way for the colony to pay for needed provisions during wartime. People could use it to pay their taxes, and gradually it would be withdrawn from circulation. The inhabitants found paper money so useful in domestic exchanges, however, that it became something of a popular political issue, and more emissions of paper money followed. In 1714 and again in 1719, a group of Boston merchants led by John Colman proposed a private bank in the English model. In order to stop Colman's plan, the General Court approved of newer, larger emissions of paper to be distributed by the towns in the form of loans against mortgages. The other New England colonies eventually followed Massachusetts' lead.

By the 1720s these public loan banks were pumping huge sums of cash and credit into the colonial economy; Massachusetts alone issued £820,000 on loan between 1715 and 1751. They also provided a source of income to the towns, which got to keep some of the interest payments to use for local improvements such as road building and schools. Paper money and public banks remained extremely controversial. Some Atlantic merchants opposed them bitterly because the legal tender bills could only be used for domestic payments, which made them useless in foreign trade. The bills also depreciated, as more and more remained in circulation. Yet among farmers, country traders, and those merchants with ties to the hinterland, the public loans were extremely popular. They helped put investment capital—and money for consumer purchases—in the hands of small proprietors, and they simplified internal exchanges. They turned the real property that constituted the bulk of most New Englanders' wealth into a liquid asset. Supporters in Massachusetts claimed that paper money increased agricultural productivity and investment in manufactures, resulting in a stronger and more diversified economy. Rhode Islanders credited their growing commercial independence from Massachusetts to the bills. Critics claimed that the bills had led to a consumer binge. All three positions were probably correct. Paper money also accustomed New Englanders to abstract concepts and representations of wealth; this may be one reason why even modest New England households invested in bank stock and insurance in the nineteenth century.

Such was the demand for paper money that despite depreciation, it commanded broad support and usage. The bills from neighboring New England colonies circulated across borders, despite the fact that they were legal tender only in the colony that issued them. The result was a regional money supply that filled a desperate need. Once again, the New England governments had acted like mercantilist states in their own right, making economic policy and charting a course toward greater economic independence. England intervened to stop a second private bank proposal in 1740, and eventually enacted the Currency Act of 1751, which forced the colonies to reduce sharply their paper money emissions. But sixty years of debating monetary policy had made colonial leaders and the general public at large invested in more than paper money. Pamphlets, speeches, and town resolutions made commonplace the idea that New England could and should pursue a diverse and developed—in other words, non-colonial—economy.

Such actions and attitudes made New England a special target of English complaint by mid-century. Pennsylvania, Maryland, and Virginia together produced more iron than New England, but English petitions and reports singled out New England as a threat to the English economy. Why? Because New England did not just export its iron; it turned it into capital goods for other trades, and it did so with the direct support of government. "Have they not set up many Looms both for Woolen and Linen Cloths, in Spite of all our Laws and Restrictions?" demanded one angry London pamphleteer in 1757. "Was not a large Premium allow'd by the Government of New-England to the American Manufacturer for Scythes, Nails, &c. out of their public Money, and is not the Demand . . . from this Country . . . so diminished annually?"[44] New England in 1770 still had a relatively undeveloped economy; its manufacturing output was minuscule compared to Britain's. And yet English policymakers were worried about New England's growing economic independence—an independence incompatible with its colonial status. The changes that overtook the region's internal economy between 1640 and 1770—the effects of linkage, the expansion of internal exchange networks, the beginnings of industry and household manufactures, and the active role of government—were overshadowed by the continued success of the Atlantic trading economy. But these changes were integral to English fears, and essential to New Englanders' ability to adjust to the next stages of industrial development.

CONCLUSION

By the mid-eighteenth century, New England had nurtured its comparative advantage so successfully that it had become both a key supplier of goods and services to other colonies and a key market in its own right: "the center of motion upon which the wheel of all the British commerce in America turns," as James Otis proudly declared in 1764.[45] The region's economic success had refuted the pessimistic forecasts of Francis Brewster and William Petty—so much so, in fact, that British bureaucrats, merchants, and industry lobbyists feared that the course of New England's economic development had put the region on a collision course with imperial interests. "So far from being a present Advantage to Britain," worried one writer, "[New England] is already the Rival and Supplantress of her Mother."[46] Parliament took action to ensure that England retained the benefits of empire.

Between 1730 and 1751, scattered legislation restricted specific types of manufactures and radically curtailed the New England colonies' ability to form banks and issue currency. Beginning in 1763, a new round of imperial regulations and tax levies affected New England's European and Caribbean trade in ways that were unprecedented, and in the colonists' eyes, damaging. In pamphlets, newspapers, and resolutions between 1763 and 1770, the colonists challenged these policies and charged that New England's dependence upon the mother country threatened the colonies' future development. As tensions escalated, anti-English agitators turned to economic weapons—particularly boycotts of English goods and calls for home manufactures—to express their displeasure.

New England became a hotbed of pre-Revolutionary protest, and this was no accident. To paraphrase historian Edmund Morgan, New Englanders had already been developing an economy that was not colonial. A sense of the region's economic viability made it possible for many of the inhabitants to confront the drastic economic consequences of separation from England, and even to believe that continued prosperity was compatible with—even contingent upon—political independence. In doing so they laid the groundwork not only for revolution, but for a vital nineteenth-century economy.

CHAPTER 2

The Invention of American Capitalism: The Economy of New England in the Federal Period

WINIFRED BARR ROTHENBERG

[T]he 1780s were . . . the most critical moment in the entire history of America. The few years following the end of the War of Independence clearly revealed for the first time all the latent commercial and enterprising power of America's emerging democratic society. In the 1780s we can actually sense the shift from a premodern traditional society to a modern one . . . Something momentous was happening in the society and culture that released the aspirations and energies of common people as never before in American history, or perhaps in world history.

THE AUDACITY OF THIS PASSAGE captures the spirit of the age. In rural New England, the Federal period was the era of capitalist transformation.[1] Which is not to say that capitalism "began" in the 1780s—as we learned in the previous essay, the earliest colonists had come from a society already undergoing a capitalist transformation—but that the lineaments of the world created during this period became visible. By the 1830s it had become clear to what extent capitalism would penetrate the society and shape all the institutions in its path: the distribution of income, wealth, and land; "the path of the law"; the nature and pace of technological change; the sources of authority; family size; the gender composition of the labor force; attitudes toward work and leisure; the forms and functions of money; the social relations of production; the tenets of religious belief; the agenda of politics; and the boundaries between public and private, secular and sacred, urban and rural, the individual and the state. Above all, in this period the market emerged as the principal agent of economic transformation.

Why in New England? Because the institutions of that culture were ready to effect a relatively seamless transition to modern industrial society. Population growth had moderated. There had long been in place a value system that privileged saving and capital accumulation. There were minimal institutional restraints on the mobility of labor and capital and the sale of land. Town settlement patterns abetted the proliferation of central places. There also were representative political institutions, common law protections of liberty and property, a relatively egalitarian distribution of income and wealth, secure land tenure, a permeable class structure, a public philosophy of individual agency, and, some historians emphasize, a Revolution to unseat political and social elites in favor of the bourgeoisie. All these elements were peculiarly congenial to the creation of what Joyce Appleby has called "a popular culture of enterprise."[2] New England at the end of the eighteenth century could claim all these in abundance. No wonder that the region's people saw themselves as the handiwork of a wonder-working Providence.

There are those who would argue that, far from unseating the elites, the American Revolution had in fact bound them to the country and its people with chains of mutual self-preservation. And indeed, the previous essay left us with so promising a portrait of colonial New England's flourishing economy that one might well ask, why unseat the elites? And why, for that matter, leave the Empire?

The New England colonies chafed most against the mercantilist impediments the Empire had thrown up against the workings of colonial markets both here and abroad. Although many scholars today consider the benefits of Empire trade to have been well worth the costs, the prevailing opinion in New England at the time was that the Navigation Acts were a burden, the chronic shortage of specie was deflationary, Parliament's disallowance of paper money and land-banking was crippling, the Currency Acts were inequitable, and the ill-timed assertion by the British of their "virtual" authority to tax stamps, sugar, molasses, all legal transactions, paper, lead paint, tea, glass, and various other necessities was tyranny. As Edmund Burke explained to his countrymen, "Liberty inheres in some sensible object, and every nation has formed to itself some favorite point which by way of eminence becomes the criterion of their happiness . . . Liberty might be safe or endangered in twenty other particulars without their being much pleased or alarmed. *Here* they felt its pulse; and as they found that beat, they thought themselves sick or sound."[3]

Of all the colonies, the burden of imperial policy probably fell least heavily on New England, yet it was New Englanders who "found that beat" and thought themselves most sick, who spearheaded the several non-importation initiatives between 1764 and 1770, and who wrung from the British the repeal of all but the tea tax.

The trade war continued during the first two years of the shooting war. The British blockaded New England's ports, attacked its merchant shipping, crippled its fisheries, and intercepted its important trade routes to the West Indies. These depredations affected the region's exports more than its imports, worsening its trade imbalance. But by mid-1778, American privateers had seized British merchant ships and cargo worth an estimated £18 million in attacks that diverted the Royal Navy sufficiently to weaken the British blockade.

In 1778, the French, Spanish, and Dutch declared themselves for the American cause and entered the war. For them, the American war was merely Act V (out of VII) in their second Hundred Years War against England. Dutch investors, who throughout the eighteenth century had been the principal holders of East India Company debt, Bank of England stock, and England's public debt, withdrew their funds from British consuls in 1780 and lent the United States 10 million guilders. At 5 percent, Dutch investors did far better than if they had invested at home, but France would pay dearly for its contribution to the American cause. The intolerable drain it placed upon the French public purse led directly to the fateful calling of the Estates-General in 1789.[4]

Valuable as they were to the American war effort, foreign loans accounted for less than 8 percent of the funds necessary to prosecute the war. Domestic loans provided another 10 percent, state debt issues contributed 18 percent, and state seizures of (Tory? tax delinquent?) properties provided 17 percent. Only 6 percent of the moneys to finance the war came from taxes (tariffs and excise taxes). Lacking the power to levy direct taxes *before* the Articles of Confederation (1777), and denied the power to do so *after*, Congress paid the remaining 40 percent of the costs of the war by printing money.[5]

The colonies had gone into the crisis with a currency supply of $10 million in specie equivalent, as well as $18 million in fiat money issued by the states and strongly backed by a commitment on their part to fund redemption out of taxes.[6] In May 1775, the Continental Congress authorized the emission of $6 million worth of paper "continentals," which initially exchanged with specie at par on the promise of their tax-funded convertibility. But with the issue of another $9 million within the year, the continental began—slowly at first—to slide. Although it was legal tender, the states would not accept it in payment of state taxes, nor would they vest the Confederation government with the power to tax for their redemption in specie. By the time new emissions ceased in January 1780, the $241.5 million of bills outstanding were exchanging with specie at 40:1; when they stopped circulating altogether in April 1781, the continental dollar was worth two-thirds of a cent. Congress eventually retired them at 100:1.

The farmers of Massachusetts came home from the war to a serious depression. Evidence of their straitened circumstances can be seen in the frequency of "dooming" in the town tax valuations of 1784–1786. "Dooming" was the name given to the consistent evasion, underreporting, and downgrading of land quality. To assessors, farmers characterized their unimproved land as "unimproveable," their meadow as pasture, and their valuable salt-marshes as "land under water." Assessed valuations plunged.

A depression is, of course, to be anticipated in any postwar adjustment. But in this case the adjustment was made more difficult because of fiscal mismanagement on both the national and state levels. Funding the national debt privileged the holders of government bonds at the expense of both taxpayers and holders of continentals. While establishing the nation's credit in European bond markets had the highest priority, the vanishing purchasing power of the continental became an "inflation tax" of $12 million a year on those left holding them.

Massachusetts taxpayers bore a still greater burden. Every state with the exception of Rhode Island (always a rogue elephant when fiscal restraint was called for) came out of the Revolution committed to accelerated repayment of its war debt, but had then been forced to yield to voters' demand for relief from oppressive taxation and fiscal austerity. In Massachusetts, however, "the extremist wing of the urgency faction" had control of the state senate and in 1785 pushed through an excessively harsh program of fiscal restraint and high property and excise taxes in an "impossible" attempt to pay off its $5 million war debt and redeem its fiat currency by the end of the decade, that is, within four or five years.[7] The state's tax burden had increased fivefold over prewar levels—a burden nearly doubled by deflation, a depreciated state note issue, specie conversion, and the export of specie to Congress (which had requisitioned it) and abroad. Edwin J. Perkins estimates that the state's per capita debt to holders of state bonds and state securities amounted to about one-third of what he calls "prevailing incomes."[8]

To get the cash to pay their taxes, Massachusetts residents were forced to sell property and their means of livelihood. County sheriffs, held personally responsible for tax collecting, pursued delinquent taxpayers through the courts with writs of execution against their real and personal property.[9] Farms, farm equipment, and animals were seized for nonpayment of taxes and default on loans, and were auctioned at fire-sale prices. Farmers in the western counties of Hampshire, Worcester, and Berkshire were the most hard-pressed: "Petitions for relief poured into the state legislature in the first half of 1786, all to no avail."[10] Shays's Rebellion broke out in August. As an insurrection of beleaguered farmers it was easily quelled, but as a demonstration of populist politics it had considerably more significance. It forced a complete relaxation of the state's punishing fiscal austerity,[11] and its dire implications loomed over the constitutional debates in Philadelphia that soon followed.[12]

A closer look at Shays's Rebellion will help us better understand the link between the Revolution and the changing agricultural economy of Massachusetts. Agricultural productivity, measured with selected data from the 1786 state tax valuation, was discovered to be significantly higher in those towns opposing the rebellion than in those supporting it. The rebellion was a consequence of the transformation taking place in the rural economy of New England, where the transition to capitalism was being played out. In the remainder of this essay, I shall explore that process and its consequences for economic growth.

THE TRANSFORMATION OF THE RURAL ECONOMY

We begin to understand the transition to capitalism in the rural economy of eighteenth-century New England by moving from the Revolution and its discontents to a consideration of the structural changes that brought it about. One of the initial conditions of a successful shift to capitalism is a demographic transition—that is, population growth generated by a rapidly declining mortality rate, moderated by a declining fertility rate. The fundamental (but complex) relationship between a population system—its size, rate of growth, age structure, sex ratio, fertility, mortality, morbidity, migration, nuptiality, life expectancy—and its economic system is so intimately reciprocal that it is often modeled as a feedback loop, a metaphor borrowed from automatic machinery to underscore the mutual codetermination of the two systems. But the determinants of population have never been entirely endogenous, and the dynamics of their interaction with the economy have never been entirely automatic. There are "veto points" all along the loop where changes in institutions, culture, and household preferences intervene to check the responses dictated from within the loop.[13] New England, and particularly Massachusetts, have been of special interest to historical demographers because the link between "modernization" and the demographic transition that began there at the end of the eighteenth century provides evidence of the effectiveness of these veto points.

We learned in the previous essay that fertility in seventeenth-century New England was extremely high, "higher even than in the England the settlers left." Thereafter, all settled regions of the country, led by New

England, experienced a steady decline in the rate of population growth from a high of 5 percent per year in the seventeenth century to 3 percent in the eighteenth and nineteenth centuries.[14] But the population growth rate is too aggregate a measure to capture the most relevant "veto point," the decisions of individual couples about family size.

The most careful family-level study for Massachusetts is Daniel Scott Smith's dissertation on Hingham.[15] In the seventeenth century, Hingham women all married and had a minimum of 6.5 children and an average of 7.6 children. The average fell sharply to 4.6 between 1691 and 1715, an instance of "astounding" fertility control in response to "foreclosed opportunities," Indian wars, and the out-migration of propertyless young men. The decline continued through a devastating smallpox epidemic in 1751, and by the mid-nineteenth century, Hingham women were having on average only 2.8 children. By the mid-eighteenth century, there are many signs of a profound alteration in the rural family. Daughters marrying out of birth order, sons marrying before the death of their fathers, decreasing intergenerational property mobility, and the pronounced decline in the naming of babies after parents or biblical figures, all signal, says Smith, the shift from "family of orientation" to "family of procreation" that is the precursor of both modernization and demographic transition.

Maris Vinovskis explains that the fertility decline in Massachusetts was caused by the adoption of modern attitudes and instrumental values: efficiency, diligence, orderliness, punctuality, frugality, honesty, rationality, experimentation, integrity, self-reliance, responsibility for consequences to others, and postponed gratification. "Most of the available research suggests that those individuals and families that have these characteristics that we might call 'modern' may also have lower fertility—even after controlling for their socioeconomic backgrounds."[16]

Modern values are nourished in urban settings, and by 1800, fully one-third of Massachusetts' population lived in what the Census defines as an urban place (at least 2,500 people). But a parallel fertility decline took place in rural places as well (Table 2.1). Vermont experienced a drop in the crude birth rate even more precipitous than that in Massachusetts, although as late as 1850 fully 98 percent of its population was still living on

TABLE 2.1   Number of children under age 5 per 1,000 white women, 20–44

Region	1800	1810	1820	1830
United States	1,281	1,290	1,236	1,134
Urban	845	900	831	708
Rural	1,319	1,329	1,276	1,189
New England	1,098	1,052	930	812
Urban	827	845	764	614
Rural	1,126	1,079	952	851
Mid-Atlantic	1,279	1,289	1,183	1,036
Urban	852	924	842	722
Rural	1,339	1,344	1,235	1,100
South Atlantic	1,345	1,325	1,280	1,174
Urban	861	936	881	767
Rural	1,365	1,347	1,310	1,209

Source: Donald Bogue, *The Population of the United States* (Glencoe, Ill.: Free Press, 1959).

farms. From 1800 to 1830, New England as a whole had the lowest refined birth rate (defined as number of children under age five per 1,000 white women ages 20–44) of any region in the United States. It also had the lowest urban and the lowest rural birth rates in the country, and experienced the most rapid fertility decline of any region across these four decades. This suggests that region effects and sector effects played a major role in the determination of fertility, but all regions and all sectors succumbed to period effects. The *times* they were a-changin'.

The changing times can be observed through measurable proxies of those values we are calling "modern": school attendance (especially of women) and literacy (see Table 2.2).

Perhaps the most significant predictor of declining marital fertility rates is the increase in the female labor force participation rate. Vinovskis estimates that at any one time, approximately one-quarter of Massachusetts girls ages fifteen and sixteen were in the labor force in this period, and given the high turnover rate of female employment, the proportion ever employed would have been much larger. As a case in point, the employment of women at home began during our period, and by 1831, there were already more females than males employed as outworkers in the Lynn boot and shoe industry.[17]

Industrial outwork as a stage in the modernization process will be discussed at some length later in this essay, and in still greater detail in the essay to follow, but there is a kind of "modernization" that is neither education, nor urbanization, nor industrialization, although it drove them all: market orientation. Lee A. Craig's analysis of the fertility transition across the rural North is in fact a market model in which household fertility decisions are driven by relative prices in three markets: land, labor, and capital.[18] In Craig's model, the farm family's decision about family size is determined by a calculation of the *net* benefits—that is, benefits minus costs—of an additional child to the family economy. The benefit of children in the farm family is the value they add to family production or household income; the cost of children is "the costs of endowing [them] with either a start in adult life or a bequest in exchange for old age security," that is, the costs of giving them either a new farm or the family farm.[19]

Relative to the Midwest or the frontier, rural New England offered the most opportunities for children to contribute to household income either on the family farm or by working for others. But the high price of land made New England children costly to endow; so much more costly than in

TABLE 2.2 Education

	NE	MA	NC	SC	SA
Percent of all whites 5–9 in school, 1840	82	50	28	14	16
Percent of white females in school, 1850	76	60	56	40	35
Percent of free black females in school, 1850	49	19	18	7	2
Percent illiterate over 20, 1850	1	5	7	15	14

Source: Constructed from data in Maris Vinovskis, *Fertility in Massachusetts from the Revolution to the Civil War* (New York: Academic Press, 1981), pp. 122–129 and fig. 8.1.

Notes: NE = New England; MA = Middle Atlantic; NC = North Central; SC = South Central; SA = South Atlantic.

the Midwest or on the frontier that it can explain why farm family fertility was lower in New England than in any other agricultural region of the country. Thus we can use Craig's model to forge the link between the fertility decline and the emergence of a market economy in New England.

The concept of a market economy is difficult to render unambiguously because the word "market" is used to denote diverse and contradictory things. The neighborhood flea market is a market, as were the medieval "markets ouverts," the village haymarkets and cornmarkets, the 800 market fairs that took place annually in seventeenth-century England, and the old Faneuil Hall Market in Boston. In this essay, I will call these "marketplaces."

We also use "market" to speak of world currency markets, the common market, the market in porkbelly futures, the bond market, the stock market. Or we speak more abstractly of "the labor market" and "the capital market," and, on still another level, "the free market." The market idea becomes larger, and as it does it becomes more abstract and more hegemonic, until as the "market economy" it comes close to being a synonym for capitalism.

A market economy is not a place or even a thing, but a *process* by which the economies of distinct marketplaces get folded in to one another. By folded in, I mean that the separate prices that prevail in each marketplace for the same good, labor, and risk tend to approach, mesh with, and converge toward those in other marketplaces. The price differentials between marketplaces narrow over time as buyers seek cheap markets and sellers seek dear markets. As the market expands, it widens the opportunities for productive employment at higher returns, generates increasing returns to specialization and division of labor, exploits economies of scale, and expands the reach of the market again.

If that which we call a market economy is a process of price convergence, let us then use that as its working definition: a market economy is a region within which differences in the prices of the same good, net of transportation costs, tend to narrow and eventually vanish in a process of convergence toward a single price. We now have an empirical test: from annual observations, over time, of the variance of prices for each commodity, the onset of convergence dates the onset of the market process. In the case of corn, English hay, potatoes, and rye, the convergence began between 1785 and 1795.

We would consider it even more persuasive if we could "catch" New England farmers in the act of making decisions about crop mix and land use on the basis of past, present, and expected future prices. But with the records those farmers left, this has not been possible. This kind of supply-elasticity can be inferred, however, at least for one kind of "crop," when it can be shown that the slaughter weight of hogs is correlated with the ratio of pork prices to corn prices. This relationship, although weak in the late eighteenth century, grows stronger over time, and is convincing by 1820. Although a hog was always butchered for the Christmas ham, farmers by 1820 will embed that decision in a market calculation.

The process of convergence depends on the willingness of buyers and sellers to travel between marketplaces. As "the journeying travellers joined village to village and enlightened the farms as they went," price differentials were arbitraged away.[20] But the high cost of hauling a wagon long distances over poor roads to unfamiliar places on the basis of little information, much uncertainty, and unlikely credit, together with the opportunity cost of man-days lost from work at home, all worked to impede mobility, delay convergence, and limit the size of the market. The emergence of a market economy depends upon evidence that these impediments were surmounted.

From the wealth of information in farmers' account books, we discover that farmers with a wagon and a team or two of oxen hauled their goods an average of about twenty to twenty-five miles per trip, but there were also long trips of well over one hundred miles. Mapping their journeys, it appears that each farmer moved out from his farm along a multitude of vectors like the spokes of an eccentric wheel radiating in a star pattern around his farm (Figure 2.1). It is the search pattern one would expect from farmers who were looking around to make the best deal—as they literally were, "it being the common rule that most men walked by in all their commerce, to buy as cheap as they could and to sell as dear."[21] Despite much that has been written to the contrary, farmers' account books show that transport

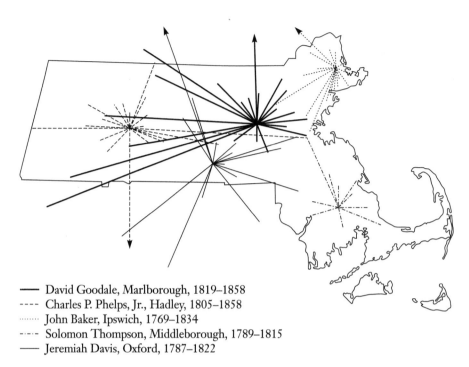

— David Goodale, Marlborough, 1819–1858
---- Charles P. Phelps, Jr., Hadley, 1805–1858
······ John Baker, Ipswich, 1769–1834
–··– Solomon Thompson, Middleborough, 1789–1815
— Jeremiah Davis, Oxford, 1787–1822

FIGURE 2.1   The pattern of hauling trips with load and wagon: five Massachusetts farmers.

Source: Winifred Barr Rothenberg, *From Market-Places to a Market Economy: The Transformation of Rural Massachusetts, 1750–1850* (Chicago: University of Chicago Press, 1992).

costs were not prohibitive and were unlikely to have isolated farmers from markets. At transport costs averaging between 15 and 17 cents a ton-mile in this period, farmers could afford to travel considerable distances, and they did.

Having established that marketing was only minimally constrained by transport costs, we turn our attention to the market towns that were the destinations of these hauling trips. New England's landscape was a profusion of small towns and villages, each of which may well have been set off in the seventeenth and early eighteenth centuries as "a space to plant community," but by 1800, each of them had evolved into "a place to support commerce."[22] Shrewsbury, Springfield, Leicester, Hadley, Dedham, Ipswich, Braintree, Roxbury, Worcester, Northampton, Providence, Woodstock (Connecticut), Northborough, Bolton, Grafton, Princeton, Westborough, Taunton, Acton, Cambridge, Concord, Groton, Harvard, Littleton, Lunenburg, Sutton, Easthampton, Southampton, Wendell, Williamsburg, Templeton, Pepperell, Sudbury, Mansfield, Newton, Marlborough, Brighton, Ware, Kingston, Waltham, Petersham, Westfield, Suffield (Connecticut), Andover, Lancaster, and Duxbury—these towns were the creation of farmers' marketing patterns. The smaller towns remained nodes in an extensive marketing pattern that reached from inland villages to world markets.[23] In each strategically located town, increasing population density gave rise to a more highly elaborated matrix of linkages, economies of scale, falling transaction costs, and new marketing institutions that tended to cluster in central places.

Among the new market institutions to emerge in the rural hinterlands of Boston immediately after the Revolution was a rural capital market. The emergence of a rural capital market is arguably even more important to the making of a market economy and the economic development of the countryside than is the emergence of a commodity market. On the eve of the Revolution, New England had the lowest per capita wealth and "the most dismal outlook" of Britain's American colonies.[24] Yet so rapid was its rate of growth following independence that by 1840 per capita income in the North was over 30 percent higher than in the South. Much of that impressive growth was due to the development of effective mechanisms and institutions for collateralizing land, for motivating the accumulation of savings in the farm economy, and for channeling those savings out of declining sectors and toward higher returns in the commercial, manufacturing, and infrastructure sectors. The dominant mechanism driving that transformation was a capital market.

Some credit instruments, like promissory notes, penal bonds, and mortgages, were familiar to the earliest settlers, but after 1781, under the usury ceiling, interest rates behaved more like prices, endorsed notes were more negotiable, credit networks were larger and more far-flung, and an entirely new menu of investment opportunities became available to rural residents.

Analysis of a sample of rural probates in Middlesex County, Massachusetts, finds that after 1781, decedents had held state and federal government securities, as well as shares in bridges, turnpikes, and the Middlesex Canal; marine, fire, and life insurance companies; banks; the Boston Manufacturing Company; the Boston Hat Manufactory; the Glass Manufactory; Newton Iron Works; Hamilton Manufacturing Company; Merrimack Manufacturing Company; Boott Cotton Mills; Lawrence Manufacturing Company; Tremont Mills; Otcheco Manufacturing Company; Nashua Manufacturing Company; several early railroads; the Boston Type and Stenotype Foundry; and the Massachusetts Hospital Life Insurance Company. In addition to industrial stocks, the investments that rural investors made in banks and insurance companies—particularly the Massachusetts Hospital Life Insurance Company—would have found their way through the secondary market into industrial stocks.

It is particularly significant that decedents' holdings of farm physical capital—implements and livestock—declined sharply as a share of their total wealth after 1781, while the share of wealth they held in the form of financial assets tripled for even the poorest quarter of the sample; rose four- and fivefold for the third and second quartiles, respectively; and increased by a factor of thirteen for the wealthiest rural wealthholders.

Perhaps most indicative is the finding that for the sample as a whole, the wealth elasticity of demand for financial assets—the percentage increase in financial asset holdings consequent on a 1 percent increase in wealth—rose from 0.4 before the Revolution to 2.0 after 1781. This is evidence of the endogenous process by which the growth of wealth itself tends to increase the liquidity of financial assets and enhance the efficiency of the capital market.

To establish when a labor market in Massachusetts agriculture emerged, it is necessary to submit the wage rates that farmers paid their day laborers to a test of convergence. By using a process similar to that used for commodity prices, one can use the onset of wage convergence to date the beginnings of a farm labor market.

We learn what farm work in New England was like from the diary of Abner Sanger, a New Hampshire farm laborer whose extraordinary journal records his every transaction between October 1774 and December

Advertisement for Boston Agricultural Warehouse and Seed Store, Quincy Hall, South Market Street, Boston. *(Boston Athenæum.)*

Most New Englanders continued to farm in the Revolutionary years. This picture shows a more typical scene than the "Onion Maidens" in Chapter 1. Here a farmer is using draft animals to plow and haul materials. Farmers increasingly were linked into markets in these years, as they traveled and sold their products within New England. Adam Smith wrote that the division of labor is limited by the extent of the market, and as agricultural markets expanded significantly at this time, farmers specialized in particular cash crops and used the proceeds to invest and to buy goods.

1794. In the fall, he raked, heaped, and burned debris and worked into the night watching the fires from trees that were burned for the ashes. The greater part of every winter day he hewed logs, peeled bark, chopped wood, and carried it on his back to the house. During the following year, he planted, hilled, hoed, gathered, husked, shelled, and threshed corn; poled beans; threshed oats and rye; took grain and provender to the mill;

planted potatoes and dug them up; winnowed beans; sawed shingles; pulled and swingled flax; and shoveled, carted, and spread dung. He mowed, raked, and stacked hay, turning it to dry and putting fence up around the stacks because the barn was too small to hold it. He made a hog pen, crafted a rack for drying pumpkins, and heaped up chip dung around the house for winter insulation. He felled brouse (very coarse forage) for the cattle and horses and trained them to eat it. He built a soap trough and a sugar trough, tapped sugar maples, and boiled syrup. He made and repaired shoes. He laid a floor. He did masonry work on the chimney and helped frame a new house and barn. He cleared the brook of brush and logs. He made brooms, carted clay, and butchered the hogs. He harrowed and sowed and went from farm to farm trying to get someone to come over to plow. He repaired roads and bridges, mortared and plastered, mended tackle, bottomed chairs, and made a log fence.

One presumes that every New England farm laborer was hired to do these tasks. But the reader will want to learn more about Abner Sanger. He learned surveying from *Batchellor's Manual*, kept accounts for his brother, and read *Paradise Lost*, Edmund Burke, John Locke, Bishop Butler's *Analogy*, John Adams's letters, Daniel Leonard's *Massachusettensis*, and Jonathan Edwards's "Careful and Strict Enquiry into the Modern Prevailing Notions of Freedom of the Will." One morning he "spent a while talking about Verses," and he wrote in his journal every day for all but six of 968 consecutive days. When he was imprisoned as a Tory in 1777, the Committee of Safety released him without the £500 bond required of Loyalists because, they wrote, he is "very poor and of a lo make."[25] Sanger continued to reap for 3 shillings a day even after he learned that reaping was paying 4 shillings. In that, as in much else, he was idiosyncratic, but the labor market emerged without him. The onset of wage convergence dates the emergence of a labor market process between 1795 and 1808, roughly simultaneous with the emergence of a farm commodity market between 1785 and 1795, and a rural capital market after 1781.[26]

With commodity markets, capital markets, and labor markets in place in much of rural Massachusetts by the late eighteenth century, it remains to forge the link between the increasing dominion of the market and the improvement of an agriculture with little if any mechanization or technological change, no exploitation of scale economies, and little increase in the capital invested in farming over the region and time period of this essay.

In a predominantly agricultural economy in which labor is the principal input, the growth rate of farm labor productivity may be used to measure the growth rate of the economy. Farm labor productivity (measured as the ratio of an index of farm wages to an index of prices at the farm gate) was fairly stable from 1750 to 1775, fell during the war years, but in the late 1780s, *simultaneous* with the demonstrably improved performance of commodity, labor, and capital markets, began to rise steadily at about 1 percent annually throughout this period and into the 1840s (see Figure 2.2).

Index

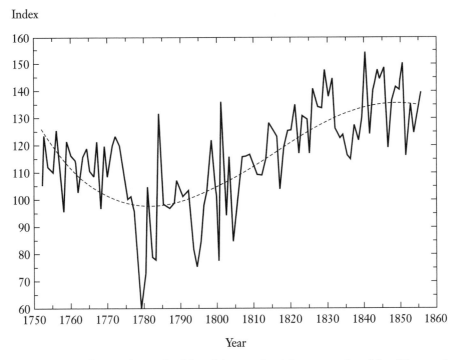

Year

FIGURE 2.2 The trend growth of farm labor productivity, 1750–1850. *Note:* The trend was regressed on a ratio of farm wages to farm commodity prices.

Source: Winifred Barr Rothenberg, *From Market-Places to a Market Economy: The Transformation of Rural Massachusetts, 1750–1850* (Chicago: University of Chicago Press, 1992).

That productivity growth and improved market integration were simultaneous is the core thesis of this essay. The increasingly hegemonic market acted as both carrot and stick, promising to reward effort and to punish error. Those New England farms that survived the competition of the western grains, meats, and livestock that came through the Erie Canal after 1825 did so by a painful adjustment to the production of a new mix of crops, a fundamental reorganization of the production process, and increased labor effort. In return, the expanding market proffered, as the carrot, the "Smithian" growth made possible by increased specialization.

Specializing away from grains was one of a number of "surviving strategies" that New England farmers adopted in response to western penetration.[27] Farms close to proliferating urban places grew hops, flax, herbs, celery, rutabaga, beets, winter squashes, pumpkins, carrots, parsnips, turnips, cabbages, onions, tomatoes, asparagus, string beans, and peas, as well as peaches, pears, rhubarb, a variety of apples, strawberries, cherries, damson plums, quinces, cranberries, and wine grapes.[28] Many farms in close proximity to their markets specialized in milk, butter, and cheese. The cultivation of broomcorn, first for cattle feed and then for the factory manufacture of brooms, began in Hadley and in parts of Connecticut during the first decade of the nineteenth century when brooms, shipped down the Connecticut River to New York City, became an important export from Hampshire County.[29] After 1845, cigar leaf tobacco would become the major export crop of Connecticut River valley farms in Massachusetts and Connecticut. Because none of these commodities is enumerated in tax valuations, their quantitative importance remains in doubt, but the diversification and commercialization of crops testify to "the manifestation of a powerful will to succeed by farming."[30]

More important as a strategy for survival than new tillage crops was the shift from tillage crops to hays and from natural hay (fresh and salt-marsh) to the cultivated and consistently more valuable English hay. As early as 1786, English or upland meadow had become the most highly assessed use of farm land. Because hay is too cheap and bulky to bear transport costs, local farms in close proximity to urban places secured uncontested access to livery stables, a reliable source of demand that grew as urbanization expanded.

Complementing the specialization in hay was an increased emphasis on livestock production and dairying. By 1801 the number of grazing animals (cattle, oxen, and horses; sheep were seldom enumerated) was more than two and a half times what it had been in 1771. Under market incentives, the better care of livestock generated positive feedback for the whole farm enterprise. Stabling and stall feeding produced, at a stroke, more and better manure, better hays, improved crop yields, shortened fallow, leguminous feeds in rotation, more selective breeding, fatter stock with a higher proportion of edible weight, and higher quality dairy products. Connecticut River valley farmers built up their herds and sent the excess stock up to summer pastures in the hill country of western and northern New England, where pastoral agriculture was fast becoming the region's most important enterprise.

It is far truer of the hill country of northern New England than it is of the Connecticut landscape for which it was written that "Nature out of her boundless store / Threw rocks together and did no more."[31] Vermont and sheep are peculiarly adapted to each other, and between 1809, when the first merino sheep were introduced from Spain, to the 1840s when, for a number of reasons, the price of wool plunged, most of the farms in Vermont, New Hampshire, and Maine were given over to sheep. "Except for a few remote districts . . . every town had more than 1,000 sheep, while some of them possessed 5,000, and a few in the Connecticut Valley and the Champlain Valley had been transformed into vast sheep runs where the numbers totaled more than 10,000 per town."[32] By 1830, the wool clipped from Vermont sheep alone sold for $1.2 million.

According to Robert Livingston, upon whose "Essay on Sheep" this paragraph draws, merino sheep are thickly clad down to their ankles in a greasy coat described as "so much finer and softer than the common wool as to bear no part of comparison with it."[33] On the animal, the wool is twisted into a corkscrew about three inches long, but untwisted it draws out to nearly six inches. The average clip from one of Livingston's rams weighed over six pounds washed, three times as much as that from a common sheep. Thereafter, so zealously were they bred that by mid-century many of Vermont's prize rams were shearing as much as twelve pounds of unwashed (nine pounds of washed) wool.[34]

Before the fall of wool prices, a full-blooded extra-fine merino breeding ram would sell for "as much as $3,500 to $5,000 per head," and their service at stud for $2,000 to $3,000 per season.[35] By the mid-1840s, however, too many farms had been turned into sheep runs—Vermont had more than six times as many sheep as people—the protective tariff had been removed, and cheaper western wool had come east through the Erie Canal.[36] The price of Vermont wool dropped from 58 cents to 25 cents a pound, and the merino mania, indeed the sheep mania, gradually subsided.

Yet the New England north country remained a robust agricultural economy, at least through our period of study. Despite the blows rained upon the hill towns by the exceptionally cold year of 1816, the threat of British invasion through Canada during the War of 1812, the bankruptcy of small textile mills after 1815, and the opening of the Erie Canal in 1825 (which toppled Vermont from its place as the leading wool- and wheat-growing state), Harold Wilson calls 1790–1830 the "summer" of the region's economic history. New Hampshire's population nearly doubled, Vermont's more than tripled, and Maine's grew fourfold.

For many farmers, the most promising survival strategy was to leave the family farm and pursue other opportunities provided by the workings of the rural labor and capital markets. In a single entry in Abner Sanger's diary, we are given a glimpse of how it came about, not as a macroeconomic process of intersectoral shift, but one man, one boy, one girl at a time.

> September 13, 1777: Young Isaac [Wyman] come to me . . . he talk of not working any more for his Father till he has a Deed of ye New Farm. Also Young Thos Barker come along by and has talk about it.

Abner says no more about it, but we have been vouchsafed a glimpse of the process by which the emerging labor market posed a threat to patriarchal authority, the primary institution of rural culture, and scattered its young.

Did Young Isaac leave home? Did he persuade Young Tom to go too? If so, where did they go? To do what? What did they know how to do? What skills did they have?

The versatility of Yankee farm boys is legendary:

A New England farmer, having finished his attention to autumnal duties, thought of going to Europe to dispose of the timber cut from his last new field. His eldest son received the following orders to be observed during his absence. "John, you may work in the smith's shop till you have iron shod the plow and the cart wheels you have made, after which you may either build a saw or grist mill for yourself, on your own place. If I should not return in three months, you may repair and adjust the old quadrant, and take charge of the old sloop, after you have new decked her. Joseph will help you spin the new rigging the sloop will want, after he has finished the loom for your mother to weave a top-sail on which; after turning the rounds for the spinning wheel, he may plow the old field, and then go on a voyage to Labradore for cod, or a-whaling to Falklands Island, just as he likes. You must take command of the sloop yourself, load her for the West Indies, unless you find that governor Phillips' last price will do for young stock and provisions; if so go to New Holland, and I shall be home, God willing, to welcome your return. My son, Joseph, it is time to leave off making wooden clocks and fiddles, tan the hides and make shoes for the family."

Samuel Blodget continues: "This is not beyond the character of the people, however it may agree in the minutiae with any known incidents."[37]

This excerpt is apocryphal, but not entirely so. In the probate inventories of yeomen and husbandmen, in addition to farm implements, can be found mill rights, shops, leather, tanyards, tanbark, shoemaking tools, woodworking tools, coopering tools, hoops, winches, fishing nets, wherries, bricks, looms, spinning wheels, beetles and wedges, cards for carding wool and cotton, and breaks and hackles for cleaning flax. If technology is defined as "the tools, skills and knowledge needed to make and do things," then the New England farmer was technologically equipped to move from the farm to the shop, and from the shop to the factory (where the next essay will pick up his story and add that of New England women as well).[38]

We can recover something of the role of individual agency in the transition out of agriculture from the collected autobiographies of a cohort of men born in the last quarter of the eighteenth century.[39] All of the men had quit the farm, and each of their stories could probably begin as Chauncey Jerome's did: "On the Monday morning that I took my little bundle of clothes, and with a bursting heart bid my poor mother good bye . . . and I perhaps never to see any of them again."[40]

> *Chauncy Jerome* began by "letting" himself to a farmer, "there being no manufacturing of any account in the country." He was then apprenticed to a clockmaker and shortly thereafter had his own clock factory in Litchfield County, Connecticut, where he soon made a fortune shipping five-dollar clocks to England.
>
> *John Ball* was the tenth child of an impoverished farm family on the Vermont frontier. He left home in his teen years, acquired some knowledge of business and law, ran a school in the South, traveled the Oregon Trail to the Pacific, and finally settled in Michigan where he speculated in real estate, administered the school system, and prospered.
>
> *Bronson Alcott*, Louisa's father, left his father's New Hampshire farm to peddle books throughout the South until he could afford to open his own school.
>
> *Arial Bragg* was orphaned at age eight and apprenticed to a shoemaker where he managed to save enough to buy back his indenture. He obtained tools and leather on credit and "went to work for the market" making shoes for slaves.
>
> *Asa Sheldon* was released from an indenture and worked as a house servant, farm laborer, and lumberman. He spent much of his later life as a teamster hauling goods to the South and hauling back cotton to markets in Baltimore, Philadelphia, New York, and Boston.
>
> *David Dodge's* father lost his savings in the Revolutionary War inflation and could not pay his debts, but he refused to move to the frontier. David left home, became a teacher and then a store clerk,

bought a store that failed, and invested in textile mills, all of which
failed.

Allen Trimble's father was among the first settlers to move his family
to Kentucky in 1784, where Allen learned to be a livestock drover.
Determined to take advantage of a wide price differential, he
drove hundreds of hogs through the wilderness to Virginia, where
he sold them at a profit of $8.00 per hundredweight.[41]

The young men who left the family farm made their lives hostages
to fortune. Not all of them prospered. Paul Johnson has plucked Mayo
Greenleaf Patch out of ignominious obscurity in order to make the point
that many who quit the farm did so because they had utterly failed within a
rural society that, at the beginnings of industrialization, was itself in crisis.[42] And having quit the farm, these "little traders," as Appleby calls them,
"however battered, had no place to turn except the market."[43]

Skilled artisans as a rule were better positioned to survive. Many kept a
farm as a hedge against the vicissitudes of commerce, thus playing a transitional role in the industrialization of New England. Deeply rooted as they
were in traditional rural society, artisans were also poised on the edge of
the modern world.

A recent study of joiners and woodworkers in two Connecticut towns
casts light on the responses of artisans to market opportunities.[44] These
joiners made chairs, desks, tables, bureaus, and chests of drawers. Some of
the surviving pieces are of museum quality. They also framed houses,
finished interiors, and made window sashes and doors. The shops were
small, 200 to 400 square feet, with two benches, two skilled journeymen,
and four young apprentices. Woodworking meshed well with farming, and
men and boys moved between the two easily as the seasons dictated. After
the Revolution, one of the towns (Woodbury) "became increasingly involved in the North Atlantic commercial world"; the other (Newtown)
chose to remain aloof from it, considering their furniture-making not so
much commodity production as what Cooke calls "familial or communal
reification."[45]

Sink in a cellar in Salem, Massachusetts. *(Courtesy of the Society for the Preservation of New England Antiquities.)*

New England cities began to have urban water systems in the early nineteenth century. They used wooden pipes, which did not last long but were far cheaper than expensive, imported iron. While most people continued to live in simple houses in the countryside, conditions of life were beginning to change for a fortunate few. The faucet was in the cellar so that water would flow through it by gravity.

By 1820 the two towns, eighteen miles apart, had drawn a world apart because Woodbury had become a magnet for artisans. The artisan, firmly anchored in rural society, can choose to make the mode, scale, and relations of production in his shop part of a household strategy that limits his market participation and determines the allocation of his labor between craft production and farm production. An artisan has that option because his farm is a hedge against the market, and because, without a heavy investment in fixed capital, he has no compelling scale economies that dictate the level of output. In short, with his farm as his safety net, the artisan will only produce an amount of his craft that will sell at a good price.

Newtown paid a heavy price for opting out of this commerce: in 1798, the two towns had almost the same number of males over twenty-one, but Newtown had only two-thirds as many males ages eighteen to twenty-one.[46] The young men had left Newtown.

EARLY INDUSTRIAL CAPITALISM

It has been estimated that nearly two-thirds of the growth of per capita output in the United States between 1800 and 1840 can be attributed to the westward movement of agriculture, which by itself gave each man so much more land to work with that it must have appeared to push the point of diminishing returns to the infinitely receding horizon. But in New England, where crowding and land scarcity were facts of life, the growth of per capita output would come principally from manufacturing. The next essay treats this subject in far more detail; we deal here only with the beginnings of America's industrial revolution.[47]

By 1800, New England's landscape was already dotted with small industries: Paul Revere's copper-rolling mill in Canton;[48] cotton and wool textiles in the Blackstone, Merrimac, Connecticut, and Saco River valleys; boots and shoes in Lynn; glassware in Braintree; hats and caps in Danbury; paper in Norwich; wooden clocks in New Haven; pottery in Roxbury and Concord; cast-bronze, brass, and other metal trades in Bridgeport, Wallingford, New Britain, Waterbury, and Meriden; shovels and axes in North Easton; jewelry in Providence; mousetraps in Sharon and Watertown; and flour milling, distilling, iron foundries, and tanning scattered throughout. By 1850, New England had invested 75 percent more capital, employed 75 percent more workers, and produced 45 percent more output per manufacturing firm than the mid-Atlantic region, which had three times the population.[49]

The mechanized factory system of manufactures is associated with a wider scope for specialization and division of labor; higher real wages; enhanced mobility of labor and capital; the possibility of increasing returns; the agglomeration economies of urbanization; linkages to "ramifying nests of symbiotic enterprises";[50] increased labor force participation rates, particularly for women; incentives to improve the skills, education, and health (human capital) of the labor force; learning-by-doing; more machine power per worker and more workers with machines; and scope for technological innovation.

But a radical critique of capitalism argues that the alleged superiority of the factory mode of production derives from a *mis*-measure of the labor input; that if labor's input were measured properly, not in man-hour inputs per unit of output, but in human effort or energy per unit output, the mechanized, disciplined, coordinated, and ultimately coercive mode of factory production might well be found to use more labor (measured in units of human effort), and hence to be less rather than more efficient than nonmechanized production.[51]

One need not agree with this critique to appreciate it for raising one of the more important questions in the economic history of capitalist production: what was the principal source of labor productivity growth in the early factory system? Was it the fixed capital that labor had to work with? Was it the more efficient ordering of the factory environment? Or was it factory discipline, which at its most coercive enlisted (or "extracted") a level of sustained human effort that had never before been demanded of free persons?

Kenneth Sokoloff's study of thirteen early industries in the Northeast concludes that while machine-intensive technologies did indeed fundamentally alter the production process, the major source of productivity growth came from the growth of "total factor productivity," a residual input that includes both environmental factors—such as plant layout, material flows, and the degree of division of labor—and those things that are properly called "managerial," among which is the management of worker effort, or "what bosses do."[52]

But the "whiff of brimstone" that attaches to this mode of production has tended to come less from the ratcheting-up of worker effort than from the "expropriation of labor's surplus value"—that is, from the charge that labor was exploited. Exploitation here has to do not with labor's productivity per se, but with the relation between it and the wage rate.[53]

The issues raised here are important, and just because they are it is consoling that in fact many of the early industries "eased into" factory production via outwork. The first mechanized textile mill in the United States was Samuel Slater's water-powered spinning mill, built on the Blackstone River in Pawtucket, Rhode Island, in 1790. The spinning was done in the mill, but Slater "put out" webs of spun yarn to local households to be woven into cloth. All weaving in New England was done this way, by outworkers, before 1813.

Outwork in New England was a labor system that adapted easily to a variety of production methods. In the textile industry, spun yarn was put out by the spinning mill to be woven at home on handlooms and sold back to the mill for finishing. Palm-leaf hat braiding was more complex: Boston wholesalers imported the leaves from Cuba and the Virgin Islands, sold them to storekeepers (especially in New Hampshire and in Worcester County, Massachusetts, which became centers of the trade). The storekeepers split the leaf and sold it to their customers (on credit), who wove or braided it into hats that were sold back to the storekeeper (for store credits). The finished hats were sold to a Boston wholesaler, who in turn sold them to the plantation market in the South and in the West Indies.[54]

In the case of shoemaking, tanned leather was put out to women and children to be sewed at home into "uppers," which were then returned to the shop where male "bottomers" "lasted" and attached the sole. Because the sewing machine was not adapted to leather until 1860, outwork lasted longest in shoemaking. In 1831, the outwork shoe industry employed more than two-thirds of the entire population of Lynn.[55]

In every industry in which it figured, the use of outwork, particularly after 1810, testified to how the division of labor could answer an enormous expansion of market demand when a technology had not yet been developed to accommodate it. But the outworker was a transitional figure who occupied an anomalous position at the center of a system of linkages between farm and factory, household labor and hired labor, debtor and creditor, buyer and seller, manufacturer and retailer, artisan and laborer, middleman and producer. To minimize transaction costs, storekeepers opened spinning mills and mill owners opened stores, both thereby accommodating (or "locking-in") store customers who paid in outwork and outworkers who were paid in "truck." It was also a credit system that, by preempting or circumventing the use of cash, provided the mill with working capital at no interest in the form of workers' uncollected pay.[56] The function of outwork, then, was not to sustain and complement the agricultural economy, but to sustain and complement early industrialization.[57]

This it did with considerable success. In 1807, Massachusetts had 15 Slater-type cotton mills and 8,000 operating spindles; by the end of the following year there were 31,000 spindles; and by 1810 there were 109 mills in New England, more than half of which were in Massachusetts.[58] The prolonged interdiction of U.S. foreign trade mandated by Jefferson's Embargo of 1808, the Non-Intercourse Acts, and Macon's Bill No. 2 had depressed the price of southern cotton and inflated the price of domestic yarns and cloth, creating a widening margin between them in which Boston investors could profit.

Nathan Appleton and Francis Cabot Lowell rushed to seize the opportunity. The two men, who had made their money in shipping, importing dry goods, exporting pot- and pearl-ash, land speculation in Maine, compensation from the Spanish Claims Commission (see Chapter 6), and Boston real estate and wharf development, met in Edinburgh in 1810 to talk about introducing "improved manufacture" into New England textile manufacture. "Improved manufacture" meant machine weaving and the end of outwork weavers. It meant obtaining the Cartwright power loom, "the crowning glory of Britain's textile technology," whose export was forbidden by English law.[59] Lowell went to Manchester to observe it carefully and carried it back to Boston in his memory.

While in Britain, Lowell and Appleton observed as well the enlightened planning in Scotland of new industrial towns and rural mill villages, which were built to reflect a "climate of Improvement." Appleton had been appalled when he first saw Manchester in 1802, and had wished "for the hap-

Early view of Lowell, painted by Benjamin Mather in 1825. *(Courtesy Lowell Historical Society.)*

The Boston Associates—a group of merchants who used their capital from commercial ventures to found industrial joint-stock companies in the first few decades of the nineteenth century—developed this cotton textile complex at the falls of the Merrimack River. Named after Francis Lowell, one of the "associates," these Boston entrepreneurs built an entire town with water-powered spinning and weaving mills and machine shops, as well as housing for workers and managers.

piness of our country" that it "be long" without manufacturing.[60] But the encounter with Scottish improvement held out hope that an American industrial revolution could be designed "by human reason and human will."[61]

Upon his return to Boston, Francis Lowell gathered around him twelve carefully chosen men to subscribe $1,000 a share in $100 installments, building up "in measured increments" an initial capital of $400,000 for a mill to be located on the Charles River at Waltham, to begin operating in 1813. It would not be a proprietorship or a partnership, the forms of business organization familiar at the time, but a joint-stock company, assuring that the enterprise would outlive the lifetime of any or all of its owners and the liquidation of any investor's assets in it. And they carefully chose their market niche: heavy or "brown" sheeting, shirting and twills of no. 4 yarn, 44 picks to the inch (the finer British cloth averaged 50 and went as high as 180) and 2.75 yards to the pound (more than twice as heavy as fine British cloth, which exceeded 6 yards to the pound).

By 1845, the Boston Associates would become 80 men with interests in 31 textile companies controlling one-fifth of the total capacity of the American textile industry. Meanwhile, seventeen of them would serve as directors of seven Boston banks commanding over 40 percent of the city's authorized banking capital, twenty would be directors of six insurance companies carrying 41 percent of the state's marine insurance and 77 percent of its fire insurance, and eleven members would serve on the boards of five railroads operating in New England. Nathan Appleton alone served as president or director of 22 companies in the textile industry, was director of the Boston Bank and the Suffolk Bank, and was at one time or another the president, director, and finance commissioner of the Massachusetts Hospital Life Insurance Company, "the largest financial institution in New England." As if their overlapping business interests were not enough to knit them together, the Appletons, Lawrences, Cabots, Lowells, Jacksons, Brookses, Amorys, Thorndikes, Gorhams, and Duttons were all linked by marriage and cousinhood as well.[62]

The Boston Associates pioneered lasting innovations and fundamental change in area after area of business enterprise. The Cartwright power loom was not only "an important cost-saving innovation[;] it was in fact virtually a life-saving innovation."[63] With it in place, the vertical integration of the entire production process was possible. Water power (the associates owned the Locks and Canal Company), the machine shop (they pioneered the machine tool industry in New England), carding, flubbing, roving, spinning, weaving, bleaching, dyeing, calico printing, and finishing were brought under one roof, and the sale of the final product was commissioned through their own marketing house. Vertical integration alone resulted in substantial savings on transaction costs at every stage.[64]

The Boston Associates revived the corporation, "an all-but-moribund institution in late eighteenth century England," and exploited its almost limitless possibilities.[65] They renegotiated the balance between the public interest (which state-chartered corporations had been required, before 1800, to serve), and private interests (which, after 1900, they were permitted to serve). And they pioneered the separation of ownership and management that is characteristic of the modern corporation.

They developed new strategies of corporate finance and, by the not illegitimate use of "insider borrowing" and "insider lending," shaped banking institutions in their own image. Indeed, the conjunction of banking with the associates' corporate and manufacturing interests was so intimate that their privileged access to capital should be included in their vertical integration of the production process.

Naomi Lamoreaux has explained how the Boston Associates recruited capital for their mills, banks, and intermediary financial institutions. With immense skill, they perfected a circular process of self-financing that worked like "an alchemist's dream come true."[66] (1) The associates set up a new mill on a large water-power site for which they need a loan. (2) They obtain a corporate charter to open a new bank. (3) They subscribe a controlling interest in the new bank's capital stock. (4) They pay for the stock with a loan from another bank in which they hold a controlling interest. (5) They deposit the loan in the new bank. (6) They borrow back the deposit from the new bank to pay the debts of the new mill, using their shares of the new bank's stock as collateral. But this leaves the new bank without funds. (7) They sell stock in the new bank to their own insurance companies and charitable institutions (Massachusetts Hospital Life Insurance Company, for example), and/or the new bank issues its own notes (subject to the reserve requirement at the Suffolk Bank—also theirs) as currency.[67] Perhaps more Indian rope trick than alchemy, they created their own facts.

The associates made innovations in labor management that are in sharp contrast to the management style at the Slater mills. They planned livable industrial villages in the countryside (which did not last). They eased the transition of women into full and respectable participation in the industrial labor force. And in establishing the model for a labor force that was paid, not in truck or in credit, but in cash wages, they freed their workforce of the common-law taint of "servant," rendering them free to contract for work, and free to quit.[68] In all these respects, the Boston Associates played a critical role in what Robert J. Steinfeld has called "the invention of free labor."[69]

Not least, of course, they presided over a prodigious expansion of the industry. According to Robert Zevin, the annual production of the New England cotton textile industry increased from 46,000 yards of cloth in 1805 to nearly 142,000,000 yards in 1830. Value added from the cloth alone (apart from spun yarn and candle wicks) increased in the same period from $2,000 to $7,435,000. Indeed, cotton textiles, which accounted for less than 10 percent of manufacturing output in 1810, made up 67 percent of value added in all large-scale manufacturing in New England by the 1830s.[70] To accommodate growth of this magnitude, manufacturers had developed large water power sites on every river of any size in New England: the Housatonic, Connecticut, Quinebaug, Chicopee, Merrimack, Salmon Falls, Nashua, Saco, Androscoggin, Kennebec, Cocheco, and Penobscot, as well as Waltham-type mills built at Lowell, Lawrence, Manchester, Holyoke, Biddeford, Lewiston, Brunswick, Waterville, Augusta, Chicopee, Dover, and Newmarket.[71]

The expansion of cotton textile production carried with it the expansion of woolens, cast iron steam boilers, foundries, water wheels, and the machine-tool industries tied to it by forward and backward linkages. Carried with it, too, were the expansion and proliferation of city building and urban public services.

Think for a moment what the Boston Associates might have been—the robber barons who made America's second industrial revolution, or the "Mafia" who are *un*making Russia's. It is appropriate to reflect that not least among the many blessings New England received from a "wonder-working Providence" was that for several generations a remarkable group of honorable men, concerned above all for their reputations among honorable men, presided over the capitalist transformation of New England.

But a stubborn question haunts this celebration of the associates and the world they made. If the cotton textile industry they created in New England was so advanced, why did its survival depend upon prohibitive rates of tariff protection against England?

Cotton manufacturing in Massachusetts had been buffered against British competition since 1807, first by the Embargo and the Non-Intercourse Acts, and then by the British blockades and war. The resumption of trade in 1816 threatened the survival of every spinning and textile mill in New England. In that year, Congress, persuaded by Francis Lowell, imposed an ad valorem tariff of 25 percent on the value of imported cotton cloths with a specific tariff of 6.25 cents a yard; that is, any fabric that came in below 25 cents a yard would be taxed as though it were 25 cents a yard.

In 1828, the so-called Tariff of Abominations left the ad valorem rate at 25 percent but raised the floor to 35 cents a yard, a minimum tariff of 8.75 cents a yard. The average British cotton cloth entered the U.S. at 12.77 cents; the tariff on it was therefore not 25 percent but 68.5 percent (8.75/12.77).

Congressional action on a protective tariff against British cloth was Lowell's paramount interest. Peter Temin contends that Lowell's choice of low-count fabrics was a political strategy to defuse southern opposition in Congress. Robert Zevin argues that the choice of market niche was technologically determined, that New England's power looms were not yet adapted to produce the higher-end ginghams and fancy weaves that we imported from England. Both arguments imply a segmented market, which, if true, would have minimized the need for a tariff. Yet it is estimated that had the tariff been removed, even as late as 1833, it "would have reduced value added in [New England] textiles by, at a minimum, three-quarters . . . [and] about half of the industrial sector of New England would have been bankrupted."[72]

The question, then, still stands: why did textile production in New England need tariff protection from England when, in the niche it chose, it would appear to have been the more advantaged producer? The New England mills were integrated "from the ground up," whereas the industry in Lancashire was astonishingly disintegrated: spinning and weaving, as well as the spinning of coarse and fine yarns, were done not only in different mills but in different towns. The New England mills used ring spinning, a technology considered superior to the power mule used in Lancashire. The New England industry, it is true, was faced with far higher wage rates (Mark Bils estimates that they were 84 percent above the British pay scale), but as a consequence American mills hired a workforce that was 60 percent female, paid them 40 percent of the male wage, and adapted the machinery to accommodate them. And finally, the cost of shipping cotton from New Orleans to New England was one-third the cost of shipping it from New Orleans to Liverpool. Notwithstanding, writes Knick Harley, "British firms could have supplied Americans with the American industry's dominant fabrics about 20 percent more cheaply than they were made domestically."[73]

Three explanations have been offered. For Bils, the most telling cost advantage of English cotton cloth over American was the wage differential, a gap that even the altered gender mix could not close. Harley attributes Britain's cost advantage, curiously enough, to Lancashire's technological superiority. But a new study by Timothy Leunig attributes the British cost advantage to the superior productivity of the Lancashire workers. Even with what he concedes was an inferior technology, Lancashire mule spinners were 10 percent more productive than New England's ring spinners. "We know that *experience* was the primary determinant of labor productivity in cotton spinning . . . The New England cotton industry was never a successful exporter . . . This lack of success was caused not just by high wages but also by low levels of labor productivity."[74]

Which provokes another question: if the British could have undersold New England manufacturers in the American market, then why not let them do it? What compelling interests was the tariff protecting?

The best case that can be made for a protective tariff is that it promotes learning and the accumulation of knowledge, "the primary sources of economic development."[75] A protective tariff used in this way is part of a development strategy called import-substituting industrialization, in which participants deliberately fly in the face of comparative advantage in the furtherance of a more compelling long-run goal. In his well-known study estimating the sources of productivity growth in the cotton textile industry, Paul David wrote, "During the period 1833–39, learning-by-doing accounted for virtually eight-tenths of the average annual growth rate of total productivity, and was nearly three times as important as the rise of capital-intensity in maintaining the rather impressively rapid rate of increase [6.67 percent per annum] in output per man-hour."[76]

FOREIGN TRADE, SHIPPING, AND WHALING

"Protecting learning-by-doing" dresses up in new language the old "infant industry" argument for tariffs, but it cannot conceal their trade distortions and regressive distributional effects. The alternative would have been the "outward-oriented" development strategy of an open economy based on the export of the goods and services for which New England had a comparative advantage. It is possible to infer which commodities these would have been in the absence of a protective tariff from the composition of Massachusetts' exports in 1787.[77] Of exports, which totaled $3.5 million in that year, 10 percent was timber and wood products, nearly 30 percent was fish, another 10 percent was the re-export of wine and spirits, about 13 percent was whale oil and its derivatives, 8 percent was foodstuffs (flour, meat, potatoes, butter, corn, and beans), and the rest was livestock, potash and pearl ash, leather, cheese, hemp, naval stores, shoes, soap, and the re-export of sugar, tobacco, ginseng, and chocolate. These are, for the most part, primary products with very little value added, and in the production of which we would soon have lost any comparative advantage we may have had in 1787.

In the brief and glorious quarter-century between 1784 and 1807, "maritime commerce was the breath of life for Massachusetts."[78] The *Columbia* out of Boston established the trade route for silks, pepper, teas, seal skins, otter skins, sandalwood, and furs to and from Boston, the American Northwest, Nagasaki, and Canton—perhaps stopping on the way at the Falkland Islands for sea-elephant oil.

Thomas Lechmere established a trading post in Bombay; Augustine Heard of Ipswich, who would later be our preeminent trader in Canton, was already plying the trade routes to India in 1812. Vessels out of

View of Canton factories, ca. 1810. *(Courtesy Peabody Essex Museum, Salem, Mass.)*

    The flags of many European countries and the United States flew over these port buildings in China. New England merchants were very active in the China trade, and many fine houses in New England contained Chinese objects of various sorts. The arrival of New England merchant ships in China in the 1790s in a sense completes the impulse that drew Columbus out of Europe three hundred years earlier — the desire to find not a New World, but a new route to Asia.

Newburyport and Beverly opened trade with Russia in 1784. George Cabot sent tea, coffee, rum, and flour to the Baltic and St. Petersburg and brought back canvas, duck, hemp, and Russian and Swedish iron. Massachusetts vessels carried well over half of the American trade with St. Petersburg. Salem vessels sailed to Arabia for coffee, then rounded the coasts of Africa and continued on to Manila, Mauritius, the Dutch East Indies, and Sumatra, where in one year, 1793, the pepper trade earned the Salem merchant-adventurers a 700 percent profit.

> A few steps from the merchant's mansion [in Salem] lies his counting-room and wharf, where his favorite vessel is loading Russia duck, West India sugar, New England rum and French brandy for anywhere beyond the Cape of Good Hope; to return with goodness knows what produce of Asia, Africa and the Malay Archipelago . . . A Salem boy in those days . . . saw Demerara and St. Petersburg before he set foot in Boston, and if he had the right stuff in him, commanded an East-Indiaman before he was 25.[79]

The Far East trade went a long way toward resurrecting New England's maritime economy after the Revolution, but by 1816 the trade winds, so to speak, were no longer blowing out to sea. "The center of interest in Massachusetts shift[ed] from wharf to waterfall," and with it went the venture capital.[80]

Even the fisheries, restored and expanded by high prices and Congressional bounties after the Revolution, were in decline. The settlement of Newfoundland during the War of 1812 as a resident fishery for the British, and the competition of cheap Norwegian fish, came close to shutting the New England fisheries out of European markets. By 1840, the bulk of the New England catch was marketed within the United States and depended upon tariffs for its protection.[81] The fishermen of Marblehead, the premier fishing port of Massachusetts in 1807, were, by the end of our period, "producing shoes worth twice the average catch of the fishing fleet."[82]

While the wars and interwar period left much of the maritime economy hobbled, whaling prospered. At the beginning of the nineteenth century only Nantucket and New Bedford regularly sent out whalers, but by 1820 there were 16 whaling ports in New England, and 35 by 1835, the largest of which was New Bedford, home to half of all American whalers. Between 1816 and 1830, out of the New Bedford port alone, sperm oil production increased from 1,150 barrels to over 37,000 barrels, whale oil from zero to 34,000 barrels, and whalebone from zero to 295,000 pounds.

But the risks of whaling—uninsurable risks with all or nothing outcomes—were appalling. "Of the 763 vessels that can be traced, almost 40 percent were lost at sea."[83] With risks that huge, the calculation of profit rates is key to understanding the growth of the industry. The reports of profits on individual whaling voyages run the gamut from 363 percent to 1.3 percent. Alexander Starbuck estimated that two-thirds of the voyages expected to arrive at New Bedford would actually *lose* at least $1 million.

It comes as no surprise that the rate of return was neither the 363 percent Samuel Eliot Morison cited, nor the 1.3 percent attributed to Charles Enderby.[84] Nor is much credence given to Starbuck's estimate that 65 percent of the voyages expected to arrive at New Bedford in mid-century actually lost money. To explain the growth of whaling in the antebellum period, Lance Davis, Robert Gallman, and Karin Gleiter recalculated the returns to whaling (in 1850) relative to investment in other sectors. With the exception of steamboats on inland rivers, whaling offered returns as good as any (Table 2.3).

If it was possible for capital to earn as high a return in whaling as in any alternative investment, that is not true of labor. Converting the fractional "lays" of whaling crews into money wages and comparing them across sectors, "the wages of skilled, semi-skilled and unskilled seamen were less than 60 percent of the wages of workers ashore."[85] By the end of our period, an unskilled seaman made about $8.66 a month, whereas cotton mill operatives earned an average of 58 cents a day at the time, which is about $14 a month for a six-day week and a four-week month.[86] As early as 1820, a marked deterioration was observable in the quality of crews, which signaled a measurable decline in labor productivity. Higher wages in manufacturing had begun to draw seamen back to shore, bridging the great cultural divide that has, since time immemorial, separated landlubbers and seamen, farmers and fishermen, sailors and factory hands. Which is to

TABLE 2.3 Rates of return for whaling and other industrial sectors, 1850 (percent)

Sector	Percent
New Bedford whaling	15.2–24.0
Manufacturing	15.4
Agriculture, North	8.0
Agriculture, South, cotton	10.0
Steamboats, tributary	24.1
Steamboats, trunk	8.5
Central Pacific Railroad	13.4

Source: Lance E. Davis, Robert E. Gallman, and Karin Gleiter, *In Pursuit of Leviathan: Technology, Institutions, Productivity, and Profits in American Whaling, 1816–1906* (Chicago: University of Chicago Press, 1997), p. 456.

say that they became folded into the same, increasingly hegemonic labor market.

After 1816, and with the decline of seafaring of all kinds—maritime commerce, the fisheries, and whaling—it was no wonder that import-substituting industrialization was seen by the merchant-investors in the cotton textile industry to be more profitable than a staple economy organized around the production for export of commodities with declining value added.

CONCLUSION

"The invention of capitalism" in New England took place within a national economy that was not only growing but expanding.[87] The expansion of settlement westward provided an avid, continent-sized market, a vent for underpaid labor, and an agriculture where the most rapid growth of labor productivity in the economy took place.

But the years 1770 to 1830 have shape and coherence because they were a critical turning point in the economic history of New England. There were other turning points, to be sure. But it was in New England, in these transformative years, that the market economy emerged hegemonic over the relations of production and exchange in the rural economy.[88] Market-driven alterations in the family—declining marital fertility, female participation in the labor force, and the younger ages at which children left home—delivered labor from the farm to manufacturing. Market-driven alterations in credit markets enhanced liquidity and delivered capital accumulated in agriculture, shipping, and commerce to the burgeoning insurance, banking, manufacturing, financial, and infrastructure sectors. Markets worked to "unleash powerful forces that acted to raise productivity . . . without major additions to the stock of capital equipment."[89] And markets worked endogenously to nurture complementary industries in a way that ignited and fueled economic growth.

CHAPTER 3

The Industrialization of New England, 1830–1880

PETER TEMIN

IN 1830, MOST NEW ENGLANDERS lived on farms and grew much of the food they ate. By 1880, most New Englanders lived in cities, worked for wages, and bought their food. How and why did this happen? It was not that the farmers of 1830 were outside markets, as Winifred Rothenberg has shown in her description of the years before 1830. It was instead due to a shift of many, many workers from agriculture to industry, with all the adaptations in location and lifestyle that went with the change of work. We call this process industrialization, and this essay will describe its manifestation in New England.

The transformation of the New England economy in the middle fifty years of the nineteenth century was comparable in scope and intensity to the Asian "miracles" of Korea and Taiwan in the half century since World War II. In each case, a predominantly agricultural and rural society marked by older methods of production, transportation, and communication was replaced by a largely urban, industrial society utilizing the most modern of these methods. Although the United States as a whole experienced many of these changes, New England underwent an accelerated revolution that recreated patterns of life.

Agriculture played a small and passive role in these developments, contrasting sharply with its central role in the New England economy before 1830. The admirable progress of American agriculture in these years took place largely outside New England, in the Midwest and then on the Great Plains. The great expansion of agriculture and later, mining in the West created opportunities for New England to play a role in transporting the agricultural surplus to Europe and financing investments in the West, but they also caused hardship for New England agriculture. Displaced agricultural workers in New England were thus a ready reservoir of labor for the industrialization of the next half century.

WHY INDUSTRY GREW IN NEW ENGLAND

What led to this transformation of the New England economy? What were the forces that set this radical change in motion? One important factor is Anglo-American culture.[1] The Puritans who settled New England long before industrialization created an environment in which new enterprises could flourish—one that consisted partly of a stable government with clear laws and a judicial process that allowed laws to adapt to new problems undreamed of by the original legislators. Also important was the region's commitment to education. This provided a numerous entrepreneurial class with access to the latest knowledge, and it also was reflected in the high educational level of the Lowell workers and the creation of the Massachusetts Board of Education. New Englanders were well suited to take advantage of this favorable economic and legal environment. Nathan Appleton and Kirk Boott were not beloved by the cotton operatives who worked so hard for them in Lowell and other nearby cities, but they had the perseverance and skill to deploy large numbers of workers in the use of new technology. The synergy between the skill of industrial leaders and of the educated, hard-working machine operators made for industrialization in New England.

In addition to the factors that were unique to New England, industrialization in this region was part of the development of the United States as a whole. New England benefited from being part of this country—even though its cotton-textile industry suffered greatly during the Civil War. New England gained in two ways. First, the legal framework that allowed investors to have confidence in long-run commitments was strengthened by the commonality of laws in different states. The federal government did not engage in massive spending at this time, but it had an extremely important effect on economic activity by creating uniform rules of conduct for business behavior. Second, New England could exploit its comparative advantage within the United States. People in New England could engage in the activities that they performed best in the confidence that their products could be traded for other goods that were more expensive to make in New England. The United States was important, therefore, for New England both as a federal government and as a free-trade area.

The patent system illustrates the advantage of being in the United States. Patents were provided for in the Constitution, and Congress constructed a patent immediately. The Patent Office, however, was only created in the time period considered here. Patents create property rights in new knowledge. The existence of these rights encourages all sorts of people to direct their energy toward the invention of new methods and products because they know that if their discoveries are valuable, they can reap the benefits. This apparently simple arrangement depends on a complex network of laws, administration (to keep track of patents), courts (to adjudicate conflicts and enforce the scope of patents), and commerce. The United States was an extensive national market not only for goods, but also for ideas. New England quickly became the prime location of patent activity, leading the nation throughout the first half of the nineteenth century in the number of patents granted per person.[2]

Even with these legal advantages, British visitors who observed industrial establishments in New England in the 1850s were amazed. The United States was an agricultural country with very productive farms. Labor on these farms was paid well, and Americans were surprisingly tall and healthy as a result. How could fledgling industrial enterprises compete with established agriculture for labor? The British visitors answered that "on account of the high price of labour the whole energy of the people is directed in improving and inventing labour-saving machinery."[3]

This statement has been discussed extensively in the century and a half since it was written. But what did the visitors mean by "the high price of labor"? And what did they mean by "labor-saving machinery"? Note this famous restatement of the British visitors' position: "In any country where land is readily available in large quantities, labour is likely to be expensive."[4] Both the British visitors and this analyst a century later argued that it would be hard to attract labor away from the prosperous American agriculture to work in industry.

One way to rephrase this observation is to say that the United States had a comparative advantage in agriculture. That is, there was so much good land in the United States that it made sense for the United States to produce and export wheat and raw cotton in return for manufactured imports. In fact, this argument holds that the United States had so much good land that it should have specialized completely in agriculture; there was no sense in producing any other tradable good. All this, it should be remembered, is to describe the antebellum United States when most workers in the country were in fact agricultural—not the far more industrial United States of 1880 and later years.

This is a good argument. The United States had so much land per person compared to Europe that it could well have made sense for the United States to specialize completely in agriculture. But if so, how can we explain the existence of industry? The British visitors said it was because of labor-saving machinery. Such machinery used few workers per machine and therefore could justify paying high wages to each worker. In the language of economics, a high ratio of capital to labor raises wages. Higher wages in industry then would allow industry to attract workers from the prosperous American agriculture.[5]

This reasoning has sounded tenable to generations of analysts, but it is wrong. When people discuss agriculture, they refer to the ratio of land to labor; when they discuss industry, the ratio of capital to labor. The result of this difference is that there are various meanings for the price of labor. In agriculture, this refers primarily to wages relative to rent on land; in industry, to wages relative to the return on capital, that is, the rate of interest. For any given technology, the industrial wage can only be high if the interest rate is low. In other words, there is a trade-off between wages and the return to capital—one can only be high if the other is low. Unfortunately for the simple theory, interest rates in the United States were equal to or higher than in Britain. It follows that industrial wages relative to the return on capital in the United States were not higher than in Britain. There was no more incentive to use labor-saving machinery in America than in Britain.[6]

How then did industry get its start in the United States? The argument assumes the same output prices and technology in the United States and Britain. One or both of these assumptions must have been inaccurate for the early United States. The first assumption was violated because the United States put a tariff on the most important industrial goods of the mid-nineteenth century: cotton textiles. The tariff was a response to the influx of English manufactured goods after the end of the 1812 war with Britain. It was designed to offset America's comparative advantage in agriculture and allow manufacturing to grow.

But it was not simple to get such a tariff on cotton textiles. Southern cotton growers sold most of their output on the English market, and they would not agree to anything that would decrease the demand for English cotton textile products or that even might provoke retaliation. Francis Lowell, founder of the first integrated cotton spinning and weaving mill in America, therefore recommended a tariff of 25 percent. This was not high enough to keep out English imports and harm Southern planters. But Lowell also recommended that there be a minimum valuation of 25 cents per yard. In other words, all fabric worth less than 25 cents a yard would pay a duty of 6.25 cents a yard independent of its worth. The price of American cloth fell below 10 cents a yard in the early 1820s and stayed that low or lower for the following decades. As Winifred Rothenberg noted earlier, the tariff on cheap goods was completely prohibitive.[7]

It was quite a trick to design a tariff that would not hurt English exporters of cotton textiles, yet would allow domestic producers to thrive. The key to this complex operation was in the quality of textiles made in the two countries. English producers made high-quality fabrics that were subject to a light duty and did not compete with the rougher American cloth, which was made in the textile mills of New England and sold for a low price. The American cloth competed with imports from India, which were indeed excluded by the tariff. Lowell had threaded the needle by designing

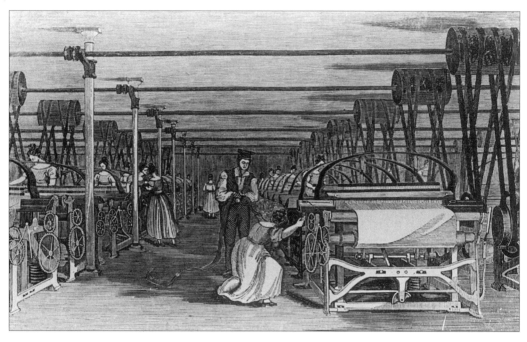

Power loom weaving. *(Courtesy New Hampshire Historical Society.)*

The cotton textile industry was expanding rapidly by 1830 as the application of power machinery to spinning and weaving proved very efficient. This picture shows the use of leather belts to transmit power from a central water wheel, possibly at Lowell, or a steam engine. The long banks of looms employed many unmarried girls of New England and turned out millions of yards of fabric that were sold around the country.

a tariff that would protect his industry while not harming the English industry or Southern planters.[8]

Another reason why American industry got its start has to do with the quality of machinery used in New England. The visitors in the 1850s noted many machines that could not be found in England, for example, the American System of Manufactures, which was built on interchangeable parts. To the extent that Yankee ingenuity outran innovators in the home of the first Industrial Revolution around Manchester, England, this provided another reason for industry to prosper in antebellum America.

Indeed, the British visitors may have meant better, rather than more, machinery when they referred to labor-saving machinery. The second assumption of the labor-scarcity argument, that of identical technology in Britain and America, was inapplicable to the early United States, although the evidence is less clear than for the first assumption (of identical product prices).[9]

Consequently, there are two reasons why the United States did not specialize completely in agriculture in the first half of the nineteenth century: the tariff on manufactures, principally cotton textiles, and technical change in America that increased the productivity of labor. The next question therefore is why New England? Why did industry take hold first in New England and only spread slowly to the rest of the country? The location and geography of New England helped. New England's coastal location made it possible to transport both raw cotton and manufactured cotton textiles cheaply by sail and steam. The rocky and hilly topography of New England created good harbors for ships and falling water for power. But these characteristics were shared by other coastal regions of the early United States. The special quality of New England had to do with the high proportion of women employed in the cotton industry.

Women were not used very intensively in New England agriculture. The primary crops were grains, hay, and dairy products, and women were not used very much in their production—even in dairying. Southern agriculture, based on cotton and tobacco, exploited more fully the work capabilities of women, partly because of the labor requirements of these crops and partly because slave women had little choice about how hard to work. The result was that the wages of women relative to men were lower in the North than in the South. New England therefore had a cost advantage within the United States as a result of its extensive use of female machine operators. The growth of industry in New England provided an opportunity for more women to work while raising women's wages relative to men's.[10]

Industrialization came early to New England because the industry that has led the way in many countries, cotton textiles, could use women who were available in New England. The early cotton industry in England used children; later cotton industries in Asia used men. New England found its own way, using the highly educated and mobile young women of northern New England. In 1860, women made up one-third of the employed workers in New England, but only one-fifth of American workers as a whole.[11]

Many other industries followed cotton textiles, but not all of them were as geographically concentrated within the United States. Steam engines, for example, were manufactured by skilled craftsmen who were found throughout the northern states. And since steam engines often needed adjustment and repair, it made sense to construct them where they would be used. The result was that each region of the country (other than the South) made most of the steam engines used there.[12]

New England therefore was both typical and atypical of regions in the United States. Typical because the laws of the United States applied to all regions—the tariff extended to North and South, and the validity of contracts extended from East to West. And atypical because local conditions made New England a leader in the progress toward an industrial economy. Both the machine tool industry and the cotton industry had their origins in this region.

THE INDUSTRIES OF NEW ENGLAND

London's Crystal Palace Exhibition in 1851 was designed to celebrate British manufacturing. But many American-made clocks, locks, and small arms appeared to be of even higher quality than the British—much to the surprise of the show's organizers. When the Americans planned an exhibit of their own in New York five years later, the British sent an interested delegation. But the Americans—however skilled at manufacturing—were less organized than the British, and the visitors arrived to find the exhibition not yet open. They therefore traveled around New England and other adjacent regions of the United States to see what they could learn on their own.

Starting and ending their tour in Boston, the British delegation toured many factories with an emphasis on those producing firearms. They missed visiting Samuel Colt's new armory in Hartford because the Connecticut River had flooded it out, but they did see many other establishments. They were very impressed and concluded:

> The contriving and making of machinery has become so common in this country, and so many heads and hands are at work with extraordinary energy, that unless the example is followed at home, notwithstanding the difference of wages, it is to be feared that American manufacturers will before long become exporters not only to foreign countries, but even to England, and should this occur, the blame must fall on the manufacturers of England, for want of energy in improving their machinery and applying it to special purposes.[13]

The American System of Manufactures, based on the use of interchangeable parts, made it possible for Americans to produce light manufactures in volumes and at prices unattainable in England. Around 1840 Chauncy Jerome, a Connecticut clock maker, used interchangeable parts to produce a one-day brass clock for less than fifty cents. He exported some to England in 1842. English customs reserved the right to confiscate goods at their invoice valuation to protect themselves against undervaluation. The clocks were clearly undervalued by English standards, and they were confiscated. This was fine for Jerome; he had sold his shipment at full price quickly and easily. He sent another, larger load, which was duly confiscated. But when he sent a third, still larger load, the customs authorities acknowledged their earlier errors and allowed it in.[14]

The American System did not, however, emerge from the private economy. It began in arms production, at U.S. government armories. The first step was taken by Thomas Blanchard at the Springfield Armory in Massachusetts, who introduced a sequence of sixteen special-purpose lathes and machines to make gun stocks out of sawn lumber. These lathes, which demonstrated the potential of the sequential use of special-purpose machines, were noted prominently by the English visitors in the 1850s. It had not occurred to the British visitors that the irregular shape of a gun stock could be made by machine. The Americans had solved this problem by using a series of machines that together produced the complex shape.

Grinding Machines, Springfield Armory, Springfield Massachusetts. (*From* Harper's New Monthly Magazine, *vol. 5, no. 26, July 1852. Courtesy U.S. Department of the Interior, National Park Service, Springfield Armory National Historic Site.*)

Arms manufacturing proved an important stimulus to the development of machine-making technology. Methods and machines introduced in the federal armories quickly found their way into private industrial plants. Although the machinery industry employed far fewer workers in New England than did the cotton textile industry, it was important for establishing a host of manufacturing enterprises throughout the region.

The next step was taken by John Hall at the Harpers Ferry Armory. Hall realized that the problem in making interchangeable parts was to keep the gauges (patterns) used to make the parts from getting worn away through use. The thousandth piece needed to be matched against a gauge that was the same as the gauge used for the first piece. But the action of comparing and filing parts to size gradually wore away the gauges, causing the pattern to "drift." Hall introduced a third level, gauges for the gauges. These would be kept safely away where they would not wear and would be brought out only periodically to recalibrate the gauges used to size the actual production. The gauges used in production then only would vary within limits set by the time period between recalibrations, assuring interchangeability.[15]

Samuel Colt used these methods in his private production of weapons. He patented his revolving method of making pistols in the 1830s and opened an armory to produce them in Hartford in 1855. This was the plant that the British visitors did not see because of the flood. The Civil War made Colt a very wealthy man, as might be imagined; he had the luck to have a new plant making the latest model firearms as the war broke out. Shortly after Colt's death in 1862, the Colt Company introduced its most famous product: the Colt .45 Peacemaker. It was the weapon of choice for most of the legends of the West, and it was made in New England.[16] Employed at the Colt works in Hartford were two men named Francis Pratt and Amos Whitney who started their own firm shortly before the Civil War. The firm of Pratt and Whitney, together with Brown and Sharpe of Providence, quickly became national leaders in the design and production of machine tools.[17] They cooperated and interacted in many ways with related firms like the Corliss Steam Engine Company of Connecticut, which made a famous patented steam engine.

These firms joined with others in and outside New England to create a fellowship of skilled machinists who visited and learned from each other. Visitors to firms like Brown and Sharpe had to show they belonged to this fellowship by engaging in technical talks or exhibiting problem-solving abilities on the shop floor. But once accepted, visitors were given tours of the plant, talked to for hours, even invited home for dinner and the night. Solutions to technical problems were shared by the managers of the host plant in the expectation that they would be treated similarly in a visit they would make. This reciprocity was the key to the fellowship of machinery-firm managers and a potent force for the dissemination of knowledge. The open-door policy was common practice among machinery firms in the later nineteenth century, and violations of the custom were criticized in the trade press the same way a lack of hospitality was scorned in many traditional cultures.[18]

As these ideas spread from Connecticut to the rest of the economy, the ability of machines to make interchangeable parts increased over time. The early practice of the armories proved hard to translate to industry; Singer sewing machines continued to be numbered until late in the century to show the order in which they were made and therefore which parts would fit together.[19] But great progress had been made by the end of the period surveyed in this essay. As stated in the 1880 Census: "Uniformity in gun-work was then, as now, a comparative term; but then it meant within a thirty-second of an inch or more, where now it means within half a thousandth of an inch. Then interchangeability may have signified a great deal of filing and fitting, and an uneven joint when fitted, where now it signifies slipping in a piece, turning a screw-driver, and having a close, even fit."[20]

Arms production and the American System of Manufactures were important for the future of both New England and the United States as a whole. They laid the foundation for American industrial expansion in both the nineteenth and twentieth centuries. The center of production moved from Connecticut to New York and then to the industrial Midwest, but the manufacturing methods used in these other regions built on the innovations made in New England.

At the time, however, machine tools were less visible parts of the New England economy than other industries because they were small, as they always are. The region's largest industry, the manufacture of cotton textiles, also was the largest industry—that is, it employed the most workers—in the United States as a whole. The second-largest industry in New England was the manufacture of boots and shoes. It too was a large industry nationally and also concentrated in New England. Other important industrial employers were important to New England and the country as a whole because they were geographically more dispersed. The manufacture of men's clothing and of sawn lumber was important throughout this period; iron foundries and machine shops became important by its end.[21]

The industry that produced cotton cloth in New England grew by using totally new techniques to produce a traditional product. Cloth is a traditional product, but cheap cotton cloth was an innovation of the nineteenth century. Wool was the traditional fabric of home production in temperate climates. Cotton only became a feasible alternative when transportation improved enough to make it economical to bring cotton from warmer climates, where it was grown, to temperate climates, where it was made into cloth. The industry also needed the cotton gin, invented by New England's Eli Whitney in the previous period, to clean the raw cotton. And the new technology used to produce cotton cloth appeared to work better with cotton than with wool.

The new techniques of the cotton industry were a blend of old and new. The machines themselves were copies of British machines made initially by Francis Lowell from his memory of visiting English factories. In this sense, the British observers were accurate when they assumed that Britain and America shared the same technology. But the organization of work was uniquely American. If we include management in our concept of technology, then the British visitors were wrong not to emphasize the way in which the machines were used in New England. The resulting industry was able to export cotton cloth to the United States as a whole, taking advantage of the free-trade area created by disallowing tariffs between states. New England had a comparative advantage within the United States in the production of cotton cloth, because of the availability of cheap transport, power, and educated young women.

The first column of Table 3.1 shows the share of cotton cloth production by Massachusetts, Rhode Island, New Hampshire, and New England at the beginning, middle, and end of our period. The states are ranked by the yards of cloth produced. In 1831, Massachusetts led the other states in cotton cloth production by a wide margin. Adding the other New England states reveals that almost three-quarters of the national production of cotton cloth was located in this region. The cotton industry was not only the largest industry in New England; it was virtually unique to New England in the United States.

This geographic concentration in New England was maintained in the following half-century. The second column of Table 3.1 shows that New England retained its dominance in cotton production on the eve of the Civil War. And the third column shows that the cotton industry was even more geographically concentrated after the war. Both Massachusetts and New England produced a larger share of cotton cloth than before the Civil

Table 3.1   Cotton textile output (millions of yards of cloth, percent)

	1831		1860		1880	
State or region	Yards (millions)	Share (percent)	Yards (millions)	Share (percent)	Yards (millions)	Share (percent)
Mass.	79	35	415	36	971	43
R.I.	37	16	148	13	264	12
N.H.	29	13	152	13	244	11
N.E.	163	71	857	75	1,813	80
U.S.	230	100	1,148	100	2,273	100

Sources: Peter Temin, "Product Quality and Vertical Integration in the Early Cotton Textile Industry," *Journal of Economic History* 48 (1988): 891–907; U.S. Census, Eighth Census, *Manufactures of the United States in 1860,* p. xxi; U.S. Census, Tenth Census, *Manufactures of the United States in the Tenth Census,* p. 956.

War, although Rhode Island and New Hampshire did not. In the half-century considered here, there were strong forces concentrating the cotton industry in New England, especially Massachusetts.

The birth of this industry and the innovations that gave it life preceded 1830 and have been described in the previous essay. Francis Lowell and Nathan Appleton were key figures in the early history; but Lowell died in 1817, and Appleton was elected to Congress in 1830. They were both gone by the beginning of the period surveyed here. The phenomenal growth of the cotton industry was the result of investments and improvements made over many years. One of the most important innovations was the exploitation of water power from the Merrimack River. The city of Lowell was established in the 1820s at an existing dam in the river, and more and more mills were built in subsequent years to use the power generated by the flowing and falling water. Kirk Boott was the superintendent of several mills in Lowell and the prime architect of the city's internal organization. Although Boott was disliked at the time as a strict disciplinarian and has a bad reputation now, he died in 1837, while the initial arrangements for staffing the mills at Lowell were working well.

The ability of one dam to power many mills created conditions that economists describe as economies of scale. One could put a single water wheel in a large river and generate power for a single mill, as the Romans put water wheels in the Arno to grind flour. One also could find a small stream and dam it to take advantage of potential as well as kinetic energy—to use an overshot instead of an undershot wheel. But it was more efficient to build a dam across a substantial river like the Merrimack and construct canals that would take the water to a variety of mills that shared the investment in the dam. The dam itself is an example of what economists call a lumpy investment; the benefits came from the whole dam, not independently from each part of it.

The result of this economy of scale was to induce entrepreneurs thinking of opening a new mill to think seriously about building their mills in Lowell. They did not think in abstract concepts, but rather that power could be purchased more cheaply in Lowell than elsewhere. The Locks and Canal Company of Lowell was able to offer these good terms because of its—for the time—large scale.

The dam at Lowell generated only a limited amount of power. The cotton industry expanded rapidly as its costs fell and demand grew. Soon there was a need for more power than Locks and Canal had to sell. The proprietors of the Lowell dam therefore decided to build another dam farther upstream and duplicate the results they had achieved in Lowell. Taking another name from a family prominent in the cotton industry, the new town was named Lawrence. It was established in the 1840s and grew rapidly in the following years.

The output of cotton cloth increased at a rate of about 5 percent a year from 1830 to the Civil War. The price of cotton cloth fell at this time relative to other prices at a rate of 1.3 percent a year. This combination of rising output and falling price implies that the supply of cotton cloth was increasing faster than the demand.[22] The demand for cotton was responsive to price because cotton textiles were lighter than wool, could be dyed and printed more easily, and could be washed more easily. But even so, the improvements in productive capacity and methods were more important in explaining the rapid growth of cotton production.

Cotton cloth made in New England was sold throughout the United States. New England both imported its raw material and exported almost all of its product. Less than 15 percent of the national population was in New England, and probably therefore about the same percentage of national consumption occurred there, while 75 percent of production was performed there. The majority of cotton textiles consumed outside New England were exports from New England. The Colt .45 Peacemaker, made in Connecticut, had an even stronger market presence in the West.

Machinery for the mills of Lowell and Lawrence was built primarily by the Locks and Canal Company of Lowell. Although in 1838 this company earned over half of its operating profits from the sale of cotton spinning and weaving machinery, it had other sources of income as well. It owned the land on which the mills at Lowell were built and received rent from them. It also had branched out into making the other dominant machine of the antebellum economy, the steam engine, and earned more revenue from this new activity than from its traditional renting activity. Unlike the products of the cotton mills themselves, the machinery and engines built at Lowell were sold primarily in New England. The proportion of sales made in Lowell declined, however, from virtually all in 1830 to about one-quarter in 1880. Southern states provided a market almost as large as Lowell by this latter date, foreshadowing the future dispersion of the cotton industry.[23]

The New England boot and shoe industry had a complex relationship with the cotton textile industry. Before 1850, shoes and boots were made primarily in people's houses or in "ten footers," workshops built onto them. The outwork system of boot and shoe production contrasted sharply with the factory work of cotton mills. Women worked at home making shoes, but in Lowell or other mill towns making cloth. Working women at mid-century greatly preferred cloth making over shoe making. One woman who made the transition wrote back that she soon would be skilled and earning good wages: "By and by . . . [I] shall have twice as much as though I were binding shoes. I guess you [won't] catch me to do that little thing again, not I! You cannot think how funny it seems to have some money."[24]

It is hard to know if the pull into outwork was stronger than the pull out of it. The mills at Lowell and Lawrence produced attractive cloth that women wanted to buy, so many women bound shoes and wove palm-leaf hats to earn money to buy it. This complex relationship endured throughout the antebellum years; but the balance of forces was changed after 1850 due to another interaction between cotton and shoes. The Singer sewing machine was adapted to sew leather around mid-century, leading shoes to be produced in factories of their own where the sewing machines were powered by steam. The boot and shoe industry increasingly provided factory employment for women. The new opportunities attracted both men and women from cotton factory work.

The boot and shoe industry was comparable to the cotton industry in many ways. It was concentrated in Massachusetts and New England throughout this period to take advantage of the available women workers and to be near the Boston market. We do not know the location of shoe production at the beginning of the period, because the early Census did not collect adequate manufacturing data and the prevalence of outwork made it hard for others to gather data by themselves. In addition, since there were no political issues involved like the tariff on cotton imports from Britain, people did not make the effort to collect data on boots and shoes. By 1860, 60 percent of American boot and shoe production (by value) was made in New England; 50 percent in Massachusetts alone. As with cotton cloth, these shares increased by 1880 to 67 and 58 percent, respectively. The two industries were roughly the same size when measured by the value of their product and the number of workers they employed. Women were important in both industries, although the proportion of female boot and shoe workers fell more rapidly over time. Half of the workers in cotton textiles were women in 1880, down from 60 percent in 1860. Only one-quarter of boot and shoe workers were women in both 1860 and 1880, fewer than in earlier years.[25]

Whaling was another industry concentrated in New England, especially New Bedford. It was a large employer, although its labor force was exclusively male, reaching its peak just before the Civil War. Whale oil, the primary product of the industry, was used for illumination, the demand for which increased as people left farming for more urban and literate activities. Whales also furnished lubricants and whale bones for women's clothing. The introduction of petroleum products in the 1850s reduced the demand for whale oil and lubricants, starting a decline from which the New Bedford industry did not recover. Only the demand for whalebone stays kept American whaling in business after the Civil War.[26]

There were many other industries that grew in New England during these years as well, although none as concentrated in this region as cotton, shoes, and whaling. The region benefited from the educated labor force of New England and grew rapidly. By the end of the period, when we have data to make a comparison, labor productivity in American industry, much of it in New England, was twice as high as in Britain. This might have been due to greater capital intensity, as the British visitors speculated, but it was not. The ratio of capital to labor was no higher in the United States than in Britain. Instead, total productivity was twice as high in America as in Britain. Better machines and organization, rather than more machines, made the difference. This may have been true before then as well, but we do not have enough data to know.[27]

People in 1830 traveled around and transported goods over land on foot, horseback, or wagons. Sea transport went by sail. There were steamboats on the Hudson and Mississippi rivers by then, but not in New England. Information traveled the same slow, arduous way as did people and goods. Newspapers reported events elsewhere in the United States that were days old, events in Europe that were weeks old.

The tempo increased dramatically in the next half-century. The instantaneous communication that we are used to today has its origin in this period. Transport also became faster, easier, and more regular. Communication within the United States was vastly accelerated by the introduction of the telegraph in the 1840s. Spreading rapidly during the next two decades, it provided a way for business communication to travel instantaneously from city to city. Messengers like the young Andrew Carnegie in Pittsburgh carried notes between the telegraph and business offices. With the laying of a cable under the Atlantic Ocean by the *Great Eastern*—the larg-

Manchester Locomotive Works. *(Courtesy New Hampshire Historical Society.)*

Because of the railroad, overland transportation changed more dramatically than at any previous time. It was now much faster, and almost as cheap, to move people and goods over land as over water. Railroads were extended throughout New England in the 1840s, before their expansion over the United States as a whole. Locomotive works like these used techniques learned in the manufacture of textile machinery and in federal armories.

est steamship of its day—in 1866, this web of communication was extended to London and Europe. Newspapers in 1880 were as up to date as they are today. Former postmaster general Amos Kendall asserted in 1847 that the telegraph had reduced by "four entire days" the time needed to transact business between Boston and Richmond.[28]

Within New England, telegraph wires followed railroads. One use of the telegraph was to schedule trains so that railroads could run with only a single track for trains in both directions. "Single tracking" was a typical American innovation that saved capital costs. Michael Chevalier, traveling in America in 1834, noted that "the railroad from Boston to Providence is in active progress; the work goes on *à l'Américaine*, that is to say, rapidly."[29] The New England railroad net was constructed rapidly in the 1840s, and New England was knit together at mid-century far more closely than a generation earlier. Henry Thoreau, celebrating the pure life in the wilderness at Walden in the mid-1840s, saw the train go by.[30]

New York was emerging as the primary point of entry for American imports of British manufactures and of exit for exports of Western agricultural products, eclipsing its rivals, Philadelphia to the south and Boston to the north. The Erie Canal opened in 1825 and provided far cheaper transport across the mountain barrier to the Mississippi Valley than had ever existed before. Boston fought back by constructing railroad links to the West to attract through traffic to its port. Its first effort, the Western Railroad, offered a connection to the Erie Canal at Albany. But although the route across New England to Boston and then across the ocean was more direct than down the Hudson to New York, it was also more expensive. Railroad transport was more expensive than rivers and canals in general, and the Western Railroad had to navigate a hilly terrain. Boston's second effort was to construct a railroad link to the St. Lawrence River and bypass the Erie Canal entirely. This had a certain political charm as defiance of New York's Erie Canal, but it made little economic sense. Despite a smoother grade than the Western, this route too had high costs deriving from the need for a longer railway link.[31]

At the same time that railroads knit New England together and revolutionized overland transportation, clipper ships and then steamboats did the same for ocean transport. Clipper ships were among the most beautiful agents of commerce ever built—their acres of billowing sails were designed to catch all possible wind and speed the ships to China and back. The *Flying Cloud*, built by Donald McKay in East Boston, was the most beautiful, fast, and famous clipper ship. It tied the record of 89 days from New York to San Francisco twice, making an average speed of ten miles an hour. And since it was built in Boston, the *Flying Cloud*'s success led to the following ditty being shouted in New York:

The clipper ship *Flying Cloud* rounding Cape Horn. Painting by J. K. Tudgay. *(Courtesy Peabody Essex Museum, Salem, Mass.)*

Proud clipper ships like this record-breaking New England beauty sailed to England, China, and India. The China trade continued to earn profits in the early years of this period, but it began to decline at the middle of the nineteenth century, as steamships superseded clipper ships. Profits from the China trade were reinvested first in textile mills, then in railroads built both within and outside of New England.

> Wide-awake Down-Easters,
> No-mistake Down-Easters,
> Old Massachusetts will carry the day![32]

Clipper ships had a short and dramatic appearance on the historical stage; they were used primarily from the 1830s through the 1850s. Demand for these highly specialized "tall ships" was fading when the opening of the Suez Canal in 1869 allowed less expensive ships to do their job as well.[33]

Much less glamorous, but more important in the long run, steamboats began in this period to make regularly scheduled trips between Boston and New York and between Boston and England. Steam engines had revolutionized ocean transport as well as land transport by 1880.

Steam engines were not only useful for transportation; they also powered factories and mills throughout America. These engines were made locally, as the sales of Lowell's Locks and Canal Company suggests. In New England around 1840, for example, 260 of the 304 stationary steam engines whose origins we know were made in New England, and only five steam engines were imported into New England. Almost all the imported steam engines came from New York, closely adjacent to New England. The skills needed to construct a steam engine had spread throughout the northern United States by the start of this period, while the ability to produce cotton textiles efficiently from southern cotton appears to have been restricted largely to New England during this time.[34]

WORKERS IN NEW INDUSTRIES AND LOCATIONS

This explosion of manufacturing activity changed New Englanders' lives in many ways. First, the new products that emerged from cotton mills and shoe factories allowed people to dress themselves and their houses in ways that could only have been imagined before. The new modes of transportation allowed these same people to move easily and quickly within New England and beyond. The railroad and steamships also brought a variety of new products to the region. Even though the price of cotton goods was falling relative to other prices, the prices of other goods were falling too: western grain became available in New England at ever more favorable prices.

The expansion of production in the new industries also required an expanding workforce in New England. Workers were attracted from the countryside to mill and factory towns by high factory wages. They were pushed from their farms as well by competition from western farms. Cheaper transportation allowed New England to exploit its comparative advantage in the production of textiles and other industrial products.

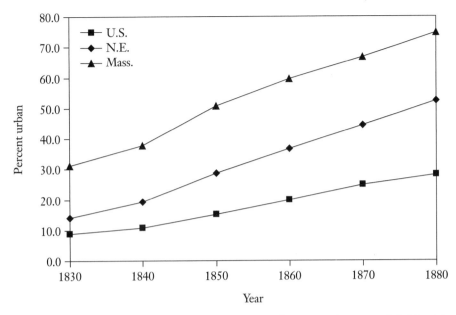

FIGURE 3.1   Percentage of population living in urban areas (> 2,500 inhabitants), United States, New England, and Massachusetts, 1830–1880.

Source: U.S. Bureau of the Census, *Historical Statistics of the United States, Colonial Times to 1970* (Washington, D.C.: Government Printing Office, 1975), pp. 11–12, 23–37.

Phrased differently, men and women chose to work in factories instead of on farms because they could use factory wages to buy goods produced at those factories and imported from other regions more cheaply than they could produce them themselves. Further, the variety of goods that could be purchased far exceeded the variety that could be grown in the hard New England ground.

With a change in work came a change in dwelling place; urbanization was a dominant characteristic of this half-century. Figure 3.1 shows the proportion of people living in urban areas in Massachusetts, New England, and the United States. It is obvious that the transition from the countryside to the city was most advanced and most rapid in Massachusetts. The transition to an urban civilization in New England was almost as rapid as in Korea and Taiwan during the last half of the twentieth century. But these countries are independent; they are not a region within a larger country. The data on the United States therefore reminds us both how unusual New England, and especially Massachusetts, was in this period and that New England industrialization was stimulated and encouraged as part of the stable, prosperous United States.

This process of urbanization can be seen clearly in the experiences of Boston, New England's largest city, and Lowell, the center of New England's largest industry. Boston grew from 60,000 to 360,000 inhabitants in the half-century from 1830 to 1880, while Lowell grew from 6,000 to 60,000.[35] Lowell grew faster, but Boston was larger. Lowell also was a one-industry town, while Boston was a metropolis with varied activities and an active port. The story of Lowell highlights the role of women in early New England industrialization, while Boston's labor force was more typical of the region as a whole. The largest employer of both men and women in Boston throughout most of this period was the men's clothing industry, although foundries and machine shops employed more men by 1880. Other large urban industries were printing and publishing, furniture, women's clothing, and—after the Civil War—slaughtering and meat packing.[36]

Boston in 1830 was the fourth largest city in the United States, behind New York, Philadelphia, and Baltimore. It was the third largest port, behind New York and New Orleans, linked during warm weather to coastal cities both north and south by semi-weekly packet (that is, scheduled) ships. It was situated on a narrow peninsula that in previous years had given good access to the city by the dominant mode of European transportation—water—and that protected it from natives who might have attacked by land. The city expanded by filling land in what is now downtown Boston, producing a virtual island city connected to the mainland by only a narrow neck.[37]

The neck that connected Boston and the rest of Massachusetts ran along what is now Washington Street. Several bridges were added to the north in the early nineteenth century, and in 1821 a dam was built along what is now Beacon Street. The purpose of the dam was to create a tidal pool in what was known as Back Bay to provide power for mills of all sorts.

This scheme proved less than fully successful for, as we have seen, the rapidly expanding cotton industry drew its power from the Merrimack River instead of the tides. In the 1830s, Back Bay was crisscrossed by two railroads running diagonally across the tidal flats, crossing near today's Back Bay railroad station.

During the later antebellum years, the road along what is now Beacon Street offered another way west from the city and a handsome drive with water on both sides. The press of population and the discomfort of having the tidal basin dry out twice a day created pressure to fill in the Back Bay, and many plans were devised for doing so. A city plan of 1856 created the Back Bay we see today with its broad Commonwealth Avenue and regular cross streets. A museum of natural history was built on Berkeley Street during the Civil War in a building that still stands today (housing a men's clothing store). The Massachusetts Institute of Technology was incorporated in 1861, adjoining the museum of natural history.

Back Bay was filled in during the next two decades using the railroad and the newly invented steam shovel. The whole Back Bay was ready for building by 1880 and has remained a defined example of Victorian town planning, bounded on the east by the Boston Public Garden, on the north by the Charles River, on the west by marshes that were later drained to make the Fenway, and on the south by railroad tracks running diagonally relative to the streets of Back Bay. Boston was unusual among large American cities in having to expand its land area as its population grew.[38]

The expansion of Lowell was completely different. In contrast to the varied occupational base of Boston's residents, Lowell's inhabitants derived their income from cotton mills. In further contrast with the long history of Boston before the nineteenth century, Lowell was a new town created in the 1820s by a small group of Boston merchants and manufacturers. Lowell was to embody the solution to two problems of the nascent cotton textile industry. The rapid expansion of production needed more power than could be obtained from the sluggish Charles River at the location of the first mill in Waltham. And the mills needed labor to run the mules and looms that produced yarn and cloth.

The problem of power was solved by purchasing land and water rights at the falls on the Merrimack River and establishing the town of Lowell. The labor problem was compounded by the low opinion of industrial activities in the predominantly agricultural society and the poor reputation of earlier workers. In Rhode Island the problem was solved the British way, by employing whole families, including children. The Lowell mills instead put to work a succession of unmarried farm girls.

These girls were available for several reasons. Agriculture in New England employed women less than did agriculture in other regions, the new cotton technology was reducing the demand for spinning and weaving work done at home, and British farm girls typically had left their families before marriage to be servants in other households. The plan was to employ these young women for a few years only, making them only transient residents of Lowell. But it was not a simple matter to attract them to Lowell. The anticipated large number of girls needed to be housed and supervised in a way different from that used for a single servant.

The initial plan of Lowell was to approximate an ideal factory town. The mills would be near the river from which they drew power. Housing would be just behind them, bounded by a main street, and the rest of the town would be across the main street. The main street would thus separate the industrial part of the town, including carefully planned mills and housing, from the bourgeois part that would grow without central planning. This plan, however, was predicated on a straight river. Although this plan was used in Manchester, New Hampshire, in the 1830s, it could not be used without alteration in Lowell for the simple reason that the Merrimack River turned sharply just below the dam.

The resulting plan of Lowell had a division between its planned and unplanned halves, but the division was nowhere near as straight or as visible as in the ideal plan. The mills were situated near the river, either parallel or perpendicular to it. The standard mill was 150 feet long and 40 feet wide, four stories high, and contained approximately 6,000 spindles on which cotton was spun. Housing for the girls operating these spindles was built directly adjacent to the mills in respectable housing. But since the girls spent twelve hours a day, six days a week, in the mills, the boarding houses were little more than dormitories.

Michael Chevalier, visiting from France in the 1830s, saw Lowell through European eyes: "Lowell, with its steeple-crowned factories, resembles a Spanish town with its convents; but with this difference, that in Lowell you meet no rags nor Madonnas, and that the nuns of Lowell, instead of working sacred hearts, spin and weave cotton. Lowell is not amusing, but it is neat, decent, peaceable, and sage."[39]

The town was rigidly hierarchical, with the corporations and its leaders at the top. The workers were differentiated sharply from them and confined to their repetitive houses. But while the buildings revealed a sharp class distinction, the people inhabiting them did not, at least at first. The workers who passed through Lowell typically worked there for about four years on their way to live lives shaped by the larger world. The rigid hierarchy of Lowell was one stage among several they passed through. Only after mid-century, when the temporary labor of Yankee girls was replaced by the more permanent labor of Irish and French Canadian immigrants, did the hierarchical structure of Lowell's buildings mirror—and help create—a social structure as well.[40] As a historian of the period has said, "Lowell was never an 'Eden,' but as the place where American women first had a chance to earn an independent living, and where the American Industrial Revolution began; the Lowell Experiment marked the beginning of a long road."[41]

Even after the passing of the original, transitory labor system, the workers in Lowell factories were far different from their counterparts in England. Anthony Trollope, visiting Lowell early in the Civil War, made the comparison: "They [Lowell machine operators] are not only better dressed, cleaner, and better mounted in every respect than the girls employed at manufactories in England, but they are so infinitely superior as to make a stranger immediately perceive that some very strong cause must have created the difference."[42]

Women were an important, even critical, part of New England industrialization, which was built on the use of their previously underutilized labor. The early stages of industrialization offered women an economic independence that was unique to this period of time. There was work in the home for both unmarried and married women, and work outside the home

TABLE 3.2   Occupational distribution of wage-earning women in Massachusetts (percent)

Industry	1837	1870
Palm-leaf hats	49	—
Textiles	17	26
Boots and shoes	14	5
Domestic service	12	34
Teaching	4	5
Men's and women's clothing	3	18
Other	1	12

Source: Thomas Dublin, *Transforming Women's Work: New England Lives in the Industrial Revolution* (Ithaca, N.Y.: Cornell University Press, 1994), pp. 20, 22.

for unmarried women. Only in the past fifty years, and in very different ways, are women again achieving economic independence, this time more thoroughly and less connected to their marital state.

Table 3.2 provides a picture of the changing fortunes of Massachusetts women during this period. In 1837, almost two-thirds of women who earned wages were working in their own homes, making hats and shoes. This outwork was part of a system known as the putting-out system in England. Initially a merchant, or putter-outer, brought raw materials to women's houses and came again to reclaim the finished product. Later women purchased the raw material at a local store and sold the product there as well.

The products made at home in Massachusetts differed sharply from the textile products made in eighteenth-century English households. The most important products in Massachusetts were palm-leaf hats and straw bonnets. The women wove and braided split palm leaves into hats. Martha Alexander, for example, braided 341 hats in the 45 months before she was married in 1834. She braided 162 hats during the next two years, maintaining her pre-wedding pace.[43] Half of the women earning wages at the beginning of this period did so by braiding hats. This work, however, vanished after the Civil War.

The other important source of outwork employed only about one-fourth of the number of women employed braiding hats. This was the boot and shoe industry, in which women "bound," that is, sewed the lining into shoes and the uppers together. This source of outwork also disappeared as industrialization advanced. The sewing machine was adapted to use with leather around mid-century, and outwork was transformed into factory labor. Women were employed in these factories, but not in the proportion that they worked in the cotton textile industry.

After domestic work, the next most important employment of Massachusetts women in the 1830s was the cotton textile industry. Unlike braiding hats at home, work in the cotton mills was only for unmarried women. Less than a quarter of working women worked in the cotton industry at any time, but they worked there for only a short time, and a far greater proportion of women passed through the cotton mills. The textile industry became a more important source of women's work during this period, and the composition of the female workforce changed. Women began to work in the mills for longer periods, not for only a few years. These long-term operatives were not Yankee girls accumulating their dowries; they were immigrants from Ireland and French Canada. The cotton mills were very different places to work at the beginning and end of the period described here.

Domestic service always offered some employment for women. Indeed, in the years after the Civil War, it offered the most opportunities for women as outwork declined. One-third of Massachusetts women who earned wages—and one-half of such women in the United States as a whole—worked in domestic service in 1870. (This national proportion was cut in half by 1900.) The needle trades offered another outlet for women as outwork declined. While employment in textiles and shoes centered in Lowell and Lynn, domestic and garment work was located most often in Boston.[44]

The experience of Mary Paul echoed that of many women in the years after 1830 who left the farm for factory work in the textile industry. Born in 1830 in Vermont, Mary left home at age fifteen to work as a farm servant in a nearby town. Not liking the work, she left to live with relatives and to appeal to her father for permission to go to Lowell or a similar place. She arrived in Lowell in 1845 and worked in the cotton mills for the next four years, and at other jobs in Lowell until 1857, when she married the son of a former boardinghouse keeper in Lowell. Mary Paul Guild moved to Lynn with her husband and had two sons in the next five years. Her work in the cotton mills was only temporary, but it set in motion a permanent move from the country to the city.[45]

The farmers' daughters lived in boardinghouses while they worked in Lowell. They wrote articles in the *Lowell Offering*, a magazine of essays about their experiences that expressed their happiness and justified their move from the farm. Susan Brown, in her eight months working as a weaver in Lowell in 1843, spent half of her earnings on food and lodging at a boardinghouse. She recorded purchases of clothes and sundries in her diary for another quarter of her income, attended fifteen plays, concerts, and lectures, and had a two-day excursion to Boston. She may have saved a bit or sent some money home, but she used most of her earnings in pursuit of a good time.[46]

It is clear that these farm girls were fully literate. They knew far more than their factory employment required. Some of the young ladies wrote and produced the *Lowell Offering*. Some of them also, like Susan Brown, went to plays, concerts, and lectures—not the activities of barely literate people. New England education prepared the ground for industrialization.

Children spent relatively little time in school during the early nineteenth century. There were thousands of schoolhouses in the countryside and even more tutorial efforts in individual houses. But learning to read and write was squeezed into myriad other activities ranging from going to church, to farming, to doing household chores. A coalition of moral reformers reconceptualized the role of schools in the 1830s and 1840s. These reformers distinguished the role of schools from other influences. They invented public schools as a way to cope with the transformations of

A New England school. (Pierpont's Second Reader, *frontispiece. Courtesy Old Sturbridge Village. Photo by Henry E. Peach.*)

Education continued to be important in New England, and the common school movement promoting education for all had its birth in the region. This early classroom shows students engaged in group reading, a typical group activity of early schools. Students learned by reciting texts, by speaking in unison, and by contests like spelling bees.

the era: of work from agriculture to industry, of residence from rural to urban, and of the student body from native-born to (partially) immigrant. This movement began in New England and spread to the rest of the country over the next century.

Public schools in the eyes of these reformers would be crucibles from which children would emerge free of provincialism and endowed with civic values and moral gyroscopes. For Anglo-American children, public schools would provide a civic vocabulary, patriotic disposition, and political knowledge. They also would initiate immigrant children into the Anglo-American cultural and political culture.[47]

Schools changed their physical appearance in pursuit of these goals. In earlier, part-time schools, students sat on benches around the periphery of the room, surrounding a central space with a stove and a teacher. Students could observe each other while remaining roughly equidistant from the stove. They stood before the teacher to say their lessons, and they often chanted their lessons in unison. In such a setting, the written word was given less importance than the spoken sociability of the community.

This structure changed first in New England cities and towns, then spread to the countryside and the rest of the country. Benches were replaced by school desks. And students no longer sat in a sort of circle, but in rows facing in the same direction. First came the two-seat desk, preserving a bit of the communal nature of the earlier school. The single desk followed, which isolated the student. Individual study of books rather than communal proclamation of moral sentiments became the norm. Age stratification increased. Grades replaced corporal punishment, report cards supplanted spelling exhibitions, and manufactured pens replaced goose quills. Schools as we know them spread over New England during this period.[48]

The public-school movement was led by a fierce New Englander. Horace Mann grew up in rural Franklin, Massachusetts, helping his mother braid palm-leaf hats and learning a stern Calvinism. He was the first secretary of the Massachusetts Board of Education, serving from 1837 to 1848, when he succeeded John Quincy Adams in the U.S. House of Representatives and turned his attention to the abolition of slavery. His annual reports to the board of education had great influence in their day and endure as classic statements of the value and function of education. The fifth annual report in 1842 explored the relationship between education and the economy.

In this report, Mann stated clearly that he felt the goals of education were broad and that the economic benefit of education was the least of them. He recognized, however, that the economic argument was needed to convince others less high-minded than he to support education in their towns and cities. So he surveyed employers in Massachusetts about the work done by educated and uneducated employees. He concluded:

> [T]he result of the investigation is a most astonishing superiority, in productive power, on the part of the educated over the uneducated laborer . . . In great establishments, and among large bodies of laboring men, where all services are rated according to their pecuniary value; where there are no extrinsic circumstances to bind a man down to a fixed position, after he has shown a capacity to rise above it; where, indeed, men pass by each other, ascending or descending in their grades of labor, just as easily and certainly as particles of water of different degrees of temperature glide by each other—there it is found as an almost invariable fact, other things being equal, that those who have been blessed with a good common-school education rise to a higher and higher point in the kinds of labor performed, and also in the rate of wages paid, while the ignorant sink like dregs, and are always found at the bottom.[49]

The recruitment of Yankee girls to work in the Lowell mills ended at mid-century. Many Irish workers had helped build Lowell in the 1820s, and there were many Irish families still in Lowell twenty years later. As cotton production revived in the 1840s, after the recession that followed the 1837 financial crisis (to be described later), mill owners decided to allow Irish women to work in the mills. This change in policy coincided with the Irish famine and subsequent emigration of many Irish to America. The mill owners found they could hire as many Irish workers as they wanted and did not need to recruit young women from the countryside. And since the Irish families lived in Lowell, there was no reason to maintain the boardinghouse system in which the Yankee girls had lived apart from their families. The *Lowell Offering* ceased publication in 1845. Lowell after mid-century was a very different place to live and work than before.[50]

The boot and shoe industry in Lynn offered an experience for women distinct from that in the cotton industry centered in Lowell. Many women working in Lynn before the Civil War had been born there, and most married and settled there. Women's work in Lynn typically was done at home by women who lived there, whereas the factory work in Lowell was done by migrants. And while most workers in Lowell were women, women in Lynn worked among male workers who attached the uppers made by women to the soles.

The shoe industry was transformed first by the use of the sewing machine in shoemaking, which increased the efficiency of the female outworkers in the 1850s. Then, a decade later, the McKay stitching machine (actually invented by Lyman Blake of Massachusetts) made factory production of the entire shoe efficient, ending the demand for outwork and sharply reducing the demand for women workers. In Lynn, the proportion of women employed in the boot and shoe industry declined from 50 percent in the 1830s to 40 percent in the 1860s. But while most workers in Lynn worked in the shoe industry, less than one-fifth of the boots and shoes made in Massachusetts were made in Lynn. For the state as a whole, the proportion of women employed in the shoe industry fell from two-fifths in the 1830s to one-quarter at the end of the Civil War industry boom.[51]

Teachers increasingly were women in this period; the proportion of teachers in Massachusetts who were women rose from 50 percent to over 85 percent.[52] They never were a large proportion of employed people, or even of employed women, in New England, as shown in Table 3.2. But teachers taught on average longer than women in other occupations. This average was composed of two quite different groups. Those teachers who followed teaching by marriage taught on average about four years, the same length of time that women typically worked in the cotton mills. But a large proportion of teachers did not marry. After the Civil War, twice as many teachers remained single than the average New England woman (30 percent as opposed to 15). These single teachers taught on average a dozen years, bringing up the average tenure of teachers.[53]

Men of course worked in a variety of jobs. The largest employers of men in 1860 were the boots and shoes, cotton goods, woolen goods, and whaling industries.[54] The result of the industrialization described in the previous section was that there were always new jobs to be filled. This pressure on labor not only brought new workers into New England; it also raised the wages of workers in New England. Real wages—that is, wages divided by the cost of living—rose about 1 percent a year on average during this period. The increases were fastest at the beginning and end of the period and slowest in the middle, when the Civil War and associated dislocations decreased the demand for labor. Real wages in New England were higher than in Europe, as the British visitors noted, and drew immigrants from Europe. They were not higher than those in the Midwest, however, and many people migrated westward as a result.[55]

Work in non-cotton manufacturing often was done under what was known as the contract system. Workers typically worked eleven or twelve hours a day, six days a week. But they did not work at standardized jobs typified by the modern assembly line. Instead, workers were paid to fill orders that were allocated to them. They could use assistants, but had to pay them from their own pay, and they could decide how and often where to produce the order. Workers signed written contracts for large orders, but smaller orders—the "peanut trade"—were handled verbally. Workers had a lot of independence *within* the factory.[56] The 1880 Census celebrated this system in the manufacture of sewing machines even as the author commented on its passing: "The system of employing head machinists by piece-work or contract may almost be esteemed a germinant principle in the development of special machinery and a higher productive efficiency in the manufacture; but works are now very commonly conducted under salaried foremen, some classes of operatives working by the piece and some by the day."[57]

Prosperity in New England was based on rising wages. The rest of the national economy was growing as well, but New England led the pack and was a rich region throughout this period. In 1840, the earliest time for which such an estimate can be made, per capita income in New England was 25 percent above the national average. The Middle Atlantic region had roughly the same income level, so New Englanders would not have appeared better off than their immediate neighbors to the west and south. Both of these wealthy regions had higher average incomes than regions to the west. In 1880, the relative income in New England was still greater than the national average. But the Middle Atlantic region had grown even faster. In New England, the lead over the national average was due mostly to the region's lead in industrialization, as opposed to its having higher wages in any given occupation.[58]

CAPITAL FOR NEW INDUSTRIES AND ACTIVITIES

The industries did not employ all of these workers in isolation. Workers needed machinery to operate and houses to live in. New machines needed to be housed in new factories, and new products had to be transported to market. Investment was the key to exploiting new technology. And just as labor was forthcoming from New England farms, capital was forthcoming from prior mercantile activity. But, unlike labor, capital invested in new ventures replenished itself and grew, so that it could be invested again in the same or other activities.

As elsewhere, the capital market in early industrial New England operated differently for large and small companies. Large companies, like the cotton mills of Lowell, were well known to potential investors. People looking for investments consequently did not need individual information about the identity of the managers or the specific nature of the business. They could get information from standard sources like newspapers and publications of the company, and they were willing to purchase standardized securities that are the antecedents of our stocks and bonds today.

Small firms, whether just starting out or in some specialized activity, did not have this wide appeal. There were too many small companies even then for a potential investor in Boston to learn about all of them, and they were too small to generate the kind of standardized information that an organized market demanded. Investors in these companies needed to have information that could only be gotten in some more intensive way—to know someone in the business or have some kind of small-scale institutional contact that would assure them of the quality of their investment.

This split still exists today. The stock market lists many companies, but still only a small subset of all companies in the United States. Large companies can be listed on one of the exchanges and be traded easily. But many other companies are too small to be traded actively or to generate the needed information for the market; they must search out capital through families, friends, banks, and venture capitalists. These two parts of the capital market are mostly distinct, but they are linked. Firms that succeed and grow can go from the informal to the more formal market; investors can go back and forth between the markets depending on their knowledge, tastes, or opportunities.

The initial investments in the cotton textile industry were made by New England merchants from Boston and Salem in an informal market. These men had earned great fortunes from trade with Europe, the Caribbean, and China. Such trade had been halted by the Embargo of 1808, however—the embargo that led to the War of 1812 with Britain—and the merchants were looking for a domestic outlet for their capital. The nascent cotton industry fit the bill. The tradition of Boston merchant families investing in cotton mills was familiar by 1830.

The cotton industry had grown substantially by 1830, and the companies started by these merchants had a track record of continuous dividend payments. New companies could draw on the established power resources of Lowell and the history of profits of the older companies to attract investors. The cotton mills therefore had moved from the informal to the formal capital market. Their shares were traded, albeit nowhere near as frequently as the shares of companies today, and the owners of these shares were recorded. The historical record contains the names of the people who furnished capital to the cotton industry. These names can be used to identify from other sources the occupations of these investors.

New cotton textile firms could issue shares for public subscription by 1830. Half of the shares were bought by merchants, following the tradition of the early informal sources of capital for the cotton industry. The major part of this half (35 percent) came from merchants outside the cotton industry, following tradition. But some (15 percent) came from cotton merchants. The industry was beginning to earn for its participants profits that could be reinvested. The continuation of the initial sources of capital is clearly visible, but these sources account for only half of the capital raised in the initial capital offering of later new companies.

Many people unrelated to the cotton industry invested in cotton mills after 1830. Professional people, people and firms engaged in non-cotton manufacturing or artisan activities, and financiers all invested in cotton firms. In addition, some shares were held by financial institutions, adding another layer of intermediation to the capital market. Women also appear on the roster of people owning shares of companies and subscribing to shares of newly formed companies, and trustees owned an increasingly large share of these firms' stock. On the eve of the Civil War, women and trustees owned one-quarter of the equity of cotton textile firms in Massachusetts. The profitability of the cotton industry and the low risk of investments in cotton firms made them a suitable investment for widows and orphans.[59]

These firms also could borrow on the markets for short-term loans established to finance trade. They raised almost all of their initial capital from selling shares. (In today's terminology, they were not levered at all.) Over time the share of equity in their total assets declined somewhat, but only from 90 percent to 60 or 70 percent.[60] Cotton firms borrowed from different sources depending on the loans' duration. Short-term loans, those for less than one year, came primarily from commercial banks. Loans longer than one year came from savings banks and trust companies; the financial institutions had specialized even then to supply different kinds of capital. Individuals were a more important source of long-term loans than of short-term loans, but they supplied less than one-quarter of even total long-term loans. As the cotton mills grew larger and more numerous, financial institutions grew also to serve their needs for loans. While each firm raised capital in many different ways, the financial institutions specialized to provide mostly one form of capital asset.[61]

The owners of cotton mills looked also for investments outside the cotton industry. There were no mutual funds in the mid-nineteenth century, and investors had to find varied investments to reduce their risks (to "diversify their portfolios," in our modern jargon). It is unlikely that these men thought in twentieth-century terms, but they acted as if they did. Despite the continuing prosperity of the cotton industry, the owners of these firms looked actively for other areas in which to invest. Even though the cotton industry was stable, it did have rough times: in the early 1840s after the financial crisis of 1837, and in the early 1860s when the Civil War interrupted the flow of Southern cotton to New England.

New England investors found many outlets for their capital; Nathan Appleton, the cotton pioneer and politician, purchased a fine house for his daughter on "Tory Row" in Cambridge on the occasion of her marriage to a Harvard professor, Henry Wadsworth Longfellow. (The imposing house on Brattle Street is operated by the park service and can be visited today.) But the most popular opportunity emerged in new railroad companies. In the early 1830s, railroads represented a new technology, as the cotton industry had over a decade before. Boston investors rushed into this new activity. The first railroad lines were intimately connected to the cotton industry. The Boston and Lowell brought cotton goods to Boston. The Boston and Providence shortened the route from Boston to New York and beyond by avoiding the long trip around Cape Cod. These railroads were joined by the attempt to reach the Hudson River and the Erie Canal over land from Boston. The Boston and Worcester was continued by the Western Railroad that went from Worcester to Albany. But while the Western had rough terrain as noted earlier, the Boston and Worcester ran over smooth ground and paid at least a 6 percent dividend every year from 1837 to 1867, when it merged with the Western.[62]

Railroads were built throughout New England in the 1840s. The mill owners were joined by more merchants as trouble in China made them look for other activities. Conflict between the British and the Chinese over opium and the extent to which Westerners could trade with China led to the Opium War of 1839–1842. Boston merchants turned away from international trade in the 1830s and 1840s as their fathers had done during the Embargo of 1808 and the War of 1812. The China trade did not employ many people in New England, but it was an important source of investment capital.

Enthusiasm for railroads was expressed by the Reverend R. C. Waterston in an 1845 poem:

> Here magic Art her mighty power reveals,
> Moves the slow beam, and plies her thousand wheels;

Through ponderous looms the rapid shuttle flies,
And weaves the web which shines with varied dyes;
Here, gliding cars, like shooting meteors run,
The mighty shuttle binding States in one![63]

The slow beam refers to the walking beam of Watt steam engines, which transferred power from the steam cylinder to a pump or other application. It is used here to refer to steam locomotion even though locomotives used high-pressure steam engines that lacked walking beams. Waterston goes on to make an elaborate analogy between the shuttle of the power loom going back and forth across the warp threads and the steam train going back and forth along its tracks.

Boston investors also began to look outside New England during the 1840s and 1850s, to railroads in Ohio, Michigan, and Illinois. The investors in western railroads included Nathan Appleton, Patrick T. Jackson, and John E. Thayer from the cotton industry, as well as John P. Cushing, John M. Forbes, and Thomas H. Perkins from the China trade.[64] Just as the New England railroads had opened up the interior and connected disparate bodies of water, these early Midwestern railroads provided outlets for farms in the interior of these states and connected the Great Lakes with each other and the Mississippi River system. Ohio railroads linked Lake Erie with the Ohio River; the Michigan Central linked Lake Erie with Lake Michigan, and the Illinois Central linked Chicago with the Ohio. The Chicago, Burlington, and Quincy linked Lake Michigan with the Mississippi River itself.

During and after the Civil War, railroads pushed across the continent to the Pacific. Boston financiers were prominent investors in the transcontinental railroads. Oakes and Oliver Ames of North Easton, Massachusetts, led a group of Boston investors into the Union Pacific, earning fabulous profits that stimulated a famous Congressional investigation into their propriety.[65] These investors differed from their New England predecessors in railroads by the source of their capital. Industrialization had progressed in New England by the Civil War to generate profits in a variety of activities, not simply trade or cotton. The Ames brothers were manufacturers of shovels and tools.

These new investors joined the older New England investors in the construction and financial manipulation of western railroads. New Englanders were presidents and major investors during the 1870s (and beyond) of the Union Pacific, the "Burlington" (as the Chicago, Burlington, and Quincy was called), and the Atchison, Topeka, and Santa Fe. Through their support of the latter railroad, Boston investors were instrumental in the development of Kansas after the Civil War.[66]

The accounts of these large investors, who operated through established financial markets, should not blind us to the investments of myriad smaller investors. There were many investments in smaller firms and industries, and in smaller New England cities and towns, that are an equally important part of New England history. These smaller, local investments were financed largely by banks, which were not like banks today. During the mid-nineteenth century, banks were precluded from engaging in interstate activity and even from having branches. Consequently, there were many small banks. In 1830, there were 172 banks in New England; by 1860, 505.

The New England banks were knit together before the Civil War in the "Suffolk System." Banks were able to issue their own notes, which were like cashier's or certified checks—that is, they were liabilities of the bank itself, not of individual depositors. Checks, which are individual rather than bank liabilities, were not used widely until late in the nineteenth century. Banks promised to pay specie—gold or silver coin—for their notes on demand.

One problem that arose in this system was determining how much specie a bank needed to hold in reserve. The bank did not earn any interest on specie, and it had an incentive to issue as many notes as it could on the basis of whatever specie it had. It also had the incentive to hope that holders of its notes would not bring them back to the bank—and to issue many, many notes as a result. The Suffolk Bank in Boston, founded by the same men who had founded the cotton industry, set out to offset this natural inclination of other banks.[67] The Suffolk Bank offered to redeem the notes of any New England bank, not just its own, at par. Since many bank notes traveled to Boston in payment for goods made or imported in the city, the Suffolk Bank had many takers on this offer. It then went to individual banks, asked them to maintain deposits at the Suffolk Bank, and threatened to bring large bunches of notes back to the banks for redemption without warning if they did not. The banks complied, and their notes circulated at or near par throughout New England as a result.

Notes are bank liabilities; the most important bank assets are loans. These were the investments that financed the expansion of industrial activity throughout New England. And loans from New England banks in the mid-nineteenth century most often were made to the banks' own directors. Instead of the arm's-length banking that we know today, New England banking at that time was dominated by "insider lending." Bank directors were not running what we now call a financial intermediary; they were raising capital for themselves.

How could this be? Such a system is ripe for abuse. There does not appear to be any reason for a person not related to the bank directors to deposit money in the bank. And yet banks multiplied and grew throughout New England. The key to understanding this apparent paradox is that this "insider lending" was attractive to the banks' depositors and investors. They knew who the bank was lending to, and they were willing to make loans on the directors' reputations.

Instead of deposits, banks raised their capital in the form of shares; people held bank shares instead of bank deposits. Unlike today's banks, in which capital is a minor liability, New England banks had roughly half their liabilities in the form of shares, that is, bank capital.[68] People invested in banks as a way of investing in the enterprises started and operated by the bank directors. The banks were more like an investment club than a bank of today.

Bank investment, then, provided a way for entrepreneurs to tap the savings of New Englanders for industrial investment. Bank directors were constrained from abusing this system by other bank directors and by the social pressures of the towns in which they lived. A small industrialist lived on his reputation, and he generally—not always—wanted to maintain his reputation so that he could borrow again in the future. The multitude of banks meant also that banks competed with each other in the sale of bank shares, and this competition created another incentive for directors to restrain themselves to good business practice.[69]

Banks loaned to directors (and others) in one of two ways. The first was commercial paper, used to finance trade. Cotton from the mills of Lowell often took a year to sell in some distant city. The cotton mill would use commercial paper from a bank to borrow money to hold these goods in the long interval from manufacture to sale. Other products had similar delays, although probably not as long because they were not made in New England for the whole country. The second way a bank loaned was with accommodation loans, which had no specified use. These loans were used to finance production and the expansion of factories. Nominally written for three or six months, accommodation loans often were renewed over and over again to become long-term loans in the guise of short-term notes.

This system worked well around the time of the Civil War, but by 1880 it was breaking down. New England had become more integrated with the rest of the country, and investments were being made farther from any bank's location. The role of reputation was diminished when loans were made at a distance. Most loans no longer went to directors, and the network of information that had made bank shares desirable before could not operate on a regional or national scale.

Although the banking system worked well over the whole period surveyed here, it had problems in the short run. As people became frightened about the safety of their banks, there were periodic bank panics, most notably in the 1830s and the 1870s. The problem of the 1830s began far away in China in the same conflicts that led to the Opium Wars and drove China merchants to invest domestically. As a result of the conflict, Americans traded less with the Chinese, and the silver normally sent to China to pay for silks and tea stayed in the United States. This silver then entered into the monetary base of the United States, that is, it was added to the existing specie reserves of banks. Banks could issue more notes and make more loans as a result, and prices rose sharply in the 1830s.

As prices rose, so did the flow of imports as they became cheap relative to goods produced at home. The United States financed these added imports by borrowing from England, the preeminent capital exporter of the nineteenth century. In 1836, the Bank of England became alarmed about the amount that British merchants were lending to America and raised its discount rate in an effort to stop it. The bank was successful, but the strain of this contraction—not unlike the reduction of loans to Thailand, Korea, and Indonesia in 1997—led to massive bank failures and then deflation in the United States. The end of the 1830s and beginning of the 1840s were difficult times for American banks and businessmen.[70]

The American economy had changed by the 1870s. Railroads had tied the country together, and the extension of railroad investment had created an opportunity for fraud. These investments were made over long distances on a national stage where the reputational constraints of New England banks were not operative. A speculative bubble burst in 1873 involving Jay Cooke, a prominent financier of the Civil War, and banks failed again. As in the 1830s, bank failures were followed by deflation and economic difficulty, though the pace of economic growth hardly faltered in the 1870s.

The railroad and the telegraph had knit the regions of the country closer together in the half-century surveyed here. Cotton goods, shoes, and revolvers were exported from New England by railroad, and capital was sent from New England to the West by telegraph. Railroads remained the dominant means of overland transport for another half-century, but the telegraph began to be supplanted by the telephone in the 1880s. On April 25, 1877, Alexander Graham Bell went to Lowell to demonstrate his new invention. He tapped his telephone into the telegraph wire to Boston where his assistant was waiting. On Bell's order from Lowell, the assistant transmitted "America" and other patriotic songs back to Lowell.[71] It was a forerunner of the next stage in the economic history of New England at the birthplace of the stage just ending.

CHAPTER 4

The Challenges of Economic Maturity: New England, 1880–1940

JOSHUA L. ROSENBLOOM

BY 1880 THE RAPID GROWTH of manufacturing industries in New England had created an urban and industrialized economy substantially different from the rest of the country. If the years before 1880 had been ones of divergence from the national pattern, however, the sixty years after 1880 were ones of convergence. After the Civil War, the rapid expansion of rail and telegraph networks gave birth to an increasingly unified national economy. As population and industry spread into the interior of the country, the gap that had previously emerged between New England and the rest of the nation narrowed. The erosion of the region's industrial leadership was especially pronounced in the industries largely responsible for New England's early industrialization: textiles, and boots and shoes. By the 1950s, the region's relatively poor economic performance had become the subject of a growing literature seeking to identify the causes of regional decline and offer suggestions about how to remedy the problem.[1]

With hindsight it is apparent that the pessimism of many studies of the 1950s was overstated.[2] Despite the relatively slow growth of the textile and boot and shoe industries from 1880 to 1920, and their absolute decline in the 1920s and 1930s, other manufacturing industries were expanding and the service sector was assuming a new level of prominence as a source of regional growth. There can be little question that the declining fortunes of mill towns tied to the textile and boot and shoe industries produced pockets of unemployment and poverty, but overall New England's economy had continued to grow at a respectable rate between 1880 and 1940.

This essay offers an account of the complex changes taking place within New England in the years after 1880, as the region adjusted to its changing position within the U.S. economy and responded to the social and political challenges posed by industrialization and urbanization. Although the forces influencing the region's economic development in this period were increasingly national or international in scope, their impact on the region was mediated by the unique set of assets—both physical and human—that had been accumulated as a result of New England's prior history. Most important, the region's early leadership in the development of textiles, boots and shoes, and machinery had encouraged the concentration of skilled labor and physical capital specific to these industries. The effect of subsequent events on these relatively immobile factors of production was largely responsible for the unique features of New England's economic history in the post-1880 period.

After 1880 a variety of developments began to erode New England's competitiveness in textiles and footwear, slowing the pace of regional economic growth and prompting a gradual reallocation of labor and capital into other areas of manufacturing—especially the machinery industry—and the service sector. Although the region's growth failed to keep pace with that of the rest of the nation, the impact of this slowdown on living standards was limited by the increasingly national scope of labor and capital markets. As the demand for labor weakened, the net migration flow into the region slowed, helping to maintain wage levels. Meanwhile, New Englanders' investments in ventures outside the region allowed them to participate in the economic opportunities created by more rapid growth elsewhere in the country.[3] As long as adjustments could be made on the margin, by varying the rate of migration into the region, the negative shocks to textiles and boots and shoes were not especially painful. After 1920, however, the shocks to the region's leading manufacturers intensified significantly, resulting for the first time in a reduction in the absolute size of the manufacturing sector. The result was high and sustained unemployment in communities dependent on these industries. These regionally specific problems were compounded in the 1930s by the onset of the Great Depression. Although the growth of employment outside textiles and footwear was not enough to offset the shocks experienced by these industries after 1920, the continued strength of the region's machinery industry and the expansion of the region's institutions of higher education were laying the foundations for postwar expansion. Meanwhile, the region's service sector absorbed a growing share of the labor force. During the 1930s, nonmanufacturing employment fell less, and recovered more quickly, in New England than in other parts of the country.

AN OVERVIEW OF THE NEW ENGLAND ECONOMY

The growth of manufacturing in New England prior to 1880 had created a regional economy substantially different from that of the rest of the nation. Most striking was the heavy concentration of manufacturing within the region. Although it accounted for just 8 percent of the U.S. population, New England was home to more than 20 percent of the nation's manufacturing workers. Over 40 percent of the region's labor force was employed in manufacturing (compared to about 20 percent nationally), while agriculture employed only about one of every five workers (compared to one of every two nationally).[4]

New England's manufacturing sector in turn was dominated by a few key industries. As Table 4.1 shows, in 1880 textiles employed more than one-third of all manufacturing workers in the region, and leather and leather products—dominated by footwear producers—employed another 14 percent of the region's manufacturing labor force. While these industries dominated regional employment totals, the table also shows that they were highly concentrated within the region. In 1880 more than one-half of all textile workers in the country and over 40 percent of leather and leather products workers were employed in New England. But even these figures understate the extent of industrial localization. Nearly 80 percent of New England's textile manufacturing capacity, for example, was concentrated within an arc of land roughly 20 to 60 miles from Boston.[5]

TABLE 4.1 Distribution of employment in selected two-digit manufacturing industries in New England, 1880–1939

Industry	Industry share of employment within New England			New England's share of industry employment		
	1880	1900	1939	1880	1900	1939
Textiles	36.9	31.0	27.5	52.2	43.5	24.1
Leather and leather products	14.0	11.6	11.3	43.3	35.3	32.7
Apparel	6.7	6.7	6.4	15.2	10.6	8.1
Lumber and wood products	6.0	4.4	2.2	13.0	8.8	4.9
Nonelectrical machinery	5.5	8.5	8.7	21.4	17.3	15.4
Fabricated metals	5.2	5.0	6.1	19.4	18.4	12.7
Miscellaneous	4.9	5.7	6.1	35.1	27.1	24.0
Primary metals	3.2	2.4	4.0	11.8	7.7	5.6
Instruments	1.0	0.8	2.0	32.4	23.8	22.5
Tobacco	0.4	0.6	0.1	2.9	3.3	1.5
Petroleum and coal products	0.1	0.6	0.3	14.3	9.4	2.5
Electrical machinery	0.1	—	3.7	21.7	—	14.3
All industries	100.0	100.0	100.0	23.8	18.0	12.1

Sources: Data for 1880 from unpublished calculations of Sukoo Kim; 1900 from Albert W. Niemi Jr., *State and Regional Patterns in American Manufacturing, 1860–1900* (Westport, Conn.: Greenwood Press, 1974), p. 130; and 1939 from U.S. Department of Commerce, Bureau of the Census, *Census of Manufactures: 1947*, vol. 1: *General Summary* (Washington, D.C.: Government Printing Office, 1950), pp. 52–65.

Note: For 1900, employment in electrical and nonelectrical machinery is reported under nonelectrical machinery.

Other important employers in the region included apparel producers, lumber and wood products manufacturers, and precision metal working industries (nonelectrical machinery, fabricated metals, and instruments). Together the precision metal working industries accounted for close to 12 percent of regional employment in 1880. In contrast to the textile and leather and leather products industries, however, none of these industries was especially highly concentrated within the region. Indeed, the region's share of national employment in these industries typically was close to its share of all manufacturing workers.

Once established, the patterns of industrial employment within the region remained remarkably persistent. The relative importance of textiles and leather and leather products fell over time, but these industries remained far and away the most important employers within the region and still employed close to 40 percent of the region's manufacturing wage earners in 1939. Reflecting New England's declining advantages in these industries, however, the region's share of national employment fell substantially, dropping by 1939 to just 24 percent for textiles and 32.7 percent for leather and leather products. In contrast to the declining shares of employment accounted for by textiles and leather and leather products, the region's machinery, metal fabricating, and instruments industries were all expanding, so that by 1939 they accounted collectively for nearly 20 percent of regional manufacturing employment. Although the machinery and metal working industries were growing in importance within the region, they continued to exhibit only a weak tendency toward geographic concentration.

After 1880 the accelerating growth of manufacturing in the rest of the country reduced the distinctiveness of New England's economic structure. By 1940 agriculture's share of national employment had fallen below 20 percent, while manufacturing employment had expanded to 29 percent of the labor force. In New England, although the absolute size of the manufacturing sector roughly doubled from 1880 to 1920, before beginning to decline, the sector's share of employment remained nearly constant at about 40 percent.[6] Despite its already small size in 1880, agricultural employment in New England continued to decline, falling to just 5 percent of the labor force in 1940. As agricultural employment fell, the service-producing sectors (trade, transportation, finance, and government) absorbed an increasing share of workers. The growth of service-sector employment reflects a broader national trend and has been paralleled in many other developed economies in the twentieth century. One reason for the growth of

TABLE 4.2   Relative regional and state income per person adjusted for differences in the cost of living, 1880–1940 (U.S. = 100 in each year)

Year	New England	Southern New England			Northern New England		
		Ct.	R.I.	Mass.	N.H.	Me.	Vt.
1880	134.0	141.1	150.3	160.0	113.1	84.6	90.3
1900	128.0	126.6	136.5	143.8	105.4	91.1	87.7
1920	118.0	112.2	120.7	129.0	97.9	95.6	84.3
1940	125.0	149.7	122.1	127.4	101.7	90.8	87.2

Source: Kris James Mitchener and Ian W. McLean, "U.S. Regional Growth and Convergence, 1880–1980," photocopy (December 1997).

services is their importance to the smooth functioning of increasingly complex market economies.

The convergence between New England and the rest of the country is clearly evident in the changing relative income per person figures reported in Table 4.2. New England's early lead in industrialization had raised regional incomes substantially above the national average by 1880. After adjusting for differences in regional costs of living, the average income per person in New England was 34 percent above the national average in 1880. By 1920, the difference in incomes had been narrowed to 18 percent. The figures for 1940 suggest that New England's relative fortunes had again improved, but the 1940 data are distorted by the effects of the Great Depression. By 1950, the regional gap in income had fallen to less than 10 percent.

Although the discussion has so far treated New England as a single entity, overall statistics mask significant differences within the region. The most pronounced division is between the three southern states—Massachusetts, Rhode Island, and Connecticut—and the three northern states— Maine, New Hampshire, and Vermont. In 1880 the three southern states already contained two-thirds of the region's population, and over the next sixty years they increased their share of regional population to roughly 80 percent. More densely settled, and much more heavily industrialized, the southern states also enjoyed substantially higher levels of income per person (see Table 4.2). Of the northern tier of states, New Hampshire was the most industrialized and enjoyed the highest income. In contrast, Maine and Vermont, the two most agricultural states, actually were below the national average in per person income. As the region's manufacturing prospects dimmed after 1880, the southern New England states were hit hardest. In contrast, Vermont and Maine experienced little change in their fortunes relative to the rest of the country.

Despite the region's decline in relative income, rising productivity both within and outside the region produced a sustained and substantial improvement in the material standard of living for most New Englanders. Figure 4.1 traces the growth of real income per person in the United States and in New England from 1880 to 1940. Expressed in 1996 dollars,

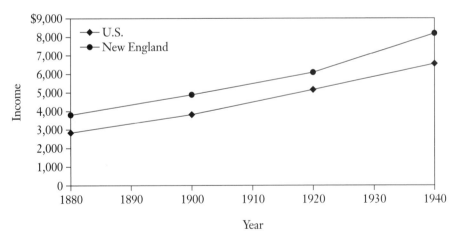

FIGURE 4.1 Real income per person, United States and New England, 1880–1940.

Source: Kris James Mitchener and Ian W. McLean, "U.S. Regional Growth and Convergence, 1880–1980," photocopy (Dec. 1997), Appendix Table A1, and Table 2; U.S. Bureau of the Census, *Historical Statistics of the United States, Colonial Times to 1970*, Bicentennial ed., 2 vols. (Washington, D.C.: Government Printing Office, 1975), series E-135; and U.S. Bureau of the Census, *Statistical Abstract of the United States, 1977* (Washington, D.C.: Government Printing Office, 1997), series 752.

average income per person in New England more than doubled, growing from $3,802 to $8,188. The benefits of this increase were not equally distributed, and the declining fortunes of the region's traditional industries resulted in considerable hardships for some residents, but the overall picture is still one of substantial improvement.

MANUFACTURING: DECLINE OR READJUSTMENT?

The concentration of textile and footwear production in New England until 1880 reflected the region's pronounced comparative advantage in these activities. After 1880, however, a series of events began to undermine the sources of this advantage. Much as the earlier shock of increased competition from more efficient Midwestern farmers had undermined the region's agricultural sector in the first half of the century, New England's manufacturers now found themselves competing against lower cost producers in other parts of the country. Meanwhile, the region's poor transportation links to the growing interior population, and limited natural resource endowments, meant that it was poorly positioned to compete in many of the rapidly growing manufacturing industries that characterized this period.[7]

In light of these events, it is not especially hard to explain the region's relative decline after 1880. Rather, what is puzzling is the relatively strong performance of the New England economy, at least until the 1920s. Although the region's growth rate lagged behind that of the nation as a whole, from 1880 to 1920 manufacturing employment more than doubled, growing from 647,000 to 1.35 million. While employment in textiles and leather and leather products grew more slowly than did manufacturing as a whole, the decline was only in relative terms. After 1920, however, the situation changed dramatically. Between 1920 and 1940, manufacturing employment fell by close to 400,000 workers, dropping to just 953,000. Of this decline, close to half was attributable to textiles alone, which saw its employment drop from 440,000 to 262,000.

This sequence of events raises a variety of questions. First, why did the trend toward the increasing concentration of the textile and leather and leather products industries in New England reverse itself after 1880? Second, why was the decline of New England's manufacturing, and especially its largest industries, so gradual from 1880 to 1920? And finally, what were the important areas of manufacturing employment growth in this period?

Economists have identified two types of explanations for the tendency of many industries to concentrate disproportionately in a few places. The first focuses on what might be termed the "natural" advantages of certain locations. Natural resources are not evenly distributed, and industries that are engaged in the processing of these resources or rely significantly on them as inputs in their production process are likely to cluster near places with favorable resource endowments. Labor and capital are more mobile than natural resources, but differences in the cost of these inputs at various sites may also influence the location of production when one or the other of these factors is an especially important determinant of costs. In instances where differences in input costs are not decisive, the decision about where to locate a factory may be driven by variation in access to markets. Locations endowed with good water transportation, or well-developed rail or road transportation connections, will become centers of activity for market-oriented producers.

The second category of explanations focuses on the "agglomeration economies" that arise when different manufacturers of similar products cluster together. Because of information sharing, the availability of specialized inputs, and/or the concentration of workers with specialized skills or knowledge, manufacturers may find it desirable to locate near each other. Where this is true it is possible for patterns of industrial concentration to arise even when the location itself offers no special advantage. Because of their self-reinforcing nature, agglomeration economies are capable of sustaining industrial concentrations long after the reasons that produced them in the first place have vanished.[8]

As Winifred Rothenberg and Peter Temin have described, New England's early leadership in the development of the textile and footwear industries can be traced to a variety of "natural" advantages that the region possessed at the beginning of the nineteenth century. Although these advantages proved largely transitory, once these industries had become established in New England, agglomeration economies developed that encouraged the continued concentration of these industries in the region.

In the textile industry, two sources of agglomeration economies were important in localizing the industry around Boston. The first involved the relationship between the textile mills and the machinery producers who equipped them. Early mills were dependent on skilled mechanics to construct and maintain complicated machinery, and all of the large mills operated their own machine shops for this purpose. As the market for textile machinery expanded in the 1840s, these machine shops spun off as independent enterprises. But as late as the 1870s much of the machinery they produced was custom built and rebuilt. Given the pace of change in textile machinery and the need for maintenance and modification of custom-built machinery, it was important for manufacturers to remain close to the machine shops.[9] Thus the concentration of textile machinery shops around Boston was an important force contributing to the localization of the textile industry. The second source of agglomeration economies operated through the labor market. While much of the labor employed in factory production of textiles was semi-skilled and required little training, a number of occupations, such as mule spinning—which was used to produce higher quality yarn—and weaving, required a higher degree of skill. Over time, the concentration of the industry around Boston helped to attract and train a significant pool of skilled machine operators that provided the region's manufacturers with an important cost advantage.

After 1880, both sources of agglomeration economies were undercut by changes in textile machinery. By this time, textile machine makers had standardized their product line. Standardized machinery produced with interchangeable parts reduced the need for sustained and close contact between manufacturers and machine builders, thus reducing the advantages of close proximity to the equipment builders. At the same time, the machinery itself was evolving in ways that greatly reduced the need for skilled labor. Unlike the mule (spinning machinery used in England and for fine cloth), which relied on highly skilled adult male workers, ring-spinning machines (used in Lowell and more generally in the United States) could be tended by relatively unskilled women and children. Ring spinning had first been introduced in the 1830s, but it was not until the introduction of the high-speed spindle in the 1870s that it became practical for anything other than the coarsest yarns. Mule spinning remained competitive for finer yarns, but gradual improvement of ring spinning continually expanded the range of counts (a measure of the fineness of cloth) that could be produced by this method. In weaving, the important turning point came in 1894 with the introduction of the Draper, or automatic, loom, which automated a number of operations that had previously required the attention of skilled weavers. With these developments it became possible to set up "turnkey" textile mills using totally inexperienced labor.[10]

As technological change undermined the forces promoting industrial concentration, labor costs loomed increasingly large in the decision of where to locate textile plants. Due to the large volume of immigration into the region, New England's wages remained competitive with other regions of the Northeast and Midwest, but by the 1880s urban manufacturing wages in the South Atlantic region were roughly 20 percent below northern levels.[11] Among cotton workers the differences were even greater, ranging by one estimate between 40 and 50 percent.[12] Given this cost advantage, it is hardly surprising that after 1880 textile production expanded rapidly in Georgia, the Carolinas, and other parts of the South Atlantic.

Figure 4.2 uses the number of spindles in operation in New England and the South Atlantic as an index of the shifting location of production. The rapid growth of the southern branch of the industry is readily apparent in the years after 1879. But the figure also shows that the capacity of the New England branch of the industry continued to grow until the 1920s. In view of the differences in labor costs between the two regions, the question is not so much why the South triumphed, but why it took so long to do so.[13]

The answer to this question has several parts. First, cotton textiles are not a homogeneous good, and New England mills were able to remain competitive in the production of higher quality fabric well after they had lost the lower quality markets. New England's advantage in higher quality fabrics derived both from its greater stock of skilled operatives and from

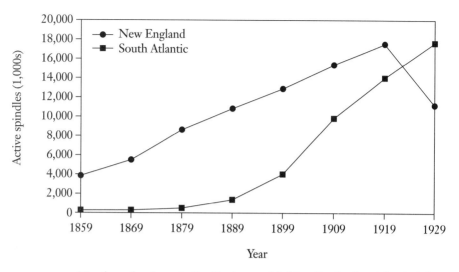

FIGURE 4.2 Number of active spindles (in thousands), New England and South Atlantic, 1859–1929.

Source: Alice Galenson, *The Migration of the Cotton Textile Industry from New England to the South: 1880–1930* (New York: Garland Publishing, 1985), p. 2.

the expertise of its mill managers. Although improvements in ring spinning were expanding the range of yarns it could be used to produce, mule spinning remained economical for higher quality yarns. At the same time, because production runs for these higher quality yarns and fabrics were shorter, and demand for particular products more variable, managers had to have a good feel for the market and the ability to adapt quickly to changing tastes.[14] Second, it appears that the imperfect integration of regional capital markets may have slowed the pace of growth in the South by limiting the access to capital to finance industrial expansion in the region. Consistent with a shortage of capital, interest rates in the South remained above those in the North, and capital-labor ratios were lower in the southern textile industries than in New England's.[15]

Over time the regional gap in skills and capital narrowed. In addition, improvements in spinning and weaving technology extended the range of fabrics that could be produced with given skills, thus allowing southern producers to extend their production into higher quality ranges. As they did so, New England producers were gradually squeezed out of the market.[16] At least at first, this trajectory must not have been predictable, which explains the continued investment in new plants and equipment in New England in the late nineteenth century. By the early twentieth century, however, investment in New England textiles was beginning to taper off. At the Boott mills in Lowell, consultants' reports in the early twentieth century repeatedly called attention to the age and poor condition of machinery and factory buildings, but the company's directors were unwilling to invest significant sums in updating the plant or equipment.[17]

Strong demand during World War I temporarily revived demand for New England textiles. But after the war, demand collapsed as a result of intensified international competition and the introduction of new synthetic fibers.[18] Meanwhile, restrictions on immigration cut off the continued inflow of labor on which the New England industry depended. This combination of shocks caused the collapse of the industry. Capacity dropped in absolute terms for the first time. Some mills simply terminated operations or declared bankruptcy; others relocated to the South. A niche for high-quality production remained, however, allowing the most adept producers to continue in the region. The economic turmoil of the Great Depression was national in scope, but New England's textile manufacturers, operating with old and often obsolete equipment, were among the more vulnerable to the resulting drop in product demand. The result of the collapse of the New England textile industry was felt most intensely in places like Fall River, New Bedford, and Lawrence, in which the industry was the dominant employer.

Like the textile industry, boot and shoe production in New England originated because of the region's "natural" advantages. In this case it was New England's favorable access to water-borne transportation in the eighteenth century, which provided access to consumer markets as well as supplies of imported skins and hides. As interior markets expanded, however, New England's location became, if anything, a disadvantage. Yet the early localization of the industry had given rise to the concentration of a large supply of skilled shoe workers. Because of the importance of skilled labor in production, access to this pool of workers became an important factor in industry location. Consequently at mid-century, the industry was actually becoming more localized.[19] Despite some progress in mechanizing shoe production, the variability of raw materials meant that considerable skill was still required in cutting and sewing shoes, especially higher-quality, fashionable shoes destined for urban markets. As a result, producers in Boston and a few other major cities continued to dominate these markets into the twentieth century.

By the late nineteenth century, however, New England producers were beginning to face growing competition from Midwestern manufacturers in the market for less fashionable but sturdy shoes for rural dwellers. These manufacturers had gotten their start as a result of Union Army contracts during the Civil War. After the war, the Midwestern manufacturers' access to an expanding supply of hides generated by the phenomenal growth of meatpacking in Chicago and other western cities, combined with greater proximity to consumers of their product, encouraged their rapid expansion. As a result, Massachusetts' share of production fell continuously after 1879. To some extent Massachusetts' losses were offset by the redistribution of production into other New England states, as manufacturers opened factories in New Hampshire and Maine in pursuit of lower-cost labor. But overall, the New England region was losing markets to new producers in Illinois, Ohio, and Missouri.

In contrast to the relatively slow growth of production and employment in New England's textile and footwear industries after 1880, a number of other manufacturing industries grew rapidly in the region. Among these, the machinery, instruments, and metal fabricating industries were among the most important for the region's future development. In the years after 1880, the region's machine shops generated a stream of new innovations that were crucial inputs for a diverse array of industries. The companies that emerged and grew in the years after 1880 would provide the foundation for the military and high-tech industries that were central to New England's renaissance in the post–World War II era.

Most of New England's machine tool makers clustered in the Connecticut and Blackstone river valleys, in close proximity to the Springfield

Crawford Induction Motors. *(Courtesy New Hampshire Historical Society.)*

Electric motors like these began to make their appearance in the early twentieth century. Water power had been displaced by steam power in the second half of the nineteenth century, and industry switched to electricity in the twentieth. In place of the leather belts that transmitted power from a central source as shown in the power loom weavers illustration in Chapter 3, small electric motors could be placed by each machine, allowing increased flexibility and efficiency in designing factories.

Armory, which had provided much of the initial impetus for their formation. Another cluster of machine producers, centered in the area north of Boston, had developed as spin-offs from the machine shops of nearby textile factories. Because the machinery and metal-using industries shared a common set of processes related to the refining, shaping, and machining of metal parts and their assembly into finished products, techniques developed in one industry could readily be applied to production in a wide range of otherwise unrelated products.[20] Methods developed in antebellum gunmaking, for example, were promptly applied to the production of sewing machines, typewriters, and agricultural implements in the post–Civil War era. In turn, solutions to production problems encountered in these industries were put to use in the production of bicycles, automobiles, and then airplanes.[21]

Like they were for textiles and boots and shoes, agglomeration economies were a crucial factor in sustaining the concentration of the machinery and metalworking industries. Unlike these industries, however, New England's machinery and metalworking industries did not dominate national production. Rather, there were important clusters of machine shops scattered throughout the nation's industrial regions. While innovations developed in New England spread rapidly to other industrial areas, New England's machine shops were also adept at absorbing innovations that arose in other parts of the country.

The early concentration of machinery and metalworking employment in New England had encouraged the development of a large supply of skilled machinists. The presence of these skilled workers in turn sustained the competitiveness of the dense network of small machine shops in New England and passed skills on to future generations of workers. Skilled machinists moved readily between shops, developing their skills and honing new ones. Their movements facilitated the rapid diffusion of knowledge about new techniques and allowed individual shops to undertake new projects by hiring workers with the necessary skills. The founders of Pratt and Whitney, for example, had learned their skills at the Colt Armory before establishing their own machine shop. In the 1920s, when the aircraft industry began to expand, the shop could easily transfer its machine-building skills to the production of aircraft motors.

The story of Henry M. Leland illustrates the facility with which machinists moved from one shop and one project to another. Leland began his career as an apprentice in the shop of Charles Crompton, a loom builder in Worcester. Later Leland moved to the Springfield Armory. After the Civil War, he worked at the Colt Armory in Hartford. When the Providence shop of Brown and Sharpe undertook a contract to produce sewing machines designed by Willcox and Gibbs, they hired Leland to run the screw machine section of the shop. Frustrated with production problems, Leland was prompted to develop the universal grinding machine, an important step in the development of techniques for accurately shaping hardened steel. Leland spent over twelve years at Brown and Sharpe before moving on to other projects and ultimately founding the Cadillac Motor Car Company.[22]

For the most part, the skilled mechanics who were the chief resource of the region's machine shops relied on practical hands-on knowledge, acquired through apprenticeship and direct observation. But as the nineteenth century drew to a close, formal academic training in science and engineering became increasingly important for machinery makers. This shift from hands-on training to scientific engineering was most pronounced in the newly emerging electrical industry. In 1879 Thomas Edison had invented the high-resistance incandescent lamp at his laboratory in Menlo Park, New Jersey. By 1882, when he opened the Pearl Street station in Manhattan, he had developed all of the elements of a complete system of electricity production and distribution.[23] Within the next five years the number of central power stations based on Edison's innovations had grown to fifty-six. By this time several competitors had also entered the field. Most prominent among them was the company founded by teacher-inventors Elihu Thomson and Edwin Houston in Lynn. While Edison focused on the use of direct current, Thomson and Houston focused on developing systems based on alternating current.

In 1892 Edison General Electric and Thomson-Houston merged, creating General Electric. Because of the company's control over most of the important patents relating to electrical equipment, General Electric possessed a commanding lead in the industry. But by the early twentieth century the company's management had come to recognize that the rapid pace of scientific progress in the field of electricity meant that the company's position could only be maintained through sustained innovation. To establish an institutional framework conducive to innovation, the company turned to Willis R. Whitney, a physicist and chemist at the Massachusetts Institute of Technology who was hired to head a newly established research laboratory.[24]

Corporate research laboratories proliferated in the first decades of the twentieth century, as more and more companies sought to institutionalize the search for new knowledge as a way of insuring their long-term competitiveness. In the manufacture of grinding wheels, for example, the Worcester-based Norton Company began in the early twentieth century to search for satisfactory man-made abrasives to replace the unreliable sources of naturally occurring abrasives on which it had previously relied. By 1912, research had been institutionalized under the leadership of Ross Purdy, who had previously been a professor of ceramic engineering at Ohio State University.[25]

Industry's rising demand for scientists and engineers was one important factor in the transformation of higher education that occurred during the half century between 1870 and 1920. It was in these years that the American research university emerged in its modern form.[26] In contrast to the fixed curriculum characteristic of small colleges—classical languages, moral philosophy, history, and general science taught largely through memorization and rote recitation—the emerging research universities placed greater emphasis on science and courses of practical utility, while integrating the production of new knowledge with teaching. Although the antecedents of this transformation can be traced back to the mid-nineteenth century, the shift was crystallized with the formation of Johns Hopkins University in 1876, followed by Clark University, in Worcester (1889), Stanford University (1891), and the University of Chicago (1892). The founding of these new institutions, combined with the expanding scale of existing institutions, contributed to increased competition between schools for faculty, students, resources, and prestige. Competition in turn accelerated the pace of institutional evolution and encouraged a growing similarity among universities in their structure and objectives.

New England institutions were important participants in this transformation.[27] Under President Charles Eliot, Harvard University had been one of the first institutions to introduce an elective plan, giving students a choice over their course of study. Harvard, Yale, and Clark were also pioneers in the expansion of scientific training and the integration of research with graduate education. The Massachusetts Institute of Technology (MIT) occupied a unique position among these emerging institutions. Founded in 1861 as a land-grant institution, MIT emerged by the 1880s as an important source of engineers and scientists for industry. MIT forged close links with many surrounding industries, and its faculty did a considerable amount of consulting in their spare time. But there was a continuing tension between the goals of providing practical training and the pursuit of research in basic science.[28] Out of this conflict a distinctive blend of applied and basic research ultimately emerged. On the one hand, industrial service and consulting became an important part of the institutional culture, and sponsored research support increased from $56,452 in 1920 to $264,797 in 1927. On the other hand, graduate education was greatly expanded, so that by the mid-1920s, MIT was awarding one-third of the country's master's degrees and one-half of its doctorates in engineering.[29]

THE LABOR MARKET:
MIGRATION, WORKING CONDITIONS, AND WAGES

At the beginning of the nineteenth century, New England's textile manufacturers had been obliged to dispatch agents to travel the countryside recruiting factory workers. By the end of the century, improvements in transportation and communication allowed the region's employers to draw on streams of labor originating in Canada and Europe. Falling costs of travel and communication also meant that New England workers were well informed about and able to respond to employment opportunities in other parts of the United States. The emergence of a well-integrated national and international labor market by the late nineteenth century created competitive pressures that effectively equalized wages and working conditions across much of the northern United States, and synchronized the growth rates (though not the levels) of wages on both sides of the Atlantic Ocean.[30]

Long-distance migration remained costly, and workers were by no means perfectly responsive to geographic differences in wages, but the extent of wage equalization in the late nineteenth century is striking. As long as New England continued to attract a net inflow of labor, as it did until the 1920s, the competitive pressures of the labor market ensured that earnings within the region would keep pace with those of the nation as a

Maria Tomacchio. *(Collection of Immigrant City Archives, Lawrence, Mass.)*

As the New England cotton textile industry expanded, the New England girls who worked there initially were soon replaced by immigrants like Maria, fifteen years old in this picture. The cotton mills still offered a way into a new life. But as many of the newer immigrants were unable to move out of the mills into other employment or activities, the mills also became oppressive and a source of industrial conflict.

whole. After 1920, however, as the region's manufacturing sector contracted, labor market adjustments became more difficult because they required a net outflow of labor from the region. Workers did move, but investments in industry and job-specific human capital, along with more intangible ties to community and family, made the adjustment a gradual process. As a result, unemployment rates in textile communities remained at remarkably high levels throughout the 1920s and 1930s.[31]

Despite the declining competitiveness of New England's leading manufacturers after 1880, the region remained attractive for immigrant job-seekers. Driven by the large volume of immigration, New England's population increased from just over 4 million in 1880 to 7.4 million in 1920, an increase of 85 percent, a rate of growth almost equal to that of the nation as a whole. After 1920, however, population growth slowed appreciably in response to the region's declining economic fortunes. Over the next two decades the region's population grew at only about half the national rate, reaching just 8.3 million in 1940.

The vast influx of foreign job-seekers between 1880 and 1920 had a profound impact on the composition of New England's population. In 1920 over one-quarter of the region's population was foreign born, about twice as large a fraction as for the entire country.[32] Immigrants were even more prominent in the region's cities, making up close to one-third of the populations of Boston, Worcester, Providence, New Haven, and Bridgeport, and more than 40 percent of the population of Lowell and Fall River.[33] Focusing only on the foreign born understates the influence of immigration, however, since the children of immigrants are counted among the native-born population. By 1920, 62 percent of New Englanders were either foreign born or had at least one parent who was an immigrant. The corresponding figure for the country as a whole was just 38 percent.[34]

The period after 1880 was also characterized by a pronounced shift in the sources of immigration. Whereas Irish, English, and French Canadian immigrants had predominated in New England prior to 1880, after this date immigrants were drawn mainly from the countries of southern and eastern Europe, especially Italy, Poland, and Lithuania. The different customs and appearance of these new arrivals, coupled with the fact that many of them were Catholic, contributed to an upsurge of nativist sentiment that flared briefly at the end of the century.[35]

The history of population movements in New England is best viewed as two distinct stories: one for the three northern states in the region—Vermont, New Hampshire, and Maine—and a second for the three more heavily industrialized southern states—Massachusetts, Rhode Island, and Connecticut. In the northern states, there was a sustained outflow of the native-born population, much of it to the more prosperous southern part of the region.[36] This outflow was offset by an approximately equivalent influx of the foreign born, but in relation to the population of these states, the volume of immigration was generally below the national average. In southern New England, on the other hand, a disproportionately high rate of foreign migration was coupled until 1900 with an influx of native-born workers drawn both from northern New England and from the mid-Atlantic region. Although foreign immigration remained relatively heavy after the turn of the century, very few, if any, native-born people moved in.[37] Reflecting these differences, the southern New England states grew much more rapidly than their northern neighbors, increasing their share of the region's population from around two-thirds in 1880 to nearly four-fifths in 1940.

Although foreign immigration created in New England an ethnically diverse population, the region remained racially quite homogeneous. In 1880 only about 1 percent of the population was black, and there was relatively little migration of blacks into the region in subsequent years. Until the beginning of the Great Migration during World War I, most of the nation's black population lived in the South. During the war northern employers began actively to recruit black workers for the first time. These early black migrants in turn provided information and assistance to a growing number of migrants during the 1920s. But the weakness of the manufacturing sector in New England meant that little of this migration was destined for the region.

Increasing population contributed to rising urbanization. Southern New England was already in 1880 a densely settled and highly urbanized place, and it only became more so with the passage of time. In 1880 nearly

80 percent of Massachusetts and Rhode Island residents lived in urban places (defined as incorporated places with populations over 2,500). In comparison, Connecticut, with just over 40 percent of its population in urban places, appears relatively rural but was still substantially more urban than the country as a whole (28 percent). By 1940 close to 90 percent of Rhode Island and Massachusetts residents lived in urban places, while urbanization had increased to about 68 percent in Connecticut.

City growth placed substantial strains on existing urban infrastructure. The density of settlement increased substantially in existing city centers, and population spread into surrounding areas, transforming them from semirural to urban places.[38] Providing safe, clean drinking water and disposing of the waste generated by an expanding urban population were significant challenges. In 1880, most cities relied on private vaults and cesspools to dispose of sewage, and drew their drinking water from the same lakes and rivers into which their sewage emptied. Unsanitary conditions and high population densities created ideal conditions for the spread of infectious diseases. Epidemics were common and mortality rates high. In Massachusetts, one of the few places for which data are available at this time, life expectancy at birth was between forty-two and forty-three years in 1880, roughly the same as it had been in 1850.[39] It was far lower than in the colonial period, as noted by Margaret Newell.

By this time, however, an adequate scientific understanding of the relationship between sewage disposal and public health existed, and over the next forty years, most American cities undertook massive investments to develop comprehensive waste disposal and water treatment systems, which dramatically reduced the incidence of disease. The introduction of water filtration in Lawrence around 1900, for example, cut typhoid death rates by 79 percent. The share of deaths attributable to infectious diseases dropped significantly, and life expectancy rose sharply. By 1920 the expectation of life at birth had increased by nearly one-third, to about fifty-five years.[40]

Another development reshaping urban life was the introduction of the electric streetcar. Until the 1880s urban settlement had been tightly constrained by the need for face-to-face contact. Commercial, manufactur-

Washington Street, Boston, 1908. *(Photo 15095 by T. E. Marr. Courtesy of the Boston Public Library, Print Department.)*

The growth of industry led to the growth of cities, which in turn led to urban congestion. Electric trolleys like those shown here ran from the city into the country, allowing urban workers for the first time to live outside the city in "streetcar suburbs." The congestion on Washington Street led to the construction of the first subway in Boston just before 1900.

ing, and residential districts coexisted in close proximity to one another, bounded by the distance a person could conveniently travel by foot within about an hour. Electric streetcars, however, tripled the distance that commuters could travel to work, and at a cheaper fare than that offered by horse-drawn carriages. The greater mobility offered by electric streetcars opened up a large peripheral area for residential settlement, allowing urban professional and clerical workers to escape the unpleasant and crowded city center for more bucolic surroundings. With this movement, the modern suburb was born.[41] Blue-collar workers remained behind in urban slums, however, because fares remained prohibitive for them and frequent job turnover made their place of work unpredictable. In the twentieth century the diffusion of the automobile and extensive road construction further expanded the distance that commuters could travel, encouraging the continued dispersion of urban population.[42]

Although the crowded and unsanitary conditions in which most blue-collar workers lived at the turn of the century appeared dangerous and threatening to many middle-class reformers, one should not paint too grim a picture. Many of the new arrivals were following friends or relatives who had provided information about employment opportunities and who assisted them in finding housing and work once they arrived.[43] The fact that these friends and relatives encouraged their migration is one indication that however bad conditions might be, they were preferable to the available alternatives. Tightly knit ethnic communities within the city also provided a network of support within which immigrants could find assistance.[44]

New England's cities were vibrant and exciting places offering a wide variety of experiences for rural migrants. Unfortunately few of their blue-collar residents have recorded their impressions. One who did was Roscoe Fillmore, who left rural New Brunswick at age sixteen to join his grandmother and several cousins in Portland, Maine. Writing in the 1950s, Fillmore recalled that although Portland was not a large city, "it was huge to my country-bred eyes and it was full of wondrous things . . . I never tired of watching the wonderful stunts, the chorus girls, the tumblers, acrobats, hypnotists and sundry other acts that made up the recreation of that day."[45]

As the disposable income of the working class increased, entrepreneurs offered a widening array of amusements to occupy city dwellers, ranging from amusement parks to skating rinks, vaudeville houses, movie theaters, and saloons.[46]

The movement from farm to city that characterized nineteenth-century industrialization was accompanied by a parallel shift in the conditions in which the typical American worked. At the beginning of the century, most New Englanders worked for themselves on family farms or in small artisanal shops. Those who were not self-employed typically worked in small family-owned and -operated businesses in close proximity to the owner. By the end of the century, the typical worker was a wage laborer in a large factory and was unlikely to have any direct contact with the establishment's owner. Although this transformation occurred continuously across the nineteenth century, the pace of technological change accelerated in the decades after the Civil War, contributing to a rapid expansion in the scale and capital-intensity of production processes in almost every sector of manufacturing.[47]

The shift from self-employment and small-scale production to factory wage labor had complex and multidimensional effects on the experience of work. The movement into factory work meant a loss of control over the pace and timing of work, as factory owners sought to control much more rigidly both the hours of work and the activities in which workers engaged during their time at work. Drinking, conversation, and other distractions often were punished with harsh fines. At the same time, as factories grew larger, management became more impersonal and hierarchical.[48] Finally, workers became more dependent upon steady employment. The self-employed were rarely idle, and while farmers might experience hard times, they rarely were unable to provide the necessities of life. In contrast, urban wage-workers, who were dependent on money income to pay their rent and purchase food, could be devastated by a lengthy interruption in their employment.[49]

As these changes progressed, labor issues gained increasing social and political prominence. In the 1880s the nation was swept by an unprecedented level of labor conflict. The number of strikes rose precipitously, peaking in 1886 and 1887. At the same time the goals of striking workers were changing. Until the 1870s strikes were primarily spontaneous, defensive responses to employer-initiated wage cuts. Increasingly thereafter, they came to be used as offensive weapons to gain recognition of labor's right to bargain collectively over wages and other working conditions.[50] Reflecting the growing political importance of labor issues, in 1870 Massachusetts became the first state to establish a bureau of labor statistics. Following Massachusetts' example, other industrialized states soon established similar agencies, and in 1885 the federal government established a labor bureau as well. Carroll D. Wright, appointed in 1873 to head the Massachusetts Bureau of Labor Statistics, quickly emerged as an influential figure in the emerging labor statistics movement and went on to serve as U.S. commissioner of labor.

Organized labor has a long history, but until the 1870s unions typically had been impermanent organizations that formed during economic expansions and collapsed during depressions. Starting after the Civil War, workers began to form stable and effective unions, and union membership began a sustained climb that continued until the mid-twentieth century. During the 1880s the Knights of Labor enjoyed a brief surge of membership following their involvement in several prominent strikes against Jay Gould's Union Pacific Railroad. Although the Knights of Labor disintegrated almost as quickly as they had grown, the American Federation of Labor (AFL) quickly replaced them as the major voice of organized labor and proved a persistent and influential force thereafter. The Massachusetts branch of the AFL was established in Boston in August 1887 at a meeting in Boston's Pythian Hall attended by AFL leader Samuel Gompers. The economic depression of 1893–1897 caused a temporary drop in membership, but by 1908 there were 1,300 union locals in Massachusetts, with a combined membership of more than 160,000. By 1915 membership had increased to around 250,000 (about 15 percent of the labor force), and by 1919 it had grown to 368,000.[51]

In contrast to the relatively inclusive ideology of the Knights of Labor, which welcomed almost everyone except bankers and lawyers, the AFL was organized along craft lines, and the bulk of its membership was drawn

from skilled trades in construction and metalworking. In the textile industry, skilled mule spinners were the most extensively unionized, while less
skilled operatives were poorly represented. Also, unlike the Knights, the
AFL focused its objectives more narrowly, concentrating on raising wages
and increasing employment opportunities for its members, rather than on
the promotion of broader social and political reforms. Such an approach
appears to have been better suited to the economic climate of the times,
for the broad mass of workers lacked significant leverage with which to
bargain. In an era of mass immigration, factory workers could be relatively
cheaply and easily replaced, which made it hard to win concessions from
employers. Indeed between 1881 and 1900 roughly one of every six striking workers in Massachusetts lost his or her job to a new employee.[52]

One of the major challenges facing workers in the late nineteenth century was the instability of employment. As the number of workers dependent on wage labor for their subsistence grew, involuntary unemployment
emerged as an increasingly important social problem. A key turning point
in the history of unemployment is evident in the wake of the financial
panic of 1873. Confronted with vast numbers of employees thrown out of
work as a result of the 1870s depression, public officials in Massachusetts
and elsewhere were forced to question their belief that individuals who
could not find a job were either incapacitated or unwilling to work. For the
first time, there was widespread recognition that many of the unemployed
were out of work through "no fault of their own."[53]

Spurred by the crisis, Massachusetts became the first state to collect
comprehensive statistics on unemployment. These data, gathered as part
of the state census, reveal a good deal about the extent of the problem facing industrial workers in New England and elsewhere. In 1885 and 1895,
both years of economic contraction, unemployment rates were 10.4 and
7.8 percent, respectively. In both years, however, roughly 30 percent of
workers reported that they had experienced at least one episode of joblessness, with the length of time spent in unemployment averaging between
three and four months. The incidence of unemployment varied considerably across occupations and was concentrated primarily among blue-collar
workers. In 1885, for example, shoe workers were more than ten times as

likely to be idled as salesmen; and all of the trades that experienced above average frequencies of unemployment involved manual labor.[54] Although the burden of involuntary idleness was borne primarily by blue-collar workers, unemployment was in other respects quite democratic, varying little with nativity, age, or sex.[55]

Although unemployment was most visible during depressions, it was a chronic problem for manual workers. Even when the economy was booming, seasonal variations in demand—or episodic events such as floods, frozen rivers, fires, or a collapsed dam—could cause factories to shut down or reduce production. In the nonrecession year of 1890, for example, when the overall unemployment rate was around 5 percent, 19 percent of males and 16 percent of females in Massachusetts experienced at least one spell of unemployment. Seasonal variations in demand were the most important source of unemployment in good times. To some extent these fluctuations could be predicted, as shoemaker T. T. Pomeroy's description of the shoe industry in Haverhill suggests:

> Haverhill is what is called a low cut town, that is we make low cut women's shoes. They are only worn in the summer, and we make them in the winter for summer wear. Now our business will commence here, that is the bulk of our business, the first of November. That is the manufacturers will commence picking out their crews, and it will gradually pick up until in December we will get a fairly comfortable living. January, February, March, and April we are rushed to death, and do a good deal more work than we ought to; then it begins to slack up again, and about the 1st of July it is very flat.[56]

But even when the seasonal rhythms of the industry could be predicted, the magnitude of the fluctuations varied considerably from year to year, and also depended on the particular fortunes of individual firms and the success of their management in securing markets for their products.

How workers coped with unemployment is not entirely clear. Few had adequate savings to tide them over, and little public relief was available for able-bodied workers. Mutual assistance, credit advanced by neighborhood shopkeepers, and the income of other family members all helped to make ends meet. But the inadequacy of these solutions is reflected in recurrent protests by the unemployed.[57] By the early twentieth century, growing awareness of the problems of the unemployed had encouraged more generous relief policies and stimulated discussion of possible governmental interventions in the labor market.[58] A bill even was introduced in the Massachusetts legislature in 1916 to create an unemployment insurance scheme, but it died as wartime demand reduced unemployment levels.

Among employers the high rates of turnover resulting from irregular employment prompted a variety of reform proposals. Henry S. Dennison, president of Dennison Manufacturing Company in Framingham, for example, urged businesses to redesign their production methods to reduce seasonal fluctuations in production and employment levels. Other companies began to experiment with methods to reduce turnover by dividing their labor force between a core of stable year-round employees and a peripheral group of temporary or seasonal workers.[59] During the 1920s a growing number of companies introduced pensions, stock ownership plans, housing subsidies, and bonuses to reduce turnover by rewarding long-time employees.[60] These changes did little to reduce the aggregate level of unemployment in the economy. But they did shift its distribution among workers by creating a privileged group of stable employees (primarily adult males) and a residual pool of temporary labor (primarily women and young men) who bore most of the burden of irregular labor demand.

Although labor interests did not win passage of unemployment insurance before the Great Depression, progressive reformers were more successful in gaining protection for another type of risk, that of death or injury on the job. Working in close proximity to dangerous equipment, accidents were an all too common threat for factory workers. Between 1888 and 1891, the Boott cotton mills in Lowell, for example, recorded seventy-one serious accidents, including two deaths and several near misses. Many of the injuries occurred while cleaning machinery that was still in operation, feeding machines by hand rather than with implements, and attempting to remove an obstruction or replace a drive belt without stopping the machinery.[61] Until the adoption of workers' compensation insurance schemes, which spread rapidly across the nation after 1911, workers bore most of the burden of these accidents.

Prior to the adoption of workers' compensation, employees generally were assumed to be aware of the risks they incurred when entering a factory, and employers were held liable only when their negligence had been a direct cause of particular accidents. Determination of this liability was left up to the courts. Even if employees wanted to purchase insurance against the risks they assumed, problems of moral hazard and adverse selection made it costly or impossible for them to do so.[62] At the same time, employers faced unpredictable and largely uncontrolled liabilities. Legislative enactment of workers' compensation schemes benefited both sides by allowing workers to insure themselves more fully while reducing the unpredictability of employer liability. Private insurers who stood to gain from the sale of additional policies were further beneficiaries of this reform. The mutually beneficial nature of this change helps to explain why forty-two of forty-eight states had adopted workers' compensation plans within a decade of the passage of the first such schemes. Among the New England states, Massachusetts and New Hampshire both enacted plans in 1911; Rhode Island and Connecticut followed in 1912 and 1913, respectively; and Vermont (1915) and Maine (1916) brought up the rear.[63]

Despite the short-run instability of employment and the erosion of textile employment after 1920, the years after 1880 were marked by significant improvements in the typical New Englander's standard of living. At root, improvements in the standard of living were the result of technological changes that raised the productivity of labor. New and better manufacturing technologies allowed New England workers to produce more and better goods while devoting less of their time to paid work. As they became more productive their incomes rose, allowing them to buy more goods and services. Not only could they buy more of the same goods, the continued introduction of new and improved products offered a much broader array of choices.

One reflection of the rising standard of living in New England is the increase in average real income per person in the region. As we have seen (Figure 4.1), from 1880 to 1940 real income per person more than doubled, increasing at an average annual rate of about 1.3 percent. What this rather dry statistic means in terms of improved comfort, convenience, and health can best be understood by what it purchased. By 1890, improvements in water supply meant that 58 percent of urban households had running water. In the other 42 percent, housewives had first to pump and then carry the more than ten thousand gallons of water that a typical household used each year for cooking, laundry, and bathing. Meanwhile, over half (54 percent) of all urban households in the United States still used earthen privies, often clustered in tenement courtyards. By 1940, 94 percent of households had running water, and 85 percent had indoor flush toilets.[64] The development of central heating produced a comparable improvement in household comfort. Until 1900 few Americans heated rooms other than their kitchen during the winter. The introduction of coal-powered central heating in the early twentieth century made it possible to heat the whole house. In the 1930s, most households shifted to oil heat, eliminating the burden of hauling coal in and out. One Boston study from around 1900 found that kitchen stoves consumed over seven tons of coal a year. In addition to reducing time spent hauling coal, the shift to oil heat substantially reduced the amount of time women had to spend cleaning coal or wood dust from floors, furniture, bedding, and clothing.[65]

After the turn of the century, electrification and the diffusion of electric appliances had a dramatic effect on everyday life. In 1900 just 3 percent of American households, and 8 percent of urban households, had electric lights. By 1920 these figures had grown to 35 and 47 percent, respectively; and by 1940, 79 percent of all households, and 96 percent of urban households, had electric lights. Electricity offered cheaper, more uniform, and substantially safer lighting. It also soon powered an array of convenient and novel appliances. Mechanical refrigerators first began to appear in the 1920s. By 1930 about 8 percent of households had them, and by 1940, 44 percent. Another new product was the radio. Nationwide the number of households with radios jumped from 10 percent in 1925 to 46 percent in 1930 and 81 percent in 1940.[66]

Automobiles also gained rapid acceptance, as Henry Ford's introduction of methods of mass production dramatically lowered their cost in the

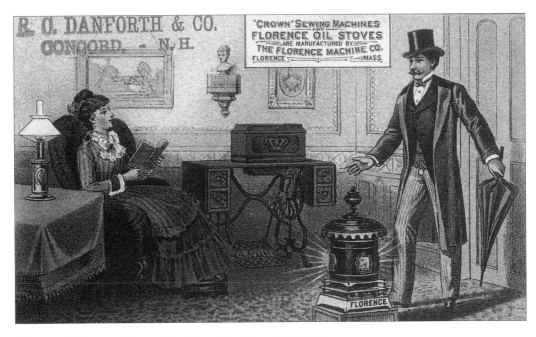

Florence Oil Stoves. *(Courtesy New Hampshire Historical Society.)*

Oil replaced coal in home heating, just as coal had replaced wood in the first half of the nineteenth century. Oil, and then natural gas and electricity, allowed people to heat their whole house without hauling the fuel and feeding the furnace. This picture shows a sewing machine as well, a ubiquitous presence used to make the voluminous clothes worn by women until World War I. As incomes rose in the early twentieth century, more and more people were able to enjoy such amenities.

1910s. Between 1915 and 1920 the number of automobiles in Connecticut tripled, rising from 40,000 to 120,000. The number of trucks grew even more quickly, rising from 7,000 to 24,000 in the same period.[67] Nationwide, 35 percent of urban households owned automobiles in 1920, a figure that grew to 44 percent in the mid-1930s and reached 55 percent in 1942. The diffusion of automobiles greatly increased mobility and allowed the continued growth and extension of residential suburbs. It also reshaped a host of other industries. Livery stables, carriage and wagon factories, harness makers, and feed stores all suffered. But gas stations and automobile dealers benefited. In addition, automobile touring spurred the growth of gift shops and country inns aimed at vacationers.[68]

The proliferation of new products was accompanied by increased leisure time in which to enjoy them. Throughout the late nineteenth century, shorter hours had been one of the most consistent objectives of organized labor. Despite considerable agitation, most workers labored about sixty hours a week in 1880, and progress toward a shorter work week was slow until the turn of the century. Some municipal governments adopted eight-hour work days for city public works projects, and in 1906, the Massachusetts legislature established an eight-hour day for state workers. But the courts generally blocked efforts to restrict hours of work for private employees, interpreting any such efforts as an infringement on the right of workers and employers to contract freely. Restrictions on hours for women and children, which were cloaked in the guise of protective legislation, were less likely to be struck down, however, and in 1911 Massachusetts adopted a 54-hour week for female employees. This limit was further lowered to forty-eight in 1919. Despite these legislative efforts, it appears that most of the movement toward a shorter work week reflects the workings of the marketplace, not regulation. By the 1920s, a 48-hour week (eight hours a day, six days a week) had become common in most industries. Hours fell further during the Great Depression, and in 1938 the Fair Labor Standards Act codified the 40-hour work week.

At the same time, more New Englanders were choosing to postpone their entry into the labor force until they had completed high school. Between 1910 and 1938 the high school graduation rate—the fraction of seventeen-year-olds graduating from high school each year—in New England rose from 16 percent to 60 percent.[69] One important reason for the spectacular rise in high school enrollment and graduation rates after 1900 was a pronounced shift in curriculum. The traditional high school curriculum, which emphasized Greek, Latin, and scientific subjects, was geared primarily to preparing students for college. After 1900, however, communities across the country began to introduce alternative vocational and technical tracks in response to the growing needs of employers for workers

Grade seven, Putnam School, Boston, 1892. *(Photograph by A. H. Folsom. Courtesy of the Boston Public Library, Print Department.)*

Schools had attained a modern look by the late nineteenth century. Students sat at individual desks, worked individually, and were graded by written work rather than oral recitations. "Practical" subjects like math and science, symbolized on the blackboard by the conic sections and the drawing of a flower, rose in importance. The most striking example of this reorientation was the Massachusetts Institute of Technology, founded in 1861.

able to "read manuals, interpret blue-prints, use complex formulas, and understand the fundamentals of geometry, chemistry, and electricity."[70] Reflecting this shift, enrollment and graduation rates in New England and other non-southern states shot upward (Figure 4.3), attaining by 1940 levels that would remain in place into the 1960s. The increase in enrollments was especially pronounced for females, many of whom could put their investment in education to immediate use in the expanding area of clerical and office jobs.[71] But the less New Englanders worked, the less they were

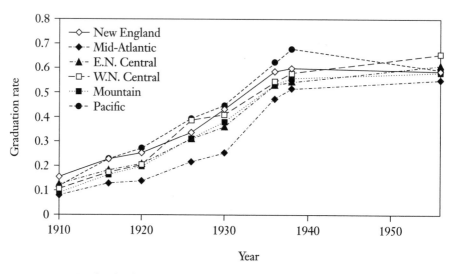

FIGURE 4.3   High school graduation rates outside the South, 1910–1956.

Source: Claudia Goldin, "How America Graduated from High School: 1910–1960," National Bureau of Economic Research, working paper 4762 (June 1994), p. 17.

paid. That New Englanders were willing to "purchase" additional leisure and education despite this opportunity cost is a compelling testament to the rising level of wealth that they enjoyed.

FINANCIAL MARKETS

Mercantile and then industrial success had enriched many New England families. The wealth they had accumulated in turn provided the basis for investment in new factories, railroads, towns, and other productive assets, which generated additional income. As the preceding essays by Margaret Newell, Winifred Rothenberg, and Peter Temin have described, one key to New England's economic success was the development of a dense and sophisticated network of financial intermediaries capable of mobilizing savings and channeling them into productive activities. Until the 1890s the Boston Stock Exchange was the leading market for industrial securities in the United States. Meanwhile the density of banks and bank deposits was higher in the region than almost anywhere else in the country, and the close connection between bank directors and manufacturers facilitated the flow of capital into manufacturing ventures.[72] Because credit relationships were quite localized, New England businesses enjoyed favorable access to industrial finance. As late as the 1880s, interest rates in the region remained as much as two or three percentage points lower than those in the Midwest, South, or West.

After 1880 progress toward a national financial market increasingly linked New England with the rest of the country, eroding the advantage New England manufacturers previously had enjoyed in access to capital (as shown by the increasing equalization of regional interest rates).[73] On balance, however, this development was favorable for the region. Increasing capital market integration broadened the scope of potential investment opportunities available, allowing savers to participate in the rapid economic growth of the country as a whole. The resulting flow of interest and dividend payments became an important source of regional income, helping to maintain the interregional differential in income per person in the face of wage equalization and the growing similarity of occupational distributions.

New England's financial institutions also played an important role in this process of institutional development that helped to break down the barriers inhibiting interregional capital flows. Much as New England's merchants in the colonial period had profited from carrying goods produced outside the region to other markets, now New England's financial intermediaries profited by helping to channel flows of investment between regions. By the 1920s, the income generated by financial service providers within the region—as well as interest payments generated by investments made outside the region—played an important part in offsetting the region's growing deficit in goods with the rest of the nation.[74]

Two of the most important institutional changes in late nineteenth-century financial markets were the development of an increasingly sophisticated market for industrial securities and the growing importance of life insurance companies as financial intermediaries. As Temin's essay describes, beginning in the 1850s New England industrialists had become involved in financing the construction of Midwestern and transcontinental railroad lines. Throughout the 1870s and 1880s the rapid expansion of the nation's railroad network created a massive demand for new capital. Between 1878 and 1893 total railroad mileage nearly tripled, and the outstanding volume of railroad bonds and stocks more than doubled, rising from $4.8 billion to $9.9 billion.[75] The railroads' needs for large-scale finance encouraged the growth of the investment banking industry. A relatively small fraternity of private, unincorporated banks handled the job of marketing this flood of new issues. Most had been established in the 1860s, either by New England industrialists or Jewish immigrants from Germany. Typical of the New England firms was Kidder Peabody, which arranged the financing of the Atchison, Topeka, and Sante Fe Railroad in the 1870s. During the 1880s, the banks also became involved in restructuring the railroads' debt burden to ensure their financial stability.[76]

In the 1880s the railroads were joined by a group of manufacturers who were introducing new capital- and scale-intensive methods of mass production.[77] As the volume of industrial securities expanded, both primary and secondary markets for them grew. At this time the New York Stock Exchange overtook the Boston Stock Exchange as the primary market for industrial securities. An important factor encouraging this shift to New York in equities trading was the concentration of bank reserves in that city. Under the provisions of the National Banking Act, New York was made the central reserve city for the nation. Other national banks could hold a fraction of their reserves as interest-earning deposits with New York banks. The New York banks in turn lent these funds on call to the investment houses syndicating new securities and to brokerage firms retailing them to the public.[78]

Among the fastest growing financial intermediaries in the late nineteenth and early twentieth centuries were insurance companies. Driven by rapidly expanding sales of life insurance policies, the insurance industry emerged as a major force in financial markets, especially as a source of mortgage loans. Because of the long-term nature of their liabilities, life insurance companies were especially well suited to make real estate loans.

For the most part, however, state regulations prohibited them from lending outside the state in which they were headquartered. The major exception to this rule was a group of five companies chartered right after the Civil War, which had been granted wider lending powers. Four of these companies—Aetna, Connecticut Mutual, Phoenix, and Travelers—were located in Hartford, Connecticut, while the fifth—Northwestern Mutual—was based in Wisconsin. During the 1870s, these five companies developed effective methods of interregional lending. Especially important was their development of methods to manage properties on which they had been obliged to foreclose. As a result they were able to weather the collapse of property values of the early 1890s, which largely eliminated the mortgage companies and national building associations that had been their chief competitors in interregional lending.[79]

In addition to their role as financial intermediaries, banks also play a central part in determining the size of the nation's money supply, and consequently in determining the level of macroeconomic activity. Banks are able to create money by converting an individual's promise to repay into an acceptable medium of exchange, the bank's promise to repay on demand. Because people were willing to accept bank notes or checks in payment, the nation was able to economize substantially on its use of specie (that is, coins). But the system was prone to periodic episodes of instability when confidence in the credibility of the banking system's promises to repay was shaken. Because banks generally held only a fraction of their liabilities as reserves, suspicion that the system might collapse could be self-fulfilling if depositors all attempted to withdraw their funds at once.[80] Between the Civil War and World War I, there were four major financial panics—in 1873, 1893, 1907, and 1914—during which banks were obliged to suspend the convertibility of deposits, and several others—in 1884 and 1890—that required concerted action to avoid a suspension.[81]

There are a number of reasons for the banking system's instability in this period. One factor was the prevalence of unit banking rules, which prevented banks from diversifying their deposit base and loan portfolios. As a result, banks were vulnerable to local economic shocks that might undermine their borrowers' ability to pay. A second factor was the system of correspondent banking that had been created by the National Banking Act. Under this system, country banks were permitted to hold a fraction of their reserves as deposits with city banks, and the city banks, in turn, could hold a fraction of their reserves as deposits with reserve city banks located in New York or other large financial centers.[82] The problem with this arrangement was that there was no easy way to expand the supply of money in response to variations in demand. As country banks drew down deposits—as they did each fall—to provide cash for crop movements, for example, central reserve city banks were obliged to tighten credit conditions by raising interest rates, cutting back on new loans, and calling in existing ones. When New York banks called their margin loans, this in turn caused investors in the stock market to sell securities, contributing to a decline in stock prices.[83]

Bankers in major cities, including Boston, sought to remedy this problem by extending the function of clearinghouses beyond check settlements. By agreeing to accept liabilities of member banks in exchange for clearinghouse certificates, the banks were able in effect to pool their reserves. In most years these arrangements were adequate to avoid significant strains. But periodically the demand for currency was too great, and banks were obliged to suspend the convertibility of deposits. In 1907 the coincidence of seasonal currency demands with a weakening economy and an increase in European interest rates contributed to a serious financial crisis. In October, Pierpont Morgan spearheaded a private effort to rescue the banking system, intervening to provide liquidity to banks he deemed solvent while allowing others to fail. As a result of this intervention the financial system avoided a serious collapse.

The events of 1907 were worrying enough, however, to prompt Congress to establish the National Monetary Commission to study the banking and monetary system of the nation. In May 1908, Congress adopted a stopgap measure, the Aldrich-Vreeland Act, which legitimated the solution the clearinghouses had already adopted by officially granting them the authority to issue emergency currency for additional liquidity during financial crises. The commission went on to recommend major reforms in the nation's financial system, chief among them the creation of the Federal

Reserve System. Although action on these recommendations was held up by political disputes, the proposal eventually won the approval of Congress, and on December 23, 1913, it was signed into law by President Wilson. As it emerged, the scheme was a carefully crafted compromise balancing the desires of a complex set of interests. Seeking to appease smaller banks, the proposal recommended creation of a system of twelve regional reserve banks, rather than a single central bank. The Federal Reserve Board, which would oversee the operation of these regional banks, was composed of both presidential appointees and members nominated by the regional banks.[84]

Reflecting the key motivation of banking reformers, the new system was designed to provide a more elastic supply of money in response to fluctuations in currency demand. To this end, the Federal Reserve banks were given the power to rediscount notes from member banks, thus providing a source of liquidity to the banking system. In addition, the system sought to increase the speed and efficiency of check clearing, by taking over the operations of the various private clearinghouses.

Almost immediately after the Federal Reserve System was established, the outbreak of World War I confronted it with the difficulties of wartime finance. Once the United States entered the war, the Federal Reserve directed its policy largely toward helping the Treasury finance the war effort. With the conclusion of the war, it kept interest rates low to facilitate the refinancing of war debt. This policy of easy credit helped promote the brief postwar boom. The Federal Reserve's subsequent tightening of credit conditions after 1919 in turn contributed to the deep economic contraction of 1920–1921. Thereafter it seemed that managers of the central bank were becoming more adept in wielding the levers of monetary policy. In 1929, however, the country was once again plunged into depression.

NEW ENGLAND IN THE GREAT DEPRESSION

In the summer of 1929 the Federal Reserve's index of industrial production peaked and then began to decline, indicating the beginning of an economic contraction. Then in October 1929 the stock market crashed. Standard & Poor's composite stock index had peaked on September 7. For the next month it drifted gradually lower, and then on Thursday, October 24, prices dropped nearly 10 percent. After a brief lull on Friday, prices began to fall again; by October 29 the cumulative decline had reached 23 percent. These events marked the beginning of the longest and most severe economic contraction in U.S. history.[85]

Between 1929 and 1933 real output fell by 29 percent while the unemployment rate rose to around 25 percent of the labor force. Despite a relatively vigorous recovery, it was not until 1939 that real GNP once again equaled its 1929 peak. As late as 1940 more than 10 percent of the labor force remained involuntarily idle. The Great Depression marked a crucial turning point in the history of government economic policy: after the Depression, the growth of federal influence on the economy accelerated rapidly. Within New England, the economic crisis of the 1930s compounded the difficulties of a declining industrial sector and drove many struggling textile and footwear producers out of business.

The causes of the Great Depression—that is, the reasons for its exceptional depth and duration—are a matter of continuing debate among economists. But most recent analysts have agreed that the downturn was initiated by the Federal Reserve's decision to raise interest rates and tighten monetary policy in early 1928.[86] This shift was a response both to an outflow of gold from the country and to rising concern about speculation in the stock market. While this policy shift did little to curb rising stock prices, it was effective in choking off interest-sensitive demand for housing, automobiles, and other durable goods.

At first the economic contraction did not appear unusual. But in the spring of 1931, an international currency crisis spread across Europe, causing one country after another to abandon the gold standard. By the fall, the U.S. commitment to the gold standard had come into question, and speculators began to exchange dollars for gold. Committed to the gold standard, the Federal Reserve chose to raise interest rates to defend the dollar. While the U.S. commitment to gold was preserved, this policy had disastrous effects on the domestic economy, initiating a further round of spending cuts and accelerating price deflation. The loss of confidence was

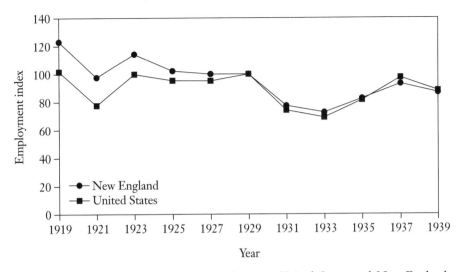

FIGURE 4.4 Index of manufacturing employment, United States and New England, 1919–1939 (1929 = 100).

Source: U.S. Department of Commerce, Bureau of the Census, *Census of Manufactures* (Washington, D.C.: Goverment Printing Office, various years).

self-reinforcing, and only a dramatic shift in policy of the sort initiated by Franklin D. Roosevelt shortly after his inauguration in March 1933 could reverse the downward spiral into which the economy had fallen.[87]

The Great Depression was a national and international crisis, but the effects of the shock varied within the United States depending on the make-up of regional economies. In New England, the 1930s Depression was overlaid on the longer-run pattern of declining manufacturing employment. Figure 4.4 traces changes in manufacturing employment in New England and the nation from 1919 through 1939. Immediately after World War I, New England's factories employed about 1.35 million wage earners. Over the next ten years, manufacturing employment fell by nearly 253,000. In contrast, the national totals remained roughly constant over the 1920s. Despite the long-run downward trend in the region's manufacturing employment, the relatively small role of cyclically volatile durable goods producers in New England's manufacturing sector actually helped to buffer the region during the contractionary phase that lasted from 1929 to 1933. On the other hand, after 1933 recovery was more rapid among durable goods producers, with the result that employment was restored more slowly in New England than elsewhere. Thus over the entire period 1929 to 1937 the experience of New England's manufacturing sector closely paralleled that of the country as a whole.[88]

Despite the difficulties of its manufacturing sector, New England fared relatively well in other respects. Nonmanufacturing employment in the region fell only about 10 percent between 1929 and 1933, and had recovered to its 1929 level by 1936. In comparison, the nation as a whole experienced a nearly 20 percent drop in nonmanufacturing employment and did not regain its 1929 peak until 1938.[89] The region's banking sector also faired comparatively well. Despite the recurrent waves of bank failures that shook the national economy, only a small number of New England banks shut their doors.[90]

Within New England, the impact of the Depression was highly uneven. Where a single industry dominated employment—as was true in textile towns like Lowell, Lawrence, Fall River, and New Bedford—unemployment rates rose well above the national average. In Boston, where there was a much more diverse set of employers, unemployment rates were not as high overall. But even within a single city, experiences could vary considerably. In January 1934, for example, a study of unemployment in Boston found that nearly 40 percent of individuals in working-class neighborhoods like East Boston and the North End were out of work, while for upper-class neighborhoods like the Back Bay, the figure was just 12 percent.[91]

In the early years of the Depression, politicians responded to the mounting problem of joblessness much as they had in the past. Boston's mayor, James Michael Curley, urged an expansion of public works spending and used some city funds to provide additional day labor jobs for unemployed workers. Faced with rising applications for relief, the city allocated additional funds to the overseers of the public welfare. But as the Depression dragged on, tax collections lagged and relief expenditures increasingly drained city resources. In Boston the number of families on relief rose from 7,463 in 1929 to 40,672 in 1932, while expenditures increased from $2.4 million to $11.9 million in the same period. In response to these pressures, the city cut salaries of municipal workers, borrowed money, and reduced the already meager amounts of aid it provided to families on relief.[92] In comparison to other cities and towns, however, Boston's resources were relatively large. Fall River, for example, was unable to meet public payrolls in July 1930, and a month later fell into the financial receivership of the state.

It was in this context that President Roosevelt undertook in 1933 the massive expansion of federal programs that has come to be referred to as the New Deal. One important element of Roosevelt's policies was a huge increase in federally funded relief and public works programs. The Federal Emergency Relief Act (FERA), signed into law in May 1933, made available $500 million in federal funds for relief, while programs like the Civilian Conservation Corps and Works Progress Administration created federally funded jobs on public works projects throughout the nation.

The New Deal is often viewed as a milestone in the expanding role of government in the economy. But this view is not entirely accurate, for the share of expenditures by all levels of government (local, state, and federal) did not grow abnormally rapidly during the 1930s.[93] There was a marked shift in the relative importance of the federal government in this total, however, and an equally striking change in the relationship between the different levels of government. At the turn of the century, local expenditures had accounted for close to 60 percent of all government purchases, while federal expenditures hovered around 30 percent. During the 1930s, these expenditure shares reversed, as the federal government assumed responsibility for funding relief expenditures and what had heretofore been viewed as primarily local programs, such as public works. As the federal government assumed these responsibilities, it did so mainly through a decentralized system that relied heavily on grants to state governments.[94] To a significant extent, grants were distributed as matching funds, making it necessary for states to spend money to get money. Thus, fiscal federalism also encouraged the expansion of state governments.

The distribution of massive amounts of money inevitably involved New

Deal officials in state and local politics. In Massachusetts, for example, control over the distribution of FERA funds was controlled by members of the state Democratic party at odds with Boston's Democratic mayor, James Michael Curley. As a result, it was not until 1935 that Boston began to receive a significant infusion of federal funds.[95] More generally, it appears that the New England states did relatively poorly in attracting New Deal expenditures. Ranked in terms of New Deal outlays per capita, only one state in the region—Vermont—was in the top half (19th). It was followed by Maine (32nd), Massachusetts (39th), New Hampshire (45th), Rhode Island (46th), and Connecticut (47th).[96] Although some of these differences reflect variations in the severity of state needs for relief, there is evidence that political motivations were also important. In particular, it appears that funds tended to be directed toward those states most likely to improve the chances of Democratic electoral victory.[97]

Although New Deal policies ended the economic contraction begun in 1929 and provided relief to many unemployed workers and their families, they were inadequate to restore full employment. Not until the military buildup at the beginning of World War II did unemployment levels fall substantially below 10 percent. While wartime demand brought new life to New England's industrial cities, there still was apprehension about what would come next for the regional economy. Looking back on the stagnation of the region's manufacturing sector since the 1920s, many observers in the late 1940s and the early 1950s can hardly be faulted for expressing their concerns about the future of New England.

Yet such pessimistic forecasts overlooked the remarkable record of flexibility that the region's economy had displayed in response to a continually shifting pattern of comparative advantage. Within the region's traditional industries, manufacturers had adeptly shifted product lines to more fully exploit the areas in which they could compete. At the same time, the growth of other manufacturing activities and an increasingly robust service sector were creating new employment opportunities and laying the foundation for the region's post–World War II recovery. Regional growth had slowed relative to the national economy after 1880, but the responsiveness of international and interregional labor migration moderated the growth of regional labor supplies in response to these diminished opportunities. Meanwhile, financial market integration enabled New Englanders to participate in the benefits of more rapid growth elsewhere in the country. The much more severe shocks that the regional economy experienced after 1920 required more significant readjustments of labor and capital supplies, and accordingly caused more pronounced hardships. Yet even in the 1930s the relatively rapid recovery of nonmanufacturing employment in the region suggests that the response to these shocks had already begun.

CHAPTER 5

The Transition from a Mill-Based to a Knowledge-Based Economy: New England, 1940–2000

LYNN ELAINE BROWNE & STEVEN SASS

NEW ENGLAND'S PRIOR ECONOMIC TROUBLES were set aside in the 1940s as the outbreak of World War II lifted New England, and the nation, out of the Great Depression. The region's mills, machine shops, and shipyards hummed during the wartime mobilization, and they turned out torrents of cloth, boots, aircraft engines, ships, guns, and other types of munitions for the military. But in 1945, the conflict came to an end. And when it did, most observers expected a quick return to the difficult times of the period between the two World Wars.

New England's manufacturing sector—the region's economic foundation since the early nineteenth century—had shown itself quite vulnerable. As detailed in the previous essay, New England's textile and shoe industries faced especially tough competitors from the South, and increasingly from overseas. While many New England textile firms had actually moved to the South or had simply closed their doors in the 1920s and 1930s, manufacturing was still the mainstay of the regional economy. The textile industry alone employed 280,000 New England workers in 1948, and the leather and shoe industry employed another 110,000; these two industries together accounted for 12 percent of total regional employment and 25 percent of New England's manufacturing jobs.[1] As the wartime boom came to an end, these industries again faced major competitive challenges.

The depth of New England's postwar difficulties was exposed in the recession of 1948–1949, the first of the postwar era. Cuts in textile employment devastated many New England communities in which the industry was the dominant employer. In 1949 unemployment rates reached roughly 12 percent in the Massachusetts towns of Fall River and Lowell, 18 percent in New Bedford, and 26 percent in Lawrence.[2]

These dislocations renewed concerns about the region's future and sparked various blue-ribbon studies of the "New England Problem." These reports, the most prominent of which was a study conducted by the president's Council of Economic Advisers (CEA), uniformly described the now familiar story. New England, they wrote, was an archaic economy beset by aggressive, low-cost competitors. The region's multistory mills, built close to water courses and railroad stations, were out of step in an economy relying on electric power and truck transportation.[3]

According to the CEA, interventions by the federal government since the 1920s had eroded further the region's competitive position. Tariff reductions had disproportionately exposed New England industries to foreign competition; federal agricultural policies had raised food and fiber prices; and labor laws had put unionized New England at a disadvantage vis-à-vis the nonunion South, the region's primary competitor in textiles and other traditional manufacturing industries. Most important, the federal government had accelerated the integration of the South into the modern U.S. economy. The government, especially as part of the war effort in the 1940s, had built airports, highways, electric power grids, and efficient, one-story manufacturing plants in the South. These facilities were closer to markets and to supplies of inexpensive labor, energy, and raw materials—and had lower production costs—than many New England mills. The rapid growth of Southern competitiveness and incomes in the 1940s was largely responsible for the decline in New England's relative per capita income, over the decade, from 126 to 107 percent of the national average.

The early postwar years were indeed difficult for New England's traditional industries. Textile employment fell to 180,000 by 1954, a loss of 100,000 jobs or 40 percent of the industry's 1948 employment and 3 percent of total New England employment. The region's shoe industry responded to competitive pressures by migrating from southern to northern New England. In Maine, in particular, an expanding leather goods industry helped soften the blow of declines in textiles. But for Massachusetts towns like Haverhill, Lynn, and Brockton, where shoemaking had been the leading employer, it was little consolation that the industry was moving to Maine rather than the Carolinas. These two industries combined would employ but 135,000 workers in 1973 and 47,000 in 1997—one-eighth of their 1948 job count.[4]

Despite this tremendous decline in these key industries, New England prospered through most of the remaining years of the twentieth century. The region did pass through periods of severe dislocation in the first half of the 1970s and again in the early 1990s. As in the years immediately following World War II, these disruptions generated considerable anxiety about the region's economic future. But despite these setbacks and renewed bouts of pessimism, New England's economic performance over the last half of the century was among the best in its entire history.

The region's economic development in many ways mirrored broad national trends. Like the rest of the country, New England passed through the baby boom and baby bust, suburbanization, the increasing involvement of women in the paid labor force, and the growth in international trade and investment. And like the nation, New England enjoyed the dramatic gains in living standards that accompanied these trends.

New England's experience, however, differed from the nation's in ways that enabled the region to overcome both the disadvantages that seemed so large at the start of the period and subsequent challenges to its economic progress. Because of these regional differences, New England unemployment averaged a half percent lower (Figure 5.1), and income grew faster than in the nation at large. At the end of the twentieth century, New England's per capita income again stood 20 percent above the U.S. average.

Population movements played an important role in New England's surprisingly good economic performance. During stressful periods, when employment opportunities in New England diminished relative to those elsewhere, out-migration rose and in-migration fell. Even in good times,

Percent

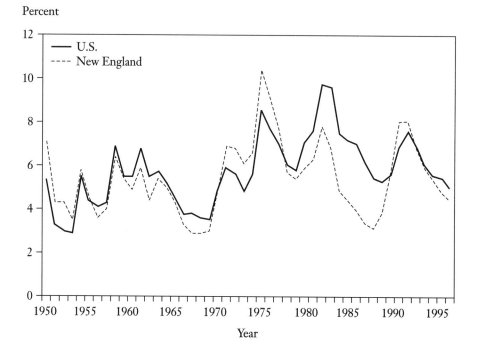

<small>FIGURE 5.1</small>　Unemployment rate, United States and New England, 1950–1997.

Source: For *1950–1981:* Anthony J. Ferrara, *Structural Change in New England Employment, 1947–1961* (U.S. Bureau of Labor Statistics, 1982). For *1982–1997: New England Economic Indicator.*

when migration into the region did increase, New England attracted relatively few low-income migrants (Figure 5.2). The major movements of low-income people in the second half of the twentieth century—African Americans moving from the South to the North in the decade after World War II, and the later immigration of Mexicans and other Central Americans—largely passed New England by. Not having to absorb an influx of job seekers helped New England cope with the hardships created by the loss of textiles and other traditional manufacturing jobs. And the region was spared a good deal of the tensions and social demands created elsewhere in the nation by high concentrations of poverty, language barriers, and racial division.

More critical to New England's postwar success, however, was its response to the successive waves of competition that struck its key industries. Periodic challenges to major employers were followed by the emergence of replacement activities with higher skill and technology content. Textiles was succeeded by aircraft engines and electronics. When defense cutbacks in the early 1970s caused these industries to falter, the minicomputer and

Percent

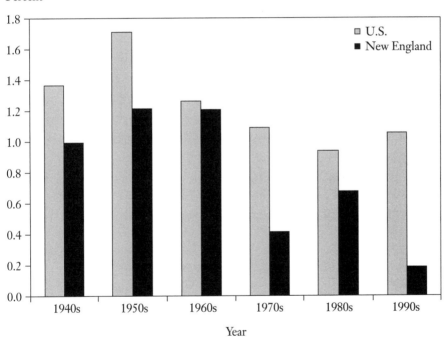

FIGURE 5.2 Annual population growth rate, United States and New England, 1940s–1990s. *Note:* 1990s through 1997.

Source: 1990 Census CPH-2-1, table 16. For 1940, http://www/census.gov/population/www/censusdata/pop-hc.html. For 1997, U.S. Census ST-97-1 Estimates of the Population of States (the figure is for July 1, 1997).

instruments industries emerged to provide a powerful impetus to growth. And when these, too, began to encounter difficulty, nonmanufacturing industries such as computer services, financial services, and health care helped sustain the economy. This succession of industries was characterized by an increasing dependence upon highly educated professionals and by-products that were increasingly less tangible.

New England's transition involved a profound shift away from manufacturing—the source of the region's prosperity since the early nineteenth century and still the foundation of its economy at the start of this period. In 1940 almost 40 percent of New England workers were employed in manufacturing, compared to 25 percent nationwide.[5] It was this specialization that had allowed New England to enjoy its relatively high income. Even though its manufacturing wages were not especially high (except in comparison with the South), productivity and wages were generally higher in New England than in nonmanufacturing industries elsewhere in the nation. By the end of the century, however, manufacturing was no longer a New England specialty; in 1996, the sector accounted for just 13 percent of employment in both New England and the nation. The services industries, in the meantime, had grown from somewhat over 20 percent of total New England and U.S. employment in 1940 to 35 percent of regional and 30 percent of national employment at the end of the century.[6]

It is far from clear, however, that success was inevitable. New Englanders were not optimistic at the time of these restructurings, and each transition was traumatic, involving substantial dislocations. In addition, the future shape of the economy was never readily apparent. During the first half of the 1970s, when New England was just starting to recover from cutbacks in defense and intensified competition in traditional industries, the 1973 oil embargo sent oil prices soaring. New England seemed especially vulnerable, with oil accounting for a larger share of the region's energy needs than the nation's. All the worries from twenty years earlier resurfaced, and people once again spoke of a mature region that might one day see its income fall below the national average.

New England's new industries built upon the intellectual, research, and financial resources created by the earlier manufacturing base. But assets from the past were not the only factors in the region's recovery. The federal government, identified by the Council of Economic Advisers as a detriment to New England's economic position at mid-century, played a critical role in its subsequent success. New England made a successful transition out of textiles and into defense and electronics, and later into computers and software, in large measure due to unprecedented levels of peacetime defense spending by the federal government. New England's defense-based prosperity during World War II turned out to be a taste of things to come.

The other critical contributors to New England's economic success were a great expansion of higher education and increased productivity resulting from collegiate training. The fraction of the population with a college degree rose dramatically after World War II, and especially after 1970. While educational attainment rose in both New England and the nation, the increase was particularly pronounced in southern New England. The resulting concentration of highly educated people in a small geographic area has created an economy in which human capital increasingly substitutes for physical capital—and in which external economies from shared inputs and knowledge spillovers are more important than firm-level economies of scale.

The dominant theme in New England's economic history from 1940 to 2000, as seen from the beginning of the period, is deindustrialization. The key industries in the region in 1940 were largely the same manufacturing industries that had dominated the regional economy one hundred years earlier. By the end of the period, the region's industrial structure looked very different. Textiles and shoes were largely gone. Manufacturing as a whole employed only a small fraction of the workforce and no longer distinguished the region.

The dominant theme as seen from the end of the period is the rise of New England's knowledge-based economy. What set the region apart in the year 2000 was the intellectual capital of its labor force and the supportive environment that its large metropolitan economies provided for such capital. New England's new economy was remarkably flexible in responding to rapidly changing circumstances. It remains to be seen, however, whether this new knowledge-based economy can provide a prosperity as durable and broad-based as the manufacturing economy offered in the past.

THE LEGACY OF WORLD WAR II
AND THE COLD WAR

The New England economy in 1950 was much more oriented to manufacturing than was the country as a whole. Although the dominant industry by far was textiles, other manufacturing industries also were important. Machinery and electrical equipment together employed about as many people as textiles; both industries accounted for a larger fraction of employment in New England than they did in the nation. Electronics was especially important in Massachusetts, while Connecticut was a center for precision machinery, metals, and a young aircraft engine industry. These industries received a powerful boost from federal defense expenditures.

The nature of defense spending and its implications for economic development differed between Connecticut and Massachusetts, however. Connecticut, unlike the rest of the region, did not have a large textile industry. Its major manufacturing industries were metals-based, and defense spending reinforced that orientation. The primary recipient of defense dollars in the state was United Technologies Corporation, which includes the aircraft engine manufacturer Pratt and Whitney, as well as various affiliates.[7]

Pratt and Whitney was a producer of machine tools and other precision-engineered products that reinvented itself in the 1920s as a manufacturer of aircraft engines. The impetus for the transformation was a group of businessmen and engineers who had been associated with Wright Aeronautical in Ohio, but who seized an opportunity to develop new, more powerful engines for the navy. Connecticut offered skilled labor and a network of machine shops that could function as subcontractors; Pratt and Whitney had cash to finance its transformation. The new engine was a success, and Hartford rather than Dayton became the nation's leading center for aircraft engine production.

Munitions workers at the U.S. Naval Torpedo Station, Newport, Rhode Island, ca. 1943. *(Courtesy The Newport Historical Society, P164.)*

Military orders, for World War II and then for the Cold War with the Soviet Union, buoyed a regional economy suffering a sharp decline in its traditional manufacturing industries. The production of ordnance, aircraft engines, and finely machined military equipment became major activities in Connecticut and Rhode Island; in Boston, military research and development, as well as its spin-off industries, transformed the metro-area economy.

Pratt and Whitney was the dominant aircraft engine supplier in World War II. After the war, the federal government decided to sponsor the development of jet engines at the large electric companies, and General Electric, with a plant in Massachusetts, emerged as an important rival. Pratt and Whitney, however, developed its own jet capabilities and succeeded in capturing the lion's share of the growing opportunities in civilian aircraft. It also benefited from the Korean War hostilities and the heightened emphasis on air power in the Cold War of the late 1950s. And it flourished during the Vietnam War buildup.

The other major defense contractor in Connecticut was Electric Boat, a maker of submarines. World War II caused a huge expansion in the Groton facility; as a result of the navy's interest in nuclear submarines in the postwar era, Electric Boat consistently was awarded a large share of the nation's shipbuilding contracts. Largely because of these two companies, Connecticut, with less than 2 percent of the nation's employment, has generally received between 4 and 5 percent of the nation's prime defense contracts since the early 1950s.

In Massachusetts, defense expenditures were distributed across a wider array of firms and industries; a substantial portion of the dollars went to support research at the state's universities, especially the Massachusetts Institute of Technology (MIT). MIT's involvement with defense owes much to Vannevar Bush, a founder of Raytheon and a professor and later dean of engineering at MIT. In 1940 Bush, then working for the government in Washington, persuaded President Roosevelt to form the National Defense Research Committee to allocate funds for military research to the universities, corporations, and laboratories that could most effectively develop promising research ideas; previously, government laboratories had been automatically given these funds. Bush himself became the head of the oversight agency.

MIT received a large share of these contracts. Apart from Bush's role, MIT had a long history of working with industry and already was engaged in work on microwaves and other subjects with military applications. Its largest project, the Radiation Lab (misnamed to obscure its true purpose) focused on improving radar systems. The British had developed the basic ideas but could not produce sufficient units because of difficulties manufacturing the copper magnetrons that generated the microwaves. MIT faculty suggested that the British collaborate with Raytheon, which already had been working with them on microwave research, and the company solved the critical magnetron production problem. The Radiation Lab went on to develop radar applications for a host of military applications. And Raytheon was transformed from a relatively minor manufacturer of vacuum tubes for radios into a major defense contractor. After the war, Raytheon applied its technology to the development of a rocket that could intercept aircraft. With the Cold War and with actual military conflicts in Korea in the 1950s and Vietnam in the 1960s, Raytheon's missile business prospered.

Another MIT facility, the Instrumentation Lab, developed a gunsight during World War II that improved the accuracy of antiaircraft guns. It later applied similar principles to the development of guidance systems for aircraft and missiles and, in the 1960s, to the Apollo moon project. Also in World War II, the Servomechanisms Laboratory took on the development of a flight simulator that could train pilots in any type of aircraft. The war ended before the simulator was developed. But Jay Forrester, the primary researcher on the project, saw great potential for the system's central computer in analyzing and reacting instantaneously to a stream of ever-changing information. The project was refocused in the early 1950s and became the basis for an air defense system along the U.S.-Canadian border that gave early warning of incoming aircraft.

MIT faculty and labs, some later spun off as independent nonprofit corporations, continued to engage in defense research throughout the post–World War II era. And the many scientists, engineers, and technicians who passed through their doors formed a pool of talent that supported the growth of a host of companies in electronics, computers, and other technologically sophisticated industries. Some of these, like Raytheon, existed prior to World War II. Others grew directly out of MIT's military research. The most prominent of these was Digital Equipment Corporation (DEC), which in the early 1980s seemed poised to challenge IBM as the nation's leading manufacturer of computers. DEC was founded in 1957 by Kenneth Olsen, who had worked with Forrester at MIT and was sent to supervise IBM's construction of the Forrester computer. Olsen saw great potential in building smaller computers for industry, and set out to prove he was right by forming his own "minicomputer" company.

Not all of the new research-based companies came out of MIT, and not all emerged from military research. An Wang, who founded Wang Laboratories in 1951, came out of Harvard's Computation Laboratory. After several shifts in focus, Wang Labs became a highly successful computer company in the 1970s and early 1980s, before falling on hard times. Itek, a defense-oriented optical company, came out of Boston University. Thermo Electron, formed to make devices converting heat directly to energy, and Bose Corporation, which makes audio systems, were both begun by MIT Ph.D.'s and professors in the 1950s.

All of these companies drew upon the pool of scientific and engineering talent that federal research fostered. And all benefited from the web of support activities that such a concentration of technologically sophisticated entities generated. Of particular importance to the formation of the Massachusetts knowledge-based economy was the emergence of financial services firms that were comfortable dealing with rapidly growing companies whose primary assets were ideas and professional workforces rather than physical capital and inventories. The building of Route 128, the circumferential highway around Boston that is now part of Interstate 95, also encouraged development by the growing firms in a space that was, on the one hand, close to the city and the universities, and on the other hand, close to attractive residential locations. Industrial parks, largely the creation of Boston's Cabot, Cabot, and Forbes, facilitated firms' relocations to the new suburbs while preserving a relatively attractive physical environment. The air force's Electronic Systems Division and MIT's Lincoln Lab were among the first to move to the Route 128 area.

By the mid-1960s, with the Vietnam War under way and efforts to send a man to the moon in full gear, Connecticut's defense business was flourishing and the cluster of research-based companies around Boston was building. University research continued to generate new companies, and existing firms began to spin off new enterprises. DEC, for example, gave rise to another minicomputer firm, Data General, when engineer Edson DeCastro, frustrated that his computer design was not pursued, struck off on his own. Employment growth in New England, while still lagging behind national levels, was strong. Unemployment rates were below the national average, and the region experienced substantial in-migration for the first time since 1920.

Defense contracting, which had emerged as the undisputed driver of the

New England economy, thus had succeeded in restoring the region's economic prospects. In Connecticut, the primary effects of defense spending were the creation of high-wage jobs at a small number of large defense contractors and the multiplier effects these jobs had on supplier networks and local economic activity. In Massachusetts, defense research at MIT gave rise to many new enterprises serving civilian and defense markets and played an important role in Massachusetts' transition from a center for textiles and shoes to a high-technology economy. In other words, defense dollars helped sustain and modernize the Connecticut economy, but helped transform the Massachusetts economy.

A HIGH-TECH ECONOMY

The winding down of the Vietnam War thus had a chilling effect on New England. Defense spending fell sharply, and funds for space research dwindled after the successful landing on the moon. The region's defense contractors made deep employment cuts. Military bases throughout the region were closed or downsized. Rhode Island was particularly severely affected by the loss of the navy's cruiser-destroyer force in 1973 and the departure of more than 20,000 navy personnel. But the seeds of the region's revival had already been planted. The late 1970s and early 1980s were to be the era of the minicomputer industry.

Although computers had their origins in the defense research of the 1940s and early 1950s, the New England computer industry was still very small in 1970. DEC employed fewer than 5,000 people, Wang fewer than 1,000. By 1974 DEC's employment had doubled, but Wang was still quite small. Over the next ten years, however, the industry exploded. By 1984 DEC employed 25,000 people in Massachusetts alone; Wang employed 13,000 in the state and Data General, Prime, and Computervision employed another 12,000.[8]

The term "high technology" was popularized, and perhaps coined, in the late 1970s by Massachusetts public officials and economists, who wanted to characterize and draw attention to computers and other industries that were then growing rapidly in the state. In addition to computers, the term encompassed electronics and communications equipment, en-

MIT computer, 1962. (Herald-Traveler *photo by George Dixon. Courtesy of the Boston Public Library, Print Department.*)

The dawn of the computer age is shown in this proud presentation of an advanced computer of the day. This machine could do in a few minutes calculations that took people years to do before. The power of computers, and information technology generally, expanded very rapidly over the remainder of the century. The Boston metro area became a major supplier of computer hardware and software, and its universities, hospitals, and investment management industries became significant users of the new information technology.

gineering and scientific instruments, measuring and controlling devices, medical instruments, photographic equipment, and drugs. Missiles, aircraft, and nondrug chemicals were included in some definitions. Computer and data processing services were also included sometimes, although high tech is associated generally with manufacturing industries.

High-tech industries were considered to be knowledge intensive and innovative; they continually developed new products and processes. They were distinguished by high fractions of scientists and engineers in their workforces and by large expenditures on research and development. Although identified with specific industries, the term high tech was closely linked to the concept of the product life cycle. High-tech industries were thought to be at the introductory stages of their respective product cycles, when product experimentation and change are frequent and production processes are not standardized. High-tech markets were also worldwide; in an economy that was becoming increasingly global, high-tech companies were active exporters.

New England's high-tech sector is most closely associated with the Route 128 area of Massachusetts. According to most definitions, however, all of the New England states except Rhode Island and Maine had larger fractions of employment in high-tech manufacturing than did the country as a whole. In Massachusetts, high-tech manufacturing accounted for 6 percent of private nonfarm employment in 1980, according to a narrow definition, and 9 percent under a relatively broad definition; nationally, the corresponding shares were 3 and 6 percent.[9]

Largely because of high tech, manufacturing employment grew substantially faster in New England than in the nation in the second half of the 1970s. This was the first time since World War II that New England's manufacturing performance had surpassed the nation's. And in the deep recessions of the early 1980s, manufacturing employment—and total employment—held up much better in New England than the nation. High tech received most of the credit. High tech, it was said, was recession-proof.

Throughout this period, employment growth was actually faster in non-manufacturing industries than in manufacturing, both in New England and the nation. It was manufacturing, however, that set New England apart from the rest of the country. Moreover, the growth in high tech directly stimulated a host of nonmanufacturing, as well as manufacturing, companies. High-tech companies were important sources of demand for activities as diverse as advertising, hotels, air transportation, and printing. High tech also went on a building spree, putting up new office and manufacturing facilities. Eastern Massachusetts derived the greatest benefit, as the high-tech companies tended to concentrate along Route 128 as well as Route 495, a second circumferential ring around Boston. After years of stagnation, the former textile town of Lowell was transformed into a high-tech center as the headquarters of Wang. Growth also spilled northward into New Hampshire, with DEC in particular locating facilities in that state.

The growth in high tech boosted New England's image, both internally and in national and even international circles. Regarded as a mature and vulnerable economy only a few years earlier, New England increasingly was seen as a dynamic and innovative region that "lived by its wits." Other regions sought to emulate New England's high-tech success.

To a large degree, New England was a beneficiary of national trends. While early computers had been very large and very costly and required armies of programmers, by the 1970s declining computer prices and advances in software had greatly expanded computers' commercial applications. No longer was demand limited to governments and large corporations. At the same time, increased national attention to pollution and energy conservation spurred the demand for instruments to measure and precisely control energy use and emissions. Advances in health care stimulated demand for medical instruments. Moreover, progress in one area led to advances in others. Computers were an integral part of more sophisticated measurement systems. Demand for computer services, such as data processing, systems integration, and software, grew along with the demand for computers.

Not all parts of the country benefited to the same degree from these developments. New England's success in capturing a disproportionate share of high-tech employment was the result of several important attributes. The research complex around Boston was a critical asset; it provided a source of cutting-edge technologies and a continuing stream of entrepreneurs eager to follow in the footsteps of Ken Olsen. The region also was home to a disproportionate number of venture capital firms, and its banks were more comfortable than institutions in other regions in dealing with high-tech companies that possessed little in the way of tangible assets.

The network of interrelated technology-based companies also was believed to be mutually reinforcing and conducive to further innovation. With technology continually changing, firms had to stay close to sources of skilled labor, cutting-edge research, and specialized services. Interactions among people working on various advanced technologies provided opportunities for cross-fertilization and the development of new ideas. Independent "job shoppers" were available to manufacture customized equipment and prototypes. Consulting firms, often including university professors, were abundant. Whatever a young firm needed was available.

Parallels were drawn between the high-tech industries of the 1970s and early 1980s and New England's early leadership in textiles and machine tools. Success then had arisen from a cluster of skilled workers and interrelated industries, the application of scientific knowledge to practical problems, and the availability of risk capital to fund new enterprises. New England, it was argued, was a fertile ground for products in early stages of development and requiring the application of science and engineering skills. But if products and processes became standardized and the focus of competition shifted from innovation to lowering costs, the region would lose its edge—as it had in textiles.

Finally, New England's labor force was an advantage. Although wages for unskilled labor were higher in New England than in the South, wages were not especially high overall. And the recessions of 1970 and 1975 had further lowered New England compensation levels relative to the rest of the nation. Average hourly earnings of New England manufacturing production workers were only 90 percent of the national average in 1980; average pay for all private workers was roughly 95 percent of the national level. At the same time, the educational level of the New England labor force was high relative to the United States as a whole. In particular, New England, especially southern New England, had a higher-than-average fraction of workers with college degrees and the engineering and technical talents needed by high tech. With the coming of age of the baby boom generation, which was far more educated than previous cohorts, the gap between New England and the nation had widened.

EMERGENCE OF THE SERVICE ECONOMY

New England's high-tech manufacturers began to encounter difficulties in the fall of 1984. Growth in world demand slowed, and competition from firms in other regions and other countries increased. Although New England firms continued to invest heavily in research and development and to win plaudits for the technical virtuosity of their products, high-tech employment in New England declined through the rest of the decade. While other parts of the country also experienced declines in high-tech employment, the reversal of fortunes was especially striking in New England. Largely because of high tech, manufacturing employment fell 10 percent in New England between 1984 and 1989, while increasing slightly nationwide.

The decline of high tech in New England remains something of a puzzle. Although various contributing factors can be identified, they do not add up to a satisfying explanation. The dominance of the minicomputer industry was certainly a major issue. The large New England computer companies all were wedded to the same technology, and all came under pressure at the same time from personal computers and later, desktops. Toward the end of the decade, the collapse of the Soviet Union led to deep cuts in defense spending and large layoffs at the region's defense contractors. Additionally, New England's venture capital companies are said to have shifted their focus from start-up companies to later-stage ventures and from a largely New England orientation to a more national perspective.

Part of the explanation may be that New England was just unusually fortunate in the early 1970s. The minicomputer was the right technology for the time, and people like Ken Olsen, An Wang, and Edson DeCastro were the right people to seize the opportunity. The likelihood of another success of that magnitude may have been small. Part of the answer may also be that some of the most innovative research and most promising investment opportunities simply did not have large employment-generating potential. A number of biotechnology companies were founded in the 1980s. Some, like Genzyme, founded in 1981, successfully developed products that enhanced the quality of life and gave value to their share-holders; but they did not create many jobs. And some promising technologies and promising companies simply did not pan out. Work at MIT's Artificial Intelligence Lab, which focused on the development of computers that could "think" like humans, led to the formation of Symbolics and Lisp Machines. But their founders were more interested in their computers' technical virtuosity than in the needs of the marketplace, and the companies were not profitable.

The initial cutbacks in high-tech manufacturing were absorbed with little pain. Employment growth remained brisk, and the unemployment rate fell to 3 percent in 1987. Wages and incomes rose much faster in New England than in the country as a whole (Figure 5.3). By 1987, average

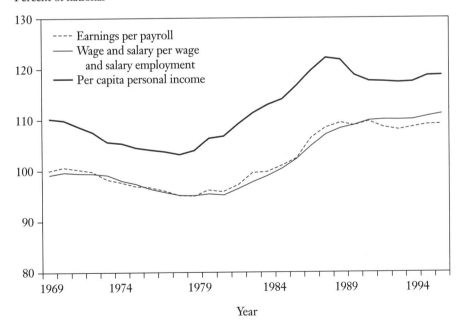

FIGURE 5.3   Personal and labor income, New England, 1969–1996.

Source: U.S. Bureau of Economic Analysis, State Personal Income Database, SA05, SA07, SA25, SA27.

earnings per worker were 5 percent higher in New England than in the country at large; and the combination of higher relative wages, low unemployment rates, and more people choosing to work or to work more than one job had pushed New England's per capita income to 20 percent above the national average.

Such prosperity at a time when manufacturing employment was declining ran counter to both past experience and the conventional view of regional growth, in which manufacturing played the role of economic driver. Yet the paradox seemed to be explained by the rapid growth in financial and business services.[10]

For the most part, and with some justification, services and related industries were regarded as less innovative than manufacturing. Productivity growth was lower, and markets were usually local rather than national or international. But while most services industries were dismissed as amounting to little more than "taking in each other's laundry," there were exceptions to this stereotype.

Insurance was a prominent New England financial services industry that served a national rather than a local market. New England's colleges and universities educated many students from other states and countries, as well as a local population. And health care, while serving a predominantly local population, certainly was innovative; it used new technologies to generate novel treatments that could stimulate demand for health care services independent of local economic conditions. Moreover, Boston was home to a number of large teaching and research hospitals that, in addition to their health care responsibilities, trained physicians for the entire country and engaged in pathbreaking research. Thus, in principle at least, certain services and financial services industries could play the role of economic driver just as manufacturing traditionally had done.

The archetype of this new concept of services was software, and Lotus, founded in 1982, was its leading representative. Software and other computer services had begun to emerge as a distinctive industry in the 1970s, but they blossomed in the 1980s. The industry was especially important in Massachusetts, where its share of employment in the late 1980s was roughly double that nationally. As in the case of computers, Massachusetts' leadership stemmed in large measure from defense-related work at MIT and Harvard.

Grace Hopper was an early software pioneer. As an officer in the U.S. Navy Reserves in the 1940s, Hopper wrote the programs that enabled Harvard's vast Mark I computer to make ballistics calculations; she later headed the development of COBOL, the first standardized language for business calculations.[11] MIT researchers developed the time-sharing concept in the 1960s and, together with the Cambridge firm of Bolt, Beranek, and Newman, laid the foundations for the Internet. The original idea was to build a telecommunications network that would not be vulnerable to nuclear attack. Lotus grew out of Visicalc, an electronic spreadsheet developed by Dan Bricklin, a student at the Harvard Business School who had been a software engineer at DEC. Even Microsoft's founders, Bill Gates and Paul Allen, got their start as Harvard undergraduates.

The other institution that seemed to symbolize the potential for business and financial services to function as regional engines of growth was the mutual fund company Fidelity. Founded in 1930, Fidelity made its reputation in the 1970s by offering money market mutual funds with check-writing capabilities and through the fabulous success of its giant Magellan Fund. With the rising stock market of the 1980s and the growth of defined contribution pension plans, in which individuals—rather than their employers—control the allocation of pension assets, Fidelity was enjoying explosive growth. The Boston papers' help-wanted pages were filled by ads for jobs at Fidelity and at other money managers and mutual fund distributors.

Wall Street was riding the same bull market, and its prosperity spilled into New England. Southwestern Connecticut benefited most directly, with many of its residents working in New York's investment banks and securities firms and many of its businesses providing support services to and competing with Wall Street. The insurance industry, which was especially important in the Hartford area, shared in the strong growth in nationally oriented financial services.

More locally oriented financial and other services also grew rapidly. Banking grew much faster in New England than it did nationwide.

Growth was very strong in engineering and architectural services. Health care was a major source of employment gains, although growth fell short of national rates.

With the benefit of hindsight, it is apparent that there was an artificial quality to some of this growth. The region's prosperity fed on itself, setting in motion a construction and real estate boom. The collapse of this boom was traumatic. Bankruptcies soared and a significant number of banks, those that were victims of bad real estate loans, failed. In the recession of 1990–1991, employment in New England fell by 10 percent—the worst job loss since demobilization after World War II. Employment in the nation fell less than 2 percent. Out-migration and withdrawal from the labor force moderated the rise in unemployment in the region and helped sustain incomes.

The New England economy that emerged in the 1990s was even more dominated by services. In this, New England's experience mirrored the nation's. Defense and computers remained in the doldrums. New England's computer makers continued to struggle, with DEC eventually being acquired by Texas-based Compaq Computer Corporation and Wang and Prime actually exiting the computer hardware business. The region's defense contractors won a smaller share of the nation's prime contract awards, a dramatic change given that defense procurement accounted for a progressively smaller share of GDP.

The industries that supported the region's expansion in the 1990s were much less distinctive and less closely identified with New England than those of the past. The bulk of the job growth was in services and related industries that, superficially at least, were little different from such industries in the rest of the country. The firms were either small, volatile, and largely unknown or parts of large national chains.

From the Industrial Revolution through the end of World War II, a handful of industries had been the foundation of the New England economy. For roughly a century, textiles, shoes, machine making, metal fabrication, and electrical equipment had been the mainstays of the region. Defense played a critical role in the region's transition from traditional pursuits in the 1950s and 1960s and contributed to the region's prosperity in the early 1980s, but by the 1990s its influence had been greatly reduced. The era of the computer industry, which helped lead New England's revival in the 1970s and came to symbolize the region's transformation, was even more fleeting. It was a cornerstone of New England's economic foundation for barely a generation. In the 1990s, no such industry stood out. The result was an amorphous economy, one not readily characterized nor understood, but prosperous nonetheless.

THE AMORPHOUS ECONOMY

The most important source of employment growth in the 1990s was business services. Two very different activities accounted for most of this growth—computer-related services and personnel supply services. By the late 1990s, the number of people employed in computer-related services in Massachusetts was roughly two and one-half times the number engaged in the actual manufacture of computers.[12] Most of the growth in computer services came from the creation of new firms rather than expansion at existing firms. With the notable exception of Lotus, which had roughly 6,000 Massachusetts employees when it was acquired by IBM in 1995, the industry was dominated by small firms, some with as few as three or four employees. These firms provided a huge variety of products, from tools to help other software companies create new software to networking programs that tie computers together, financial planning packages, and graphics and formatting capabilities to make presentations more professional.

The industry was very fluid. Firms appeared and disappeared. They were acquired and changed their names. Sometimes they changed their business. Often, the line between computer-related services and other industries was fuzzy. Firms could combine software services with telecommunications or the manufacture of computer hardware; they also could provide consulting and data management services. Indeed, systems integration was a Massachusetts specialty—an outgrowth, some claimed, of the expertise developed from work on complex weapons systems.

Personnel supply was the other major source of growth in business services in the 1990s. Firms of all kinds, both in New England and in the nation, looked to temporary workers rather than permanent hires to meet their manpower needs. The workers provided by a help supply agency were employees of the agency and thus counted as part of business services. But they actually worked in banks and insurance companies, manufacturing plants, and even software firms. The range of skills available through such agencies had grown far beyond the clerical activities traditionally associated with temporary work. Many help supply firms specialized in professional and technical workers; some offered whole teams of professionals to handle complex software design or engineering projects. The use of temporary help was the ultimate form of outsourcing, the use of outside vendors to supply services formerly provided by employees of the firm. The growth of this sector was perhaps the clearest illustration of the amorphous character of the U.S. and New England economies in the 1990s.

Also contributing to the amorphous quality of regional growth were the various service providers that did business in national and international markets, as well as within the region. Most New England law firms served only a local clientele; but some handled mergers and acquisitions or trade disputes for multinational corporations. Some physicians and hospitals, financial advisers, engineering firms, management consultants, and entertainment and recreation facilities likewise served a national clientele and brought significant income into the region. But it was difficult to discern precisely how much of these industries' resources and activities were devoted to local clients and how much were allocated to national customers. Thus the nature of their contribution to the region's prosperity remained unclear.

New England still had some of its distinctive industrial clusters. Mutual funds and asset management companies in Massachusetts and securities firms in Connecticut were clusters that fared extraordinarily well. The Massachusetts software and communications services, as well as equipment industries, can be viewed as part of a larger "information technology" sector that also included the computer makers. These industries drew on many of the same skills and resources, and with the eclipse of the minicomputer, many of the hardware resources flowed into these companion industries.

Nevertheless, reorganization and diffusion were at least as important as continuity with the industrial past. In the information technology sector, for example, the discontinuities in markets, distribution channels, and technical traditions separating the computer makers and the software and communications industries called forth new rosters of firms, even as older hardware companies struggled to compete. Moreover, the software and communications clusters themselves were divided into differentiated segments connected to still other parts of the New England industrial landscape. Within the telecommunications industry, for example, the Massachusetts Telecommunications Council listed three primary "segments"—manufacturing, software/network integration, and communications services. The Massachusetts Technology Collaborative called such clusters "fusion industries," since they "combine the strengths of several industries." Because of their amorphous quality, the collaborative continued, "fusion industries are often difficult to define and to track over time."[13]

Thus the 1990s saw a dramatic reorganization and diffusion of New England's industrial base. The patterns of industrial growth were much the same in the New England and U.S. economies. And by the end of the decade, the broad industrial contours of the region were much the same as those of the nation (Figure 5.4). Despite this similarity and despite the vicissitudes of the early 1990s, New England's per capita income remained well above that in the country as a whole.

HIGHER EDUCATION AND THE
KNOWLEDGE-BASED ECONOMY

At the beginning of the twenty-first century, the New England economy is perhaps best characterized by its universities and highly educated workforce. A tremendous increase in the nation's investment in higher education was one of the central economic developments of the last half of the twentieth century. The share of the U.S. workforce composed of managers, professionals, and technical workers grew dramatically. Despite this increase in supply, these educated workers continued to earn substantially more than workers without this "human capital." The surge in collegiate

Percent of total earnings by place of work

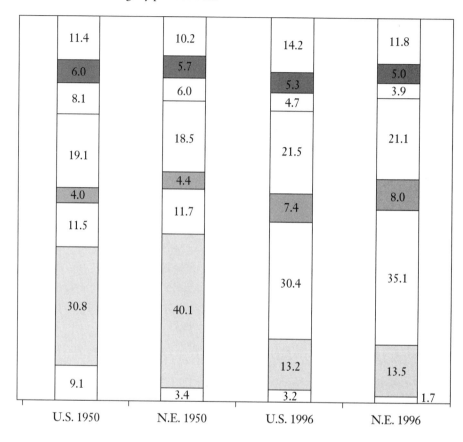

<small>□ Government and government enterprises   ■ Finance, insurance, and real estate</small>
<small>■ Construction   □ Services</small>
<small>□ Transportation and public utilities   □ Manufacturing and mining</small>
<small>□ Wholesale and retail trade   □ Farm, ag. services, forestry, fishing, other</small>

FIGURE 5.4   Earnings by industry, United States and New England, 1950, 1996.
     Source: U.S. Bureau of Economic Analysis, State Personal Income Database, sao5.

education, which affected the entire U.S. economy, was unusually important for New England. The region's role in this educational process and, in time, the disproportionate gain in the educational attainment and professional competencies of its workforce, underlay its transition from a mill-based to a knowledge-based economy.

Before World War II, workers with college educations were rare. Only 4.5 percent of U.S. workers ages twenty-five and over had college degrees in 1940. These educated workers were concentrated in upper management positions and in professional service industries such as education, health care, and law.[14] By the end of the twentieth century, however, over half of all young Americans would enter college. Nearly one in four U.S. workers would hold a baccalaureate; one in twelve, more advanced degrees.

World War II was a turning point. The wartime experience dissipated many of the social barriers to college attendance, especially for poorer whites and the children of European immigrants. Stepped-up government spending then financed the schooling of a great many young people who otherwise would not have attended college. The GI Bill—the Servicemen's Readjustment Act of 1944—stretched out the reabsorption of returning servicemen into the economy by paying their tuition at college or technical school. The program equipped these veterans with skills that raised their productivity and incomes when they reentered the workforce. The GI Bill proved extremely popular and helped push the level of school enrollment in 1950 to 13 percent of U.S. young adults (those twenty to twenty-four years of age). This fraction continued to rise as state governments—the nation's major operators and funders of collegiate institutions—kept expanding their programs.

The largest enrollment jump came in the mid-1960s, when the leading edge of the baby boom generation, those born between 1946 and 1964, reached college age. Baby boomers were much more likely to go to college than cohorts just ahead of them, and there were many more in their cohort. College attendance levels remained about the same for succeeding age groups, but the stock of human capital in the U.S. economy continued to rise as these better-educated cohorts entered the labor force and less-well-educated ones exited.

New England, with its concentration of elite private universities, had long been a national center for higher education. At the end of the nineteenth century, about one in four U.S. college graduates held degrees from New England institutions. But over the first half of the twentieth century, the growth of state colleges and universities elsewhere in the nation diminished New England's distinctive role. By 1940, college attendance and the educational attainment of the workforce essentially were identical in New England and the rest of the nation. Throughout the postwar era, state governments in New England continued to play a much smaller role in higher education than did states elsewhere in the nation.

New England's colleges and universities nevertheless flourished in the postwar years. The nation's leading universities still were located disproportionately in New England, and the status of academic learning received a significant boost in the atomic age. With the government paying the bill for returning veterans, ability to pay became a much less significant factor in college attendance. Immediately after the war, the nation's elite institutions shifted their focus from serving the nation's socioeconomic elite toward educating its intellectual elite.[15] New England's colleges and universities captured a disproportionate share of the postwar surge in enrollments as students from other parts of the country came to New England to go to school. Reflecting this migration, 16 percent of New England's young adult population was enrolled in school by 1950, versus 13 percent nationwide. This enrollment differential continued through the remainder of the century, as New England institutions continued to attract both tuition-paying students and students bringing significant financial support from the federal government.[16]

The success of New England's colleges and universities had several important economic implications. Most directly, higher education became a bigger industry in the region. In addition to its direct employment effects, the expansion of the universities stimulated the construction industry and, through the expenditures of students, various locally oriented industries such as retail trade, real estate, and amusement and recreational services. Universities, with their large endowments and other financial assets, also

The kitchen of today, 1967. *(Courtesy of the Boston Public Library, Print Department.)*

The kitchen illustrates the rise in economic well-being. Gone are the open fires of colonial days and the stand-alone appliances of the nineteenth century. Kitchens assumed their "modern" form after World War II, with ever more efficient appliances integrated into a sleek, streamlined workspace. New materials such as plastics—found throughout the modern kitchen, in items from the cabinets to the table and chairs—further increased functionality and the quality of everyday life.

became important players in the investment management community; from the start, too, they participated in venture capital funds.

Higher education functioned increasingly as an "export" industry, one that brought income into the region. This was not the case at the start of the period. A study by Penelope Hartland estimated that the net contribution from the provision of higher education and ancillary services (gross receipts less payments made for New England students studying outside the region) amounted to just 0.1 percent of regional income in 1939. By 1958, according to estimates by Francis Doody, net "exports" of higher education and ancillary services had risen to 0.8 percent of regional income.[17] This contribution most likely rose even more with the arrival of the baby boom generation. Between 1960 and 1970, the wages and salaries of people employed in private education rose from a 1.5 percent to a 2 percent share of New England personal income. By the mid-1990s, over 20 percent of entering freshmen came from outside the region, and 5 percent of total enrollments came from outside the United States.[18]

The most critical economic contribution of the region's universities—with the possible exception of the research activities discussed earlier—was the supply of labor they provided to the regional economy. The unusually large number of young people graduating from New England's colleges and universities gave the region a rich supply of educated workers equipped with the most up-to-date academic training. In 1970, for example, New England had less than 6 percent of the nation's population but produced 7 percent of the nation's bachelor's degrees and more than 8 percent of its advanced degrees. The figures at the end of the century were much the same.[19]

In the years immediately after World War II, opportunities for college graduates, particularly those in technical areas, were quite limited in New England and many left the region. "The median salary of Ph.D. scientists employed by private industry in New England in 1948 was lower than in any other region of the country except the Mountain and Plains states."[20] It is perhaps no wonder that people like Ken Olsen and An Wang decided to found their own companies. A decade later, the educational attainment of New England's labor force was much the same as that of the nation. Despite the region's higher college enrollment and graduation rates, only 8 percent of New Englanders over age twenty-five had completed college—roughly the same as in the country as a whole.

This situation changed with the baby boom. In line with trends around the nation, the number of young adults enrolled in New England schools more than doubled in the 1960s, with growth particularly strong among those seeking advanced degrees. The number of bachelor's degrees conferred by New England institutions jumped from 29,000 in 1960 to 56,000 in 1970; the number of master's and doctoral degrees from 8,000 to over 20,000.[21] With advances in the quality of professional education, many of these graduates entered the labor force with substantially improved skills.

In business education, perhaps the curriculum experiencing the most significant improvement, training in economics, statistics, and computer methods became standard. This was especially so in the increasingly popular MBA programs.[22]

The entry of the highly educated baby boomers into the labor force and the rapid growth of New England's high-technology industries in the 1970s were more than a mere coincidence. While young workers with academic training in science, engineering, business, and other professional areas were relatively abundant in New England, the demand for their services from traditional sources was limited. With defense cutbacks and intensified competition in textiles, shoes, and other older industries, the New England economy was in the doldrums in the first half of the 1970s. Meanwhile, the nationwide surge of well-educated baby boomers into the economy had overwhelmed the available supply of job opportunities, depressing the incomes of college graduates elsewhere (especially relative to high school graduates). The oil shock and the recession of 1973–1975 further dampened employer demand. By default, offers from the emerging minicomputer companies and other New England firms in high-tech and knowledge-based industries were attractive.[23]

The baby boomers provided the state-of-the-art knowledge, the drive, and the imagination that were necessary to make fledgling companies international competitors. These industries needed more than scientists and engineers. Sales and marketing people, financial analysts, technical writers, and customer service representatives were all important in high-tech firms. In the 1970s, the baby boomers also provided a workforce for other rapidly growing industries with advanced educational requirements, such as law, health care, investment management, management consulting, and computer and data processing.

It proved critical for New England that many of the newer knowledge-intensive industries were exporters. Unlike traditional employers of highly educated workers, such as law, religion, health care, and education, these new industries did not need to be geographically close to their customers. This was especially true for the high-technology manufacturers. But many firms selling business and financial services also found ways to sell their products in national and international markets. They used airplanes to travel to consulting engagements or business reviews outside the region. And they employed a host of new communications devices—from magnetic tapes, diskettes, and modems to fax machines, CD-ROMs, and the Internet—to transfer their services around the globe with speed and economy.

The blossoming of New England's high-technology and knowledge-based industries in the 1970s created a clear gap in educational attainment between the labor force in New England and that of the rest of the country. By 1980, 19 percent of New England adults ages twenty-five and over had college degrees, compared to 16 percent nationwide. And this gap continued to widen. By 1996, 30 percent of New England adults had college degrees, compared to 24 percent nationally. Almost 11 percent of New Englanders also had graduate or professional degrees, compared to 8 percent in the nation (Figure 5.5).

The current New England economy is distinctive for the high educational attainment and professional competencies of its workforce. In the "industrial age," the period from the early nineteenth century to the middle of the twentieth, New England's economy was best characterized by its industrial composition—its strong manufacturing orientation and within manufacturing, its specialization in textiles, shoes, and machinery. But after more than a century of relative stability, the industrial composition of the region changed dramatically and in the process became much more like the structure in the rest of the nation.

Meanwhile, the educational attainment and professionalism of the New England workforce grew more exceptional. The industries that served as the region's economic drivers after World War II all had relied on the highly educated workers supplied by New England's colleges and universities. The significance of the region's workforce became even more apparent at the end of the century. Information technology, biotech and medical products, mutual funds and securities firms, and professional services such as management consulting, law, engineering, and health care—all of these industries relied on highly educated professionals.

Percent of population 25 years and older

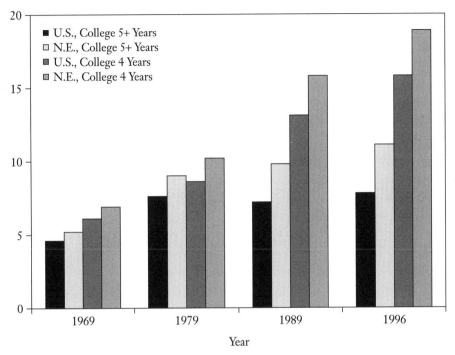

FIGURE 5.5 Baccalaureate and postbaccalaureate college graduates, United States and New England, 1969–1996.

Source: U.S. Bureau of the Census, table P27 (1996), table P28 (all other years), at www.census.gov/hhes/income/histinc/incperdet.html.

This distinctive workforce underlay key aspects of New England's postwar economic performance, and especially that of the last quarter-century.

For example, New England's highly educated labor force contributed to the region's industrial volatility by supporting the development of technically innovative firms and industries. This dynamism meant that product cycles were short and firms were exposed to technical "shocks," or unexpected technological developments, that could alter the competitive landscape for good or ill. Such shocks were especially prevalent in information technology. New England enjoyed unexpected successes in minicomputers and telecommunications. But it also suffered nasty surprises from competing technologies, like the personal computer, and from technological disappointments, like artificial intelligence. As information technology became "the tools of the trade" for essentially all highly educated workers, the dynamism of the sector produced instability throughout New England's knowledge-based economy.

Adding to the volatility of New England's knowledge-based economy was a relative lack of significant sunk costs at the enterprise level. Most firms that relied on New England's highly educated workforce did not need to make major investments in company-specific or even industry-specific capital. Specialized manufacturers, such as the aircraft engine makers, were an exception, and many knowledge-based companies invested in proprietary technologies and company-specific marketing relationships. Nevertheless, most used generic capital and rented much of what they used. They typically leased their real estate—usually standard office and research and development space. Much of their equipment was generic information technology, which, even if purchased, had a very short life span. The primary asset used in their ventures was human capital, which they "rented" by paying higher wages. Because of this lack of long-term sunk costs, firms could enter an industry, expand, contract, and exit with relative ease.

New England's distinctive workforce also helps explain the sharp jump in the region's income relative to the nation's. Earnings in New England went from 96 to 109 percent of the national average between 1980 and 1990, a remarkable rise.[24] And despite the deterioration in the region's economic performance in the early 1990s, workers in New England maintained that earnings differential.

A sharp increase in the earnings premium associated with a college education contributed to this rise in New England labor incomes. College-educated men in the United States earned about 45 percent more than high school graduates in 1980, and about 65 percent more in 1990; the rise in the education wage premium for women was much the same (Figure 5.6). Given the growing concentration of college-educated workers in New England, this rise in the nationwide returns to education, by itself, can ac-

Ratio, earnings of college graduates to earnings of high school graduates

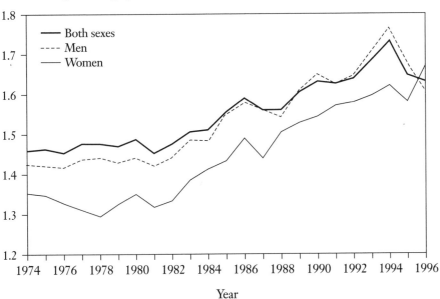

FIGURE 5.6   National college wage premium, 1974–1996.

Source: U.S. Bureau of the Census, table P27 (1996), table P28 (all other years), at www.census.gov/hhes/income/histinc/incperdet.html.

count for roughly 15 percent (or 2 percentage points) of New England's gain in relative earnings.[25]

A second factor raising New England incomes was the agglomeration economies in knowledge-based activities. Agglomeration economies are increases in productivity that result when factors of production cluster together. The fact that economic activity concentrates in cities and does not spread evenly across the landscape, or that the U.S. textile industry clustered for so many years in eastern New England, demonstrates the importance of agglomeration economies in economic history.

Clustering is not always beneficial. In economics, the standard assumption is that an increase in the supply of a factor (given fixed supplies of other factors) will diminish its productivity and its market price. Agriculture in sixteenth-century England and eighteenth-century New England are classic examples. More people on the land resulted in lower output and earnings per worker. In the mid-twentieth century, the clustering of highly educated workers seemed to have similar effects. Thus, Ph.D.'s were both abundant and cheap in New England in 1948 and limited opportunities encouraged them to disperse. But then the balance tipped in favor of concentrations of highly educated workers. By 1980 a noticeably larger proportion of the New England workforce had college degrees, and during the 1980s earnings in New England rose sharply relative to college-educated workers elsewhere in the nation. Were it not for agglomeration economies, this clustering would tend to depress, not raise, the earnings of educated workers in New England relative to educated workers elsewhere in the nation.

Agglomeration economies generally result either from the existence of economies of scale or from reductions in the cost of moving goods, people, or ideas.[26] In the last quarter of the twentieth century, both seemed important in encouraging the concentration of knowledge-based activities.

The term "economy of scale" generally refers to a large, "lumpy" asset that provides services at either lower cost or higher quality the more intensively it is used. The large research university, discussed above, was one such asset. A second was a major airport, as in Boston and nearby New York City, which provided frequent flights and extensive connections throughout the country and around the world. The falling cost of air transportation and reduced flight times facilitated the export of sophisticated, knowledge-intensive goods (which were often shipped by air) as well as services (with consultants and clients rarely traveling any other way). The rising importance of air transportation thus led to agglomeration economies and income gains that were metropolitan, more than regional, in their geography.

A second economy of scale, also operating most clearly in the large metropolitan areas of Boston and New York, arose from the opportunity to share specialized inputs. Large urban markets allow vendors to specialize, and thereby deliver products that are lower in cost, higher in quality, and more tailored to their customers' needs. In large cities, one can find sources of a wide variety of instruments, machinery, materials, and components; firms that offer targeted financial, marketing, consulting, and legal services; and workers with highly refined and esoteric skills. Support for this final form of specialization—providing a deep market for educated and experienced labor—may have been the most important contribution of large metropolitan agglomerations in the knowledge-based economy.

The ability to access specialized suppliers was vitally important to the small firms of the knowledge-based economy. The clustering of specialized resources in metropolitan areas replaced, in many ways, the internal economies of scale that had given rise to large manufacturing corporations earlier in the century, and it went hand in hand with the new vitality of small and medium-sized enterprises. As access to specialized suppliers was especially critical for start-ups, clustering enhanced an economy's ability to generate new businesses. The entrepreneurial vitality of large urban agglomerations, as well as deep markets, mitigated the risks inherent in knowledge-based economies. These agglomerations also provided the novelty and variety in consumer products that educated, well-paid workers demanded.

In addition to capturing scale economies, clustering also reduces the cost of moving goods, ideas, and people. Nineteenth-century cotton textile production had concentrated in the New England "industrial district" in part because doing so reduced the cost of moving semifinished goods through the industry's extended production process—from carding, through spinning, dyeing, weaving, fulling, printing, finishing, and packing the cloth for shipment. Sharp drops in the cost of long-distance transportation largely dissipated this advantage in the twentieth century. In determining the location of manufacturing activity, economizing on the costs of moving goods became far less important than economizing on labor and other costs. With the development of the knowledge-based economy, however, clustering produced valuable reductions in the cost of moving ideas and people. As with scale economies, these advantages were more pronounced in the large metropolitan areas of Boston and New York City than in the region as a whole.

The flow of ideas was clearly a critical issue in the knowledge-based economies of the late twentieth century. Some important types of knowledge and information—important for stimulating the development of new technologies or for improving worker skills—did not travel well. In these instances, geographic proximity improved the effectiveness of idea transfers.

Adam Jaffe, Manuel Trajtenberg, and Rebecca Henderson used patent citations to show that the transfer of technical knowledge was especially strong within metropolitan areas; while inventors cited patents from all around the globe, they cited patents from their own metropolitan area far more often than if geography had had no effect.[27] Proximity thus accelerated the flow of ideas and the process of technical invention. Jaffe and his coauthors also found that inventors often cited patents from seemingly remote technological fields; this flow of ideas across technologies no doubt contributed to the industrial volatility of knowledge-based economies.

Other studies have argued that the efficient exchange of ideas in U.S. metropolitan areas enhances worker skills and productivity in a manner similar to formal education. James Rauch showed that the presence of educated workers in a metropolitan area increased the productivity of other workers, and estimated that this "external" benefit equaled 70 percent of the income gain captured by the educated worker.[28] Edward Glaeser and David Mare found that earnings of workers moving to metropolitan areas rose over time and that these gains persisted even for workers who subsequently migrated to nonmetropolitan areas—a pattern consistent with acquisition of skills in an idea-rich urban environment.[29] Glaeser observes that cities have become postcollegiate training grounds for the knowledge-based economy.[30]

Finally, agglomeration economies arise from reductions in the cost of moving people. Clustering in cities gives people expanded access to work, stores, amusements, financial institutions, physicians, accountants, business contacts, and a host of other customers and suppliers. This broadens the "market" and erodes monopolies, and allows urban residents to capture the economies of scale, whether from international airports or access to rare-book dealers and medical specialists.

The movement of people and ideas were closely linked in the knowledge-based economy. AnnaLee Saxenian has argued that networking among people was a basic mode of communication in high-technology districts.[31] Cutting-edge technologies and skills were transferred along Boston's Route 128 and in Silicon Valley in face-to-face conversations with business acquaintances, in seminars and professional meetings, and even in job interviews. This link between the movement of people and the movement of ideas was important not just in high technology, but also in business and professional dealings throughout the knowledge-based economy. That people in metropolitan areas could network and establish face-to-face contacts with relative ease, and thereby speed the flow of technologies, skills, and business deals, helps explain the importance of agglomeration in raising productivity and incomes at the end of the twentieth century.

At the beginning of the postwar era, the widespread adoption of the automobile and extensive highway construction seemed to undercut the economic significance of cities. The economy was still driven by manufacturing, and auto and truck transportation diminished the importance of urban clusters in producing and distributing goods. With the emergence of the knowledge-based economy in the final quarter of the century, the ability of cities to speed the flow of people and ideas grew more important.

Clustering increased productivity and incomes in knowledge-based economies, but an offsetting force limiting the growth in metropolitan areas was the diseconomy in the production of urban real estate. The initial proliferation of automobiles and highways in the postwar era greatly expanded the effective supply of metropolitan real estate. But the automobile is a land-intensive form of transportation. And the taste for land-intensive suburban housing soon led builders to develop homes, stores, and office parks farther and farther from the urban core. Commuting and travel times lengthened in the most productive metropolitan agglomerations, and desirable real estate grew scarce and expensive. Congestion and real estate costs thus became both an indicator of economic success and a constraint on further expansion.

The clustering of knowledge-based firms and industries thus drove up incomes in the Boston and New York metropolitan areas, and pressed

Moving to the suburbs, 1959. *(Photo by Elliot Erwitt. Courtesy Magnum Photos.)*
    The automobile and rapid economic growth after World War II led to the rise of residential "developments," industrial and office "parks," and retail shopping "centers" in outlying areas surrounding the older urban core. The new mobility provided by cars expanded markets and opportunities in employment, consumption, and residential location.

against the availability of scarce urban land. The situation resembled the exhaustion of easily accessible water power in nineteenth-century Lowell, and the resulting spread of manufacturing to other New England mill towns. As congestion and real estate costs rose in the Boston and New York areas, competition in knowledge-based industries emerged—not within New England, but in other regions and other nations.

THE RECONFIGURED LANDSCAPE

New Englanders have tended to see themselves, and outsiders have seen them, as part of a meaningful economic region. And for the most part, the fortunes of the six New England states have tended to move together. To some degree, this reflects common industrial structures, most notably the prominence of textiles in all the New England states, except Connecticut, in the 1940s and 1950s. Moreover, because of this common dependence on textiles, much of the region had to face the challenge of economic restructuring in the postwar era. Defense production played an important role in this restructuring. The defense tie was strongest for Connecticut and Massachusetts, which received disproportionate shares of prime defense contracts over the years; but other New England states also were active in the defense business, typically as subcontractors.

In addition, in a small region like New England, prosperity and problems spill across borders. The growth in high tech along Route 128 spilled over into southern New Hampshire. Vacation areas throughout the region were affected by the swings in the economic fortunes of the region's major centers, as well as those of Wall Street. Money made by brokers and investment bankers went to build second homes in Vermont, western Connecticut, Cape Cod, and along the coast of Maine.

But while the economies of the six New England states exhibited similarities, their experiences also differed in important ways. Connecticut's population grew much faster than that in the rest of the region, faster even than in the country as a whole, during the 1940s, 1950s, and 1960s. Job opportunities at rapidly growing defense contractors and the movement of New York residents and businesses into suburbs in Connecticut (as well as in New York and New Jersey) drew people into the state. In contrast, northern New England grew slowly in the 1940s and 1950s, and more rapidly thereafter. New Hampshire made a particularly successful transition from textiles to high tech, as Nashua and other southern New Hampshire communities attracted plants from Massachusetts and elsewhere by offering proximity to Boston, easy access to mountains and lakes, low taxes, and probusiness attitudes.

At the end of the twentieth century, success in the New England economy depended to a substantial degree on links to the knowledge-based economy. Education had become central to an individual's ability to be a direct participant in this economy and earn a good living. Proximity to the large metropolitan agglomerations also was key. Most of the communities that enjoyed the greatest prosperity over the past fifty years were located in the Boston metropolitan area and in the portion of southwestern Connecticut that forms part of the New York City metropolitan area.

Boston helped create the new knowledge-based economy, and the success of the Boston metropolitan area is in many ways the central story of New England's economic history at the end of the twentieth century. Boston's network of educational and research institutions, industrial concerns, and financial institutions created a fertile environment for the generation of new firms and industries. Its industrial diversity also provided protection against economic shocks. The construction of Route 128 and the Massachusetts Turnpike, in the mid-1950s, created an economically integrated metropolitan area within which both businesses and people could move relatively freely. The turnpike also strengthened ties to the rest of the country and, via Logan airport, to the rest of the world. Communities along Route 128 grew particularly rapidly, serving both as bedroom suburbs for the city of Boston and as industrial locations. The city itself and the interior industrial communities did not fare as well, losing both people and businesses to more peripheral locations. The metropolitan area as a whole, however, generally enjoyed lower unemployment rates and higher incomes than the rest of New England.

In a similar way, southwestern Connecticut benefited from proximity to the huge concentration of financial and intellectual resources in New York City. Stamford, in particular, thrived as a headquarters location for national and multinational corporations that would otherwise have located in New York City. The area also served as home to many New York commuters. Hartford, Connecticut's major urban center, was less agglomerative, lacking the mass and the educational and research capabilities of a Boston or New York. It specialized in two major industries—aircraft engines and insurance. Largely because of the success of these industries, the Hartford area flourished through much of the period after World War II. During the 1990s, however, sharp cuts in defense spending coincided with widespread downsizing in the insurance industry, and Hartford languished.

Many communities far from the Boston and New York metro areas

Logan Airport, 1970s. *(Courtesy of the Boston Public Library, Print Department.)*

Over the last half of the twentieth century, airplanes replaced trains as the primary way people traveled long distances. People still needed to move around for business, no matter how powerful computers and electronic communications got, and business opportunities were increasingly found overseas. As a result, a major international airport, like Boston's Logan, became fundamental to the success of a modern economy.

maintained their viability by becoming recreational areas for city dwellers and suburbanites. In 1990, vacation homes accounted for 17, 11, and 15 percent of the total housing stock of Vermont, New Hampshire, and Maine, respectively, by far the highest percentages in the nation. The enormously successful Foxwoods Casino in Connecticut drew visitors from both metro areas, as well as the rest of the Northeast. The casino was established in 1992 by the Mashantucket Pequot tribe on tribal lands not far from Electric Boat's facility in Groton. Revenues from Foxwoods helped southeastern Connecticut contend with post–Cold War defense cuts at the submarine builder.

Community attitudes seem to have played a role in those localities that successfully made the transition from a mill-based to a more knowledge-based economy. Nashua, New Hampshire, faced with major layoffs when Textron shut down its local operations after World War II, aggressively sought out small, diversified replacement businesses.[32] The abrupt loss of so many jobs was an important catalyst to action. Shortly thereafter, Royden Sanders left Raytheon and founded Sanders Associates (now part of Lockheed Martin Corporation) in a Nashua mill; the defense contractor eventually became one of New Hampshire's largest employers. In Connecticut, the success of the former hat-making center of Danbury in attracting new industries in the 1960s and 1970s—most notably, the corporate headquarters of Union Carbide—was attributed at least in part to local business leaders recognizing the need for change, as well as to the flexibility of the local labor force. In other places, such as Fall River and Lewiston, Maine, however, the empty textile mills simply became home to the lower-wage apparel and shoe industries.

Serendipity also created winners. The Burlington, Vermont, area enjoyed relatively strong growth and low unemployment rates after the mid-1960s. Burlington's success owed much to the presence of a large IBM facility. In addition to its direct impact on local employment, IBM's presence attracted a large cluster of highly educated, technically sophisticated people, who launched a host of imaginative enterprises, from high tech to upscale food products. Legend has it that IBM chose Burlington because its chief executive skied in Vermont and was willing to consider an otherwise remote and unlikely location. A 1990s example was the decision of the credit card bank Maryland National Bank Corporation to open a large call center near Camden on the coast of Maine; again, the chief executive had a fondness for the area, in this case stemming from summers spent there as a child.

For many parts of New England, however, isolation from the knowledge-based economy, arising from cultural and psychological barriers as well as from sheer distance and travel time, limited a community's ability to cope with the loss of major industries. The biggest losers over the past fifty years were the one-industry communities, especially those devastated by the loss of textiles after World War II. Of these, the most important was Providence. Despite the presence of Brown University and a number of other educational institutions, the Providence economy until recently was dominated by relatively low-wage, low-skill industries. Jewelry rather than electronics or computers replaced textiles as the most important manufacturing industry in the post-textile period.

A number of smaller industrial cities, such as Fall River, New Bedford, and Lawrence in Massachusetts, also were unable to shake the legacy of the loss of textiles and suffered chronically high unemployment thereafter. Some of the metalworking communities in Connecticut, western Massachusetts, and along the Connecticut River in Vermont and New Hampshire also suffered from a lack of diversity when their dominant industries came under pressure from foreign competition and from shifts in technology favoring alternative materials.

In the more rural areas, industrial communities like Springfield, Vermont, once thrived based on access to water power. In some cases, a cluster of skills and relationships developed that extended their ability to compete long after electricity and highway transportation had superseded water power and rail. But once key employers succumbed, these locations had little to offer replacement industries. They were too remote from major centers to be attractive to most businesses and often too industrial in character to be reborn as tourist destinations.

For some, a lack of good highway linkages, not distance per se, was a problem. Providence, for example, did not have good highway ties to Boston until the late 1960s. A number of the older industrial communities inside Route 128 did not have as good access to the highway network—and therefore, to downtown Boston, the suburbs, or Logan airport—as more newly developed locations on the circumference. Because of the cost and disruptions associated with land takings, it was much easier to build highways in the less populated areas. Consequently, the major radial highways that were built to carry traffic toward and away from Boston after World War II did not penetrate inside Route 128 until well after the portions outside Route 128 were completed.

In addition to geography, racial and language barriers limited access to and participation in the region's economic success. Until recently, New England was very homogeneous in terms of race; in the three northern New England states, the population was still 98 percent white in 1990. Unlike the Great Lakes and the mid-Atlantic states, New England was not seen as an attractive destination for blacks leaving the South immediately after World War II. Connecticut, which was growing rapidly at the time and offered relatively high manufacturing wages, was something of an exception; by 1970 blacks made up 6 percent of Connecticut's population, compared to 3 percent in Massachusetts and Rhode Island. During the prosperous 1980s, in-migration to the region increased. The black population grew faster than the white population, the Hispanic population faster still. By 1990 blacks made up 8 percent of Connecticut's population and Hispanics 6 percent; in Massachusetts, blacks and Hispanics each represented 5 percent of the population; in Rhode Island, 4 percent.

New England's black and Hispanic populations resided disproportionately in communities with high poverty rates. Although the overall poverty rate in New England was 8.5 percent in 1989 compared to a national rate of just over 13 percent, seven New England cities had poverty rates in excess of 20 percent—Hartford and New Haven in Connecticut; Lawrence, Holyoke, Chelsea, and Springfield in Massachusetts; and Providence. Roughly 25 percent of New England's black and Hispanic populations lived in these seven cities, compared to less than 4 percent of whites.

In these high-poverty communities, low educational levels, language barriers, and large concentrations of single-parent families hampered participation in New England's core economy. In 1990, less than 60 percent of the adults living in Hartford and Lawrence had completed high school, compared to roughly 80 percent in the states of Connecticut and Massachusetts; fewer than 10 percent of Lawrence residents had completed college. Over 50 percent of Lawrence's population lived in homes where a language other than English was customarily spoken, compared to 15 percent in all of Massachusetts. The use of languages other than English typically, but not always, was associated with relatively large immigrant populations. And 46 percent of families in Hartford had female heads, compared to 16 percent in Connecticut as a whole.[33]

New England's problems have always been concentrated in particular localities. But the degree to which these communities have been left behind while the region as a whole has prospered is striking. To some extent, New England's fragmented political structure, with hundreds of separately incorporated cities and towns, makes these concentrations more visible. In other regions, these high-poverty communities would be part of much larger and wealthier political jurisdictions. Hartford and Boston would have annexed surrounding suburban communities; Chelsea would have been absorbed into a larger Boston. Nevertheless, the contrasts were striking, especially in Connecticut. Although the state's per capita income was the highest in the nation and the overall poverty rate was under 7 percent in 1989, more than one-quarter of the people in the city of Hartford, and more than 40 percent of the children, lived below the poverty level. The overall picture of the New England economy has thus been one of general prosperity marred by a few pockets of severe poverty.

THE FUTURE

If a blue-ribbon commission were to evaluate New England's prospects at the end of the 1990s, its report would surely be far more optimistic than the accounts issued after World War II. The region had succeeded in making the difficult transition out of its traditional mill industries and had remained one of the most prosperous economies in the world. New England's deindustrialization—its shift out of manufacturing—was not the road to ruin as so many had feared. Instead, it was the region's highway to the future.

The transition, however, was far from smooth. The region suffered several sharp economic downturns as parts of the old economy suddenly gave way, or as parts of the new failed to take hold. New England was also forced to restructure its economy not just once, but several times. None of the industries that emerged as candidates to replace textiles, shoes, or machinery—to act as the region's new economic driver—held that role very long. New England at the end of the twentieth century was no longer the vulnerable, over-mature region of the early postwar years. But neither was it the defense specialist of the 1950s and 1960s, nor the high-tech specialist of the second half of the 1970s.

In terms of broad industrial structure, New England at the end of the twentieth century looked much like the country as a whole. No small group of industries stood out as economic drivers, as had textiles, shoes, and machinery. In this regard, New England's postindustrial economy resembled the colonial economy of the seventeenth and eighteenth centuries more than it did the industrial economy of the nineteenth and early twentieth centuries. In both periods, the region relied on a broad array of exports, not one or two staple products, to earn its keep in the world. Inasmuch as the region did have a specialty, it lay in the "tertiary," or "services" sector—trade and finance in the colonial era, and education, research and development, software, consulting, and finance in the postindustrial economy. In both periods, these tertiary activities clustered in the region's largest urban areas, where they enjoyed significant agglomeration economies.

What most differentiated New England's postindustrial economy from what came before was its reliance on highly educated workers and rapidly changing technologies. These workers and the process of technical change now lay at the core of the New England economy. The region specialized not in specific industries, but in portions or aspects of those industries that were technologically dynamic or demanding. Because of the dynamism, New England's roster of industries, as well as firms, was changing continually.

While New England's prospects certainly appeared far brighter at the end of the twentieth century than they had fifty years earlier, the region's continued prosperity hardly is assured. The assets upon which this prosperity depends require continual replenishing. Rather than mills and industries that can continue for generations, New England's greatest assets are a highly educated and versatile workforce and the network of suppliers, educational institutions, and personal contacts located around its major urban centers. Federal spending on defense, education, and research had given the region tremendous assistance in building its intellectual resources, but this federal contribution declined substantially with the end of the Cold War. The task of replenishing the region's workforce and networks, and of maintaining the region's role in the technical development process, now falls to the states, corporations, households, and the universities themselves.

Finally, there is no assurance that these assets, even if amply supplied, will continue to earn ever-higher incomes. Competitors could emerge, and existing competitors could become more effective. Alternatively, the economic contribution of new technologies could fall. If the stream of promising technologies does run dry, in areas ranging from pharmaceuticals and medical procedures to new information or material technologies, the income generated by New England's knowledge-based economy may again find itself lagging behind the rest of the nation. The story of economic growth in New England is hardly finished.

CHAPTER 6

Reflections on the Origins, Development, and Future of the New England Economy

Slavery and Population Growth in Colonial New England

BERNARD BAILYN

THE LITERATURE ON THE NEW ENGLAND ECONOMY from its beginning to the eve of the Revolution is massive. In fact, one of the fullest accounts of this very large subject was written 107 years ago, by W. B. Weeden, in his two-volume *Economic and Social History of New England, 1620–1789,* a work that is still cited by historians. Since Weeden's time, year after year, the studies have multiplied. There is now a library of journal articles, books, monographs, and edited documents touching every aspect of early New England's economic history—fisheries; the timber industry; coastal, Atlantic, and inland trade; finance; banking; credit and debt; and government regulation (local, provincial, and imperial). This literature touches also the lives of the major or interesting people involved—from the Puritan merchant Robert Keayne, with his tortured conscience on gaining and using wealth, to the first non-Puritan Anglo-American Atlantic merchants of the Restoration era like Thomas Breedon; from transition figures of the early eighteenth century, such as Peter Faneuil and Jonathan Belcher, to provincial grandees of the later eighteenth century like Thomas Hancock, Nicholas Boylston, William Vassall, the Hutchinsons, and the Clarks. It also includes those wonderful models of social ascent through shrewd commercial operations, the Brown brothers of Providence, Rhode Island.

Descendants of semi-literate backwoods Baptist traders, they became respectable economic forces and founded a great fortune and a famous family.

Yet in all of this writing, documentation, and analysis there seems to be little effort to isolate the key dynamic forces at work during the period, the unique underlying conditions that energized these economic factors. There were, I believe, two such underlying conditions that had unique force in driving the region's economy forward.

Margaret Newell's basic question in this volume is: How did it happen that New England became the catalyst for America's industrial revolution? One might rephrase the inquiry to avoid the implied teleology (people of the 1760s were not working to anticipate the industrial revolution; they were trying to earn a living, to prosper and enjoy life), and simply ask the more contextual question: How was it that this unpromising, barely fertile region, incapable of producing a staple crop for the European markets, became an economic success by the eve of the Revolution? Indeed, New England was described by the most careful student of early modern wealth levels as having achieved in 1770 the highest standards of living "for the bulk of the population in any country up to that time."[1]

The most important underlying fact in this whole story, the key dynamic force, unlikely as it may seem, was slavery. New England was not a slave society. On the eve of the Revolution, blacks constituted less than 4 percent of the population in Massachusetts and Connecticut, and many of them were free. But it was slavery, nevertheless, that made the commercial economy of eighteenth-century New England possible and that drove it forward. As Barbara Solow and others have shown, the dynamic element in the region's economy was the profits from Atlantic trade, and they rested almost entirely, directly or indirectly, on the flow of New England's products to the slave plantations and the sugar and tobacco industries that they serviced.[2] The export of fish, timber, agricultural products, and cattle and horses on which the New England merchants' profits mainly depended reached markets primarily in the West Indies and secondarily in the plantation world of the mainland south. Without the sugar and tobacco industries, based on slave labor, and without the growth of the slave trade, there would not have been markets anywhere nearly sufficient to create the returns that made possible the purchase of European goods, the extended credit, and the leisured life that New Englanders enjoyed. Slavery was the ultimate source of the commercial economy of eighteenth-century New England. Only a few of New England's merchants actually engaged in the slave trade, but all of them profited by it, lived off it.

On this foundation, the merchants were able to engage in the Atlantic commercial world and to prosper. But there were problems—not just moral problems—related to slavery. Some, but not many, of the merchants worried about the moral difficulties of slavery, though their descendants would empower the abolition movement. Instead, the problems they chiefly faced in this commercial economy were more technical and elusive. What was the region's balance of payments within this complex trading system, which extended from North American coastal towns to the Caribbean plantations, Atlantic islands, and European markets? Were the profits of exports, shipbuilding, freightage, and other services sufficient to at least balance the imports from abroad? Since the economy prospered, the answer has to be yes. But the bookkeeping may suggest latent problems of some importance. The greatest profits in the basic West Indies trade were made not with the British West Indies but with the French, whose planters for various reasons could sell sugar products cheaper than the British producers could. Trade with the French in these products had ostensibly been taxed out of the market, and while Margaret Newell is right to argue that in general the British trade restrictions were as much help as hindrance, in the specifics of the sugar trade these regulations were not a help, given the profits that could be made from trade in French sugar products. The result was smuggling so systematic and so general that handbooks were printed that listed the appropriate bribes for the various customs officials in the American ports. When after 1763 the British government sought to crack down on such illegalities and to lower but enforce the taxes on foreign sugar products, the leaders of New England's commercial economy struck back with force.

The fragile balance of payments relates too to the scarcity of capital and credit in this developing economy, and hence to the highly imaginative banking schemes of the mid-eighteenth century and to the issuance of paper money by the provincial governments, both of which created not only mediums of exchange but also sources of capital for small-scale yet widespread investment. While much has been written on the early American banks—especially by Bray Hammond, a former secretary of the Federal Reserve Board—no one I know of has followed up on Richard Lester's comparative study of 1939, *Monetary Experiments: Early American and Recent Scandinavian*, which argued that these experimental banking and monetary schemes of eighteenth-century New England were almost unique in the western world—*almost*, since he found later parallels in Sweden.

New England's commercial economy in the late colonial period was a complex phenomenon, and for all of the immense scholarship devoted to it, it remains full of questions that historians have not yet answered and continue to explore: the nature and significance of the region's consumerism; the Anglo-American political networks that were shaped by commercial connections; the domestic retail marketing system for imported products, a system that wound through the region's hinterland; and the profits and losses of the processing industries, like distilleries, that were dependent on the West Indies trade. These questions spin out from the basic fact that New England's commercial economy of the pre-Revolutionary period was an annex, an offshoot, a service industry of the great powerhouse of the Atlantic economy in the pre-Revolutionary period: slave plantations and their workforce.

But not all of the region's economy was involved in Atlantic commerce, and that more parochial, rural, domestic economy too had its singular, underlying condition that propelled it forward—namely, indigenous population growth.

Little of this extraordinary growth was the result of immigration after the mid-seventeenth century. From the original migrant population that may have reached just over 20,000 in the mid-seventeenth century, the region's population rose to approximately 90,000 by 1700 and to over half a million in 1770. These figures are astonishing given that there was little immigration. While the population in the Chesapeake South in the seventeenth century failed to reproduce itself at all and grew, slowly, only by the importation of hundreds of servants and slaves each year, New England's population, by natural growth, was increasing by approximately 3 percent a year (early modern European populations rarely increased at more than 1 percent a year), thereby doubling every twenty-seven years. Decadal population growth has been estimated at 27 percent.

There can be no more important, basic, elemental fact than that. The population growth accounts, for example, for the multiplication of towns at a fabulous rate. New Englanders settled 209 new townships between 1660 and 1710. Between 1760 and 1776 the number of towns founded annually tripled—rose from an average of 6 per year before 1760 to 18 per year after 1760, a total of 283 new towns in that fifteen-year period. New England's population as a whole rose 59 percent between 1760 and 1780.

It was this remarkable population growth that made land speculation so attractive and lucrative. It explains the growth of local small-scale manufactures and of hinterland markets supplied by coastal and riverine merchants. It accounts for the increase in British exports to the region, and it explains the great increase in New England's agricultural productivity, which fed the Caribbean and Atlantic markets.

But *why* did it happen? What economic and social factors underpin these remarkable demographic facts? Some of the data are almost unbelievable. The median age at death for men of the first generation in New England was approximately what it is now—seventy-one, and one should note that even for the second generation it was sixty-five. Age of death is different from life expectancy, which is difficult to judge since we do not have good records of death in infancy. But even if unrecorded infant deaths are estimated at 20 percent, life expectancy *at birth* was over twelve years longer in seventeenth-century New England than it would be in England two hundred years later.

How can this remarkable longevity and population growth be explained? The obvious answer is simply that a typical demographic transition had set in—that is, the continuation of a traditional high birth rate or its slow decline, together with a sudden drop in the death rate due to better sanitation and medical care and an improvement in the urban conditions that lead to devastating epidemics. But in colonial New England, medical care was the same as it was in England and France, sanitation was like that found in the English countryside, and there were no urban slums. So what made the difference? Clearly the thin spread of population through the countryside helped contain the spread of disease, and the physical environment was favorable—certainly more so than the malarial swamps of the Chesapeake tidewater region. But the crucial factor was the combination of land available for family farm cultivation and a more or less balanced sex ratio. Together they made possible the relatively easy establishment of new households—and that, in turn, meant early marriages and hence long procreative cycles. The average age of first marriage in seventeenth-century England was 28 for men and 24 for women; in New England in some places it was 25 for men and 22 for women, in others it was 27 and 20. Almost everywhere in seventeenth-century New England women were marrying in their early twenties. Given the healthy environment and the low age for women at first marriage, reproduction moved toward the biological maximum and survival rates rose sharply.

But one seeks to go deeper into this question. One of the most suggestive, because counterintuitive, findings I know of is in the work of an English geographer and historian Mary Dobson, whose excellent book *Contours of Death and Disease in Early Modern England* was published recently.[3] Early in her career, Dobson came to America to make a comparative study of epidemics in southeastern England and New England, working especially with David Fischer at Brandeis. Was it not reasonable to think that New England's growth rate resulted from a lack of the epidemics that periodically scourged England's population, rural and urban? But she found that neither the *frequency* of epidemics nor their *virulence* was much different in New England from what it was in England. Savage epidemics—of smallpox, diphtheria, measles, and dysentery—in fact accounted for the death of approximately the same proportion of the population in New England as in England. But while both the frequency of epidemics and their virulence were similar to those of southeast England, the mortality levels during the healthier periods *between* epidemics were remarkably low. Her conclusion was that "in between these far-reaching epidemics New Englanders enjoyed a much healthier existence than their forefathers had ever experienced in Old England. The low base levels of mortality [not the lack of devastating epidemics] were a new and unprecedented phenomenon for the early modern age."[4]

The external, commercial economy of pre-industrial New England flourished because of the existence of a huge and growing slave labor force in the plantation world; and the interior, domestic economy was driven by the remarkable growth of the population—the result not of immigration, but of extraordinary rates of natural reproduction, which in turn was the result of early marriages made possible by the relative ease of creating new households. The combination of these forces, in my view, was the foundation of New England's prosperity in the late colonial period and explains the region's early industrial growth.

New England Industry and the Federal Government

MERRITT ROE SMITH

ON MORE THAN ONE OCCASION, MIT's distinguished metallurgist Cyril Stanley Smith argued that virtually all of the great discoveries in ceramics and metallurgy prior to the twentieth century came from artists whose imaginative and oftentimes playful manipulation of materials resulted in new insights and practical applications. Imaginative manipulation and the ability to recognize new properties and replicate them counted for everything.

I appreciate and support Smith's observation because, as a historian, I believe that the process of discovery in the use of materials and the process of discovery in historical scholarship have a good deal in common. Much depends on one's angle of vision and willingness to look at the subject matter from different perspectives.

For me, one issue lies at the center of any discussion concerning American industrial expansion during the middle decades of the nineteenth century: the role of government—local and state, but particularly the federal government. I shall argue that there were moments during the nineteenth century when government action made an enormous difference to the development of the market economy. In effect, I am advancing a variant of Carter Goodrich's old but still viable "government in/government out" thesis.[1]

Early in his essay, Peter Temin indicates that "the federal government did not engage in massive spending at this time [1830–1880], but it had an extremely important effect on economic activity by creating uniform rules of conduct for business behavior." He mentions in this context the patent system and its role in creating "property rights in new knowledge." Several pages later, he points to the minimum valuation tariff of 1816 and the introduction of "better machines that increased the productivity of labor" as two reasons why the United States did not specialize in agriculture in the first half of the nineteenth century. From there he goes on to argue persuasively that "arms production and the American System of Manufactures . . . laid the foundation for American industrial expansion in both the nineteenth and twentieth centuries." Firearms, not cotton textiles or boots and shoes—the two other industries to which he devotes considerable attention—evidently laid the foundation. But why was this so?

Those who are familiar with the work of Nathan Rosenberg and David Hounshell doubtless will recognize the linkages that existed between the American system and mass production.[2] Briefly stated, the new mechanical technologies that originated primarily in the Connecticut Valley small arms industry quickly found applications in all sorts of technically related manufacturing activities—sewing machines, pocket watches, padlocks, typewriters, business machines, farm machinery, photographic equipment, bicycles, automobiles, home appliances, and a host of mass production industries of the twentieth century. Rosenberg describes this phenomenon as "technological convergence." The critical link between the armory system and other manufacturing industries was the machine tool industry, which first appeared in and around Springfield, Massachusetts, during the 1840s and came of age during the following decade. Leading machine-tool firms such as Pratt and Whitney of Hartford, Jones and Lamson of Springfield, Vermont, and Brown and Sharpe of Providence trace their origins directly to the military small arms industry, the center of which (prior to the Civil War) was the U.S. government armory at Springfield.

But how did these machine-making firms come into being? And how did they develop their respective lines or types of machine tools? The answers can be found in the workings of the arms-contracting system that the War Department introduced after the War of 1812.[3]

Historians of technology long have known that a number of fundamentally new machine-tool designs—for milling machines, forging machines, edging machines, and turret lathes, to name but four of the most important types—first appeared in the firearms industry and that their inventors held contracts with the War Department. We also know that a number of the most important designs (like Simeon North's plain milling machine of 1816–1817) were never patented and those that were (like John H. Hall's drop forging equipment) quickly made their way into armories, machine shops, and technically related manufacturing operations around the country without any royalties being paid to the inventors.[4] This was so because the War Department, at the behest of the U.S. Army Ordinance Bureau, which oversaw the contract system, insisted that if private arms makers wished to continue as government contractors, they had to share their inventions and improvements on a royalty-free basis with the government-owned national armories at Springfield and at Harpers Ferry, Virginia. The national armories, in turn, made the new technology readily available to all comers. Virtually anyone who was interested and had a proper letter of introduction (which was easily obtained from one's congressman) could visit the national armories at Springfield and Harpers Ferry, make drawings of interesting designs, and, in some cases, even borrow patterns from the armory machine shops for a particular machine or a complete set of machinery. As a result, the new technology quickly filtered out into the larger economy. Two firms that took advantage of this open-door policy were the Ames Manufacturing Company of Chicopee, Massachusetts, and Robbins and Lawrence of Windsor, Vermont—arguably the earliest commercial builders of machine tools in the Connecticut Valley and the direct precursors of larger, more specialized "modern" machine-tool builders like Pratt and Whitney, Jones and Lamson, and Brown and Sharpe. Several privately owned "satellite" machine shops emerged at Harpers Ferry as well, but owing to their isolation in a largely rural hinterland, they never prospered to the extent that their New England counterparts did.

The War Department's contractual policy and the open door that it maintained at all of its manufacturing establishments meant that the real novelty of the American system was as much administrative as technological. The irony is that no one at the War Department or, for that matter, at the national armories fully understood the larger implications of their actions until long after the fact.[5]

Stimulated by the London Crystal Palace Exhibition of 1851, various British investigators interested in learning more about the "American system" visited the United States. The most important of these commissions visited in 1854 and ended up purchasing over $100,000 worth of machinery and tools from the Springfield Armory–influenced Ames Company and from Robbins and Lawrence. In the commission's view, the most innovative firms—those with the most novel "labor saving" machinery—were located in the Connecticut Valley, not in Lowell, Lynn, or Boston. In their final report to Parliament, the commissioners devoted most of their attention to the manufacturing processes employed at the Springfield Armory and described "best practice" arms-making firms like the newly built Sharps Rifle Company and the Colt Patent Arms Manufacturing Company, both of Hartford. Lowell and Lynn, on the other hand, received a scant four sentences. Upon visiting Lowell, the committee curtly noted that "they went over the extensive machine shop, and found that very much the same machinery was used there as in England." Lynn proved even less interesting. While the committee noted that "Howe's [sewing] machine was . . . much used in shoe-making," they "did not find machinery so extensively used as they had been led to expect."[6]

Yet federal government involvement in the private sector also had made a significant difference for the origins of Lowell. Consider the decision on the part of the Boston Associates to expand their textile manufacturing operations beyond their original mills at Waltham to the falls of the Merrimack River at East Chelmsford, which was soon to be renamed Lowell in honor of the recently deceased founder of the original Boston Manufacturing Company. In addition to the associates themselves, a key player in this expansive move was none other than Daniel Webster. At a time when conflict of interest had little or no meaning in American soci-

ety, Webster served simultaneously as a U.S. congressman (and later sena-
tor) from Massachusetts and as the chief lobbyist and legal representative
of the Boston Associates in Washington.

Of all his work for the associates, none proved more impressive or more
lucrative than his involvement with the Spanish Claims Commission,
which had been established as a result of the Transcontinental Treaty of
1819. What is best remembered about the Transcontinental Treaty is that
Spain ceded East Florida to the United States. What is often forgotten is
that the United States agreed to assume the claims of American citizens
against Spain to a maximum limit of $5 million. Since the bulk of these
claims included vessels and cargoes lost by merchants during the Napole-
onic Wars, a number of Boston Associates as well as several marine insurance companies owned by them became eligible to seek reimbursement for
their losses. They consequently lost little time in engaging Daniel Webster
to represent them before the Spanish Claims Commission. Promised a
commission of 5 percent for every dollar awarded, Webster represented
the associates' claims before the government commission and succeeded in
getting a total distribution of well over $1 million, fully 20 percent of the
total claims funds dispensed.

But there is more to this story. The Spanish claims monies arrived in
Boston between 1822 and 1825, just as the first surge of factory building
was taking place at Lowell. While one cannot prove that these claims
funds were directly applied to the building of Lowell's early mills, at the
very least they freed up capital for investment there.

As it turned out, opportunity for federal support knocked not once but
twice at the associates' doors. The second opportunity came in 1831, when
another federal claims commission was established to oversee the distribution of funds resulting from a treaty signed that year with the French republic. At issue were longstanding claims of American merchants against
France amounting to $10 million for confiscations of ships and cargoes
dating back to 1804. This time, however, the French government of Louis
Philippe agreed to pay 25 million francs, while the United States assumed
only $1.5 million. Daniel Webster again represented the Boston Associates
and their insurance companies, this time before the French Claims Com-

mission. Although the exact amount of the disbursements actually made to the associates has yet to be ascertained, it is nonetheless certain that they were made and that they corresponded with a second wave of mill building that took place at Lowell between 1832 and 1837. Seemingly inconspicuous federal government actions meant a great deal for the pocketbooks of the Boston Associates.

The federal government was important too in the development of engineering and modern management. Temin argued that public schooling "prepared the ground for industrialization" in New England. Yet when it comes to critical investments in human capital, something must be said of the U.S. military academy at West Point, New York. Modeled after the French Ecole Polytechnique, West Point became the nation's leading engineering school prior to the Civil War. Its "soldier-technologist" graduates played leading roles not only in introducing the American system of interchangeable manufacturing (itself originally a French idea), but also in planning and overseeing the construction of a national transportation system.

West Point graduates brought military management methods to the civilian world. A case in point is the career of George Washington Whistler (b. 1800). Although remembered today as the artist Whistler's father, G. W. Whistler achieved an international reputation during his lifetime as one of America's foremost civil engineers. A member of the class of 1819, he ranked a very respectable tenth in his class at West Point and, upon graduation, was commissioned a second lieutenant in the army's corps of artillerists. After serving as an instructor [appropriately enough, of mechanical drawing] at West Point and as a member of a topographical engineering team charged with surveying the U.S.-Canadian boundary in what is now northern Minnesota, his next assignment involved a radically new technology—the building of a steam-powered railroad.

Lieutenant Whistler's introduction to railroading came about as a result of the General Survey Act of 1824, a little remembered but landmark piece of federal legislation that sanctioned direct military involvement in building a national transportation system. Specifically, the Survey Act permitted the president of the United States to assign army engineers to state and privately owned transportation companies for the purpose of conducting topographical surveys, estimating costs, and supervising construction. Initially all costs associated with these services were borne by the federal government.

Whistler's activities typified those of other army engineers assigned to the private sector. Between 1828 and 1830, he served as a member of an army team seconded to the Baltimore and Ohio Railroad. During that time he conducted surveys, assisted in preparing cost estimates, spent six months in England studying construction methods and steam locomotives, and ended up supervising the construction of the first section of the new railroad from Baltimore to Ellicott's Mills, Maryland.

After leaving the Baltimore and Ohio in May 1830, Whistler moved on to survey and initiate construction on three more eastern railroads before resigning from the army in 1833. Calling himself a "consulting engineer," he next went to work for the Boston Associates as superintendent of the newly established Lowell Machine Shop. There he introduced the manufacture of steam locomotives, which he had seen during his earlier visit to England. From Lowell, he went on to supervise the construction of several New England railroads, the largest and most demanding being the Western Railroad, a 160-mile line that linked the cities of Boston and Worcester with Albany, New York, and the burgeoning trade of the Erie Canal and America's western regions. From New England, Whistler moved to Russia, where he served as chief consulting engineer in building the 420-mile St. Petersburg and Moscow Railroad, at that time the longest in the world. There he died in 1849, a victim of cholera.

Although the American railway system would experience its greatest growth and influence after the Civil War, many of its defining features were introduced prior to the conflict. Of these none proved more important than the management methods brought to the industry by West Point–trained engineers like Whistler. More than 120 West Pointers worked on American railroads prior to the Civil War, all in engineering, supervisory, or executive capacities. Indeed, one writer declares that "up to 1855, there was scarcely a railroad in this country that had not been projected and most cases managed by officers of the Corps [of Engineers]."[7]

Between 1802 and 1867, West Point produced 2,218 graduates. Of that number, according to Forrest G. Hill,

> some 139 had entered the field of education and 334 had taken up pursuits of a technical nature. Those in education included 26 presidents of universities and colleges, 23 principals of academies and schools, 5 regents and chancellors of educational institutions, and 85 professors and teachers. In specialized callings were 1 superintendent of the Coast Survey, 6 surveyors-general of states and territories, 14 chief engineers of states, and 35 presidents of railroads and other corporations, 48 chief engineers and 41 superintendents of railroads and other public works, 155 civil engineers, 30 manufacturers, and 4 architects.[8]

Given these impressive numbers, it is unlikely that any other entity in America could claim to have made a better investment in human capital than the federal government did with the U.S. military academy at West Point.

The Future
of New England

PAUL KRUGMAN

THERE IS A SMALL "JAPANTOWN" near my house in Cambridge—a cluster of noodle shops, sushi bars, groceries, and Japanese bookstores. Many of the shops are in Porter Exchange, a grand old building that used to be the Cambridge Sears outlet. The building, with its high ceilings and open floor plan, was unable to find a good use for an extended period after Sears moved out, but it turns out to be quite well suited for use as a sort of mall. The location turns out to be excellent for this use because many of the patrons are public-transit-using students at MIT and other area schools, and the mini-mall benefits from its proximity to the Porter Square stop on the Red Line subway. The cluster seems to be growing; perhaps one day Porter Exchange will be the nucleus of a large and distinctive shopping district.

How did that building become available? Sears discovered that a location with poor access to highways and limited parking could not compete with stores in suburban shopping malls. Why did they build it there in the first place? I don't know for sure, but I suspect that the location was actually a very good one when the building first went up, far enough away from downtown to offer inexpensive land and room to build, but still accessible because of the trolley line that ran up Massachusetts Avenue. And "Mass.

Ave.," as we Cantabrigians all know, began as a track for cattle drovers in the time period of Margaret Newell's essay.

Henry Ford is supposed to have said that history is just one damn thing after another. Maybe not, but explanations of economic location are almost always historical, and the history does tend to have a "one damn thing after another" character. If you try to explain why a particular region is home to a particular industry, you usually end up explaining it largely by describing the sequence of events that caused the industry to be there. A Georgia teenager makes a tufted bedspread as a wedding gift; sixty years later, that event makes Dalton, Georgia, America's carpet capital.

The essential driving force behind this historicity is, of course, the tendency of an industry to stay where it has been established, thanks to locational external economies. It remains hard to improve on Marshall's threefold classification of these externalities as arising from the ability of producers to share specialized providers of inputs; the advantages to both employers and workers of a thick labor market with many participants; and localized spillovers of knowledge, especially through personal interaction. They apply just as well to Boston's complex of world-class hospitals as they did to the nineteenth-century Sheffield cutlery district that inspired Marshall. Now, as then, such localized externalities provide a virtuous circle that tends to keep an industrial cluster locked in place.

But how do such clusters get established in the first place? You might think that the process is largely random. An accidental event, or a remarkable individual, creates the seed around which an industry grows. Reading the essay on New England after World War II by Lynn Browne and Steven Sass, however, one gets the feeling that the process is not so much random as chaotic. That is, the history of New England's changing industrial structure often seems to be a story of events that were more or less deterministic, but whose outcome nonetheless could not have been predicted.

Consider, for example, the Boston mutual-fund industry. Its existence— and the resulting ability of metropolitan Boston to benefit disproportionately from the stock market mania of the 1990s—clearly is not accidental. Browne and Sass suggest that the financing needs of high-technology start-ups built up a special sort of financial competence in the area. The high-technology industries of Massachusetts, equally clearly, did not emerge by accident; they were there largely as a legacy of World War II and Cold War research. And this research was concentrated in Cambridge because of the presence of universities, which was ultimately the product of the need of Puritans for a place to train preachers. At each stage there was a clear reason for what happened, but nobody could possibly have predicted the sequence.

The process seems to work mainly as follows. Start with a region that has a particular industrial base, itself the product of a long historical evolution. If the environment were unchanging, that industrial base would tend to persist; but things do change. The rise of new technologies makes old advantages irrelevant and offers new opportunities, but the past is not completely irrelevant. The special characteristics of regions, the consequences of their old industrial mixes, determine which new industries find them congenial soil. Machine shops set up to serve textile mills can turn to the production of components for aircraft engines; experience gained from time-shared minicomputers, having become temporarily devalued with the rise of personal computers, turns out to be relevant again with the popularity of local area networks. In other words, the regional industry structure at time t determines the structure at time $t + n$ in a non-random way (n being an additional period of time), but it does so through quirky linkages that nobody could have foreseen.

Because the linkages are so hard to foresee, the rising and falling fortunes of regions inevitably involve a large degree of luck (even though they may not involve very much true randomness—chaos theory is funny that way). And over the past fifty years New England clearly has gotten lucky. At the end of World War II, the region's industrial base appeared destined for decline. Its textile and shoe industries could no longer compete with lower-wage producers in the South, and one reasonably might have expected New England to become a permanently depressed area. Instead, however, the legacies of the region's past turned out to give it an unexpected advantage in snaring some of the industries of the future. Some of this process involved conventionally Marshallian linkages—the support network that had once served the textile industry could be transferred to new uses—but much of it also involved novel linkages, especially those having to do with the region's universities. Again, there was not really that much true randomness. Taking World War II and the Cold War as given, it was in retrospect entirely natural that MIT and some other universities along the Charles River would have played a crucial role in developing military technologies and their civilian spinoffs, and that this would give rise to a new high-technology economic base. But half a century ago nobody realized just how economically significant the kinds of things done at MIT's Radiation Lab would turn out to be.

Will New England stay lucky? This turns out to be more than a question about whether New England will retain its lead in the sectors it now dominates, or whether it will manage to seize enough new sectors to replace old advantages as they erode. For even a casual look at the current New England economy suggests that this time things are somewhat different.

Put it this way: what exactly does New England do for a living these days? As recently as the 1980s, it was not that hard to give an off-the-cuff answer. The dominant "export" sectors, those that drove the region's growth, were minicomputers and a few other high-technology manufacturing industries. Digital Equipment was both the largest area firm and the emblem of what the new New England was all about. But now we have what Browne and Sass call an "amorphous economy," in which it is hard to find any focus. New England is clearly doing very well selling *something*; but what?

I am of two minds about the putative amorphousness of the economy. One simple interpretation is that the fuzziness is not in the real economy but in our statistics. As measured, New England seems to be virtually indistinguishable from the national average employment structure; perhaps that is simply because industrial-era statistics cannot keep up with a service economy. It is easy to think of examples. Browne and Sass point to the rapid growth of "business services" as a statistical illusion. In large part it reflects the growing preference of companies for outsourcing of previously internal activities, and even for temporary over permanent employees. Yet all business services are lumped together, so that firms selling technical support for software companies in Cambridge end up in the same category as those selling technical support for oil exploration in Houston. Or consider the health care industry. The world-famous brain surgeon at Massachusetts General Hospital, who attracts clients from all over the globe, gets lumped in with general practitioners; the result is that even though Boston probably has an almost uniquely large sector exporting medical services, it is considered together with the nontradeable general health care sector, and the region's distinctiveness is obscured.

Yet it is hard to avoid the sense that the economy may have become truly more amorphous as well. To travel the cities of the United States today is to be struck by the sameness of their working worlds. Where once Chicago was a city of hog butchers and Pittsburgh one of steelworkers, today every metropolitan area is populated largely by office workers who look the same and do the same kind of jobs. Some labor economists suggest that the surprising recent ability of the U.S. economy to achieve low unemployment without inflation is partly the result of a homogenization of job requirements. Once upon a time, they suggest, being a hog butcher or steelworker was a special skill, not easily acquired; so hog butchers could push up wages even in the face of general unemployment, although they also became unemployed if the demand for their services declined. Now, however, many jobs require the same set of skills (literacy and basic computer knowledge) so that firms find it easy to replace workers (reducing the market power of current employees) and workers find it easy to switch jobs (reducing frictional unemployment).

If regions really are all pretty much the same these days, why aren't they more self-sufficient? In particular, why are hundreds of thousands of businesspeople taking plane flights every day to make presentations or attend meetings somewhere else in this apparently homogeneous economic landscape? The people they are going to see must be doing something different, or the business could be concluded locally.

At this point I believe you could tell two quite different stories depending on which view of the New England economy you choose. One is that despite all that I have said on behalf of amorphousness, in the end a region does have a set of core competencies that give it a hard-to-measure but real distinctiveness. Most residents of Southern California are not beautiful, but nonetheless the core of beautiful people gives the region a special competence in the entertainment field. Most people in greater New York are not unusually avaricious, but the core of superlatively avaricious people gives it a special competence in deal-making. Most people in greater Boston are not brilliant, but the core of brilliant people gives it a special competence in the knowledge industries. New England has a higher share of college-educated workers than other regions. What really stands out, however, is the overrepresentation of the region in the tallies of top-ranked universities—according to *U.S. News and World Report*, New England, with only about 3 percent of the nation's population, has four of the top five research universities and eight of the top twenty-five; some rarefied version of the Marshallian trinity sustains these clusters.

Alternatively, regions really are pretty much the same, and all the business between them is a matter of micro-level, almost accidental, advantages and connections. An Atlanta firm needs some specialized service; it just so happens that the firm that can supply that service is in Boston, when it could just as easily have been in Atlanta. Or perhaps there even is a firm with that competence in Atlanta, but it is easier to go with the firm you know about that is a couple of hours away by plane than to search for a local supplier.

If we believe my first story, then the way to think about New England's future is first to try to figure out what the true common denominator of its success really is, then to ask about the prospects for that newly defined "industry." If we believe the second, regional fortunes will henceforth be determined by some sort of generalized economic quality, not by the specifics of what their workers do and know. And we really don't know which is true.

I guess on general grounds that it is unlikely that the historical importance of regional specialization has truly vanished. New England probably still is driven by a few self-sustaining clusters of activities, which do not appear in our data only because we collect the data badly. Indeed, one might guess that the area's investment activities, its remaining computer industry, its exportable business services, and so on all reflect a common set of

Marshallian external economies. If so, the question is whether the region's advantages will persist.

Life is chaotic—so whatever we say is almost sure to be wrong. Still, the essay by Browne and Sass did make me feel a bit uneasy about the future value of my Cambridge house, because it struck me that many of New England's recent successes depend on the costs of transportation and communication being in a sort of Goldilocks range—not too high, but not too low, either.

Let me explain. It is a familiar point from the "new economic geography" that the impact of transportation costs on agglomeration tends to have an inverted U shape. At very high transport costs, there cannot be agglomeration; the world consists of self-sufficient peasants. At very low transport and communication costs, there is little incentive for agglomeration; necessary inputs can be delivered to wherever the factor costs are lowest. (This happened to the textile industry. Improved transportation made it unnecessary for mills to remain in the established centers and allowed them to move to lower-wage locations.) It is only in an intermediate range that agglomeration is both possible and necessary.

Many examples of recent New England successes depend on transport or communication costs having fallen enough that previously nontraded activities become possible export sectors, but not so low that localized external economies fade away. Thus specialized computer services can now be delivered at long distance via e-mail or a few plane flights, but the personalized interaction that gives New England firms their expertise still depends on face-to-face contact. People can fly to Boston for specialized medical procedures where they would once have had to rely on whomever their local hospital could provide, but the core of highly skilled doctors and staff must be concentrated in a small geographical area. And the particular state of modern transportation and communication technology seems to be especially congenial for the kinds of things that New England is currently good at.

Suppose, however, that video conferencing becomes cheap and routine, so that a working cluster of experts can form without any need for physical contact. Might the computer consulting firm of the future have only a tiny central office, consisting mainly of a coalition of geographically dispersed people who meet around virtual conference tables now and then? If so, wouldn't it be likely that many of the experts would choose to live somewhere cheaper and/or warmer than Boston? Similarly, the time is clearly not too distant when remote surgeons will guide operations—perhaps even operate robot machinery—from long distance. In that case, why can't the great surgeon do it all from his seaside estate, with no need to deal with Boston traffic?

As you might guess, this observation is based partly on personal experience. Over the past twenty years, I have watched the physical location of an academic researcher steadily diminish in importance. One's important colleagues in a specialty are increasingly likely to be scattered across the world, rather than concentrated in one's own university. To take a nonrandom example, Cambridge has far more experts in international finance than anyplace else on earth, but most of the international-finance community nonetheless is someplace else. Intellectual interaction takes place mainly at conferences, via e-mail, or—especially since the onset of the Asian crisis—via Internet postings. When I recently spent a couple of weeks in a rented house several hours' flight from Cambridge, I found it possible to do most of what I normally do quite well—and I suspect that most of the people who correspond with me via e-mail, or look for my work in cyberspace, had no idea I was away. And perhaps the same is true of many "knowledge workers," which means that the kind of cluster of such workers that New England now offers will soon dissolve.

Or maybe not. For the one overwhelming lesson of New England's economic history is that while each successive stage reflects forces that are obvious in retrospect, attempts at prediction nearly always get it wrong.

Notes

I THE BIRTH OF NEW ENGLAND IN THE ATLANTIC ECONOMY

Some of the material in this essay appeared previously in Margaret Ellen Newell, *From Dependency to Independence: Economic Revolution in Colonial New England* (Ithaca, N.Y.: Cornell University Press, 1998), and is used by permission of the publisher, Cornell University Press.

1. Sir Francis Brewster, *Essays on Trade and Navigation. In Five Parts* (London, 1654–1655), pp. 88, 91; Sir William Petty, *Political Arithmetic* (London, 1691), pp. 75–84.

2. Thomas M. Doerflinger, *A Vigorous Spirit of Enterprise: Merchants and Economic Development in Revolutionary Philadelphia* (New York: W. W. Norton, 1986), p. 4.

3. D. C. Coleman, *The Economy of England, 1450–1750* (Oxford: Oxford University Press, 1977), pp. 12–29; Keith Wrightson, *English Society, 1580–1680* (New Brunswick, N.J.: Rutgers University Press, 1982), pp. 121–125.

4. John Winthrop to ? [1629], in *Winthrop Papers*, 6 vols. to date (Boston: Massachusetts Historical Society, 1929–), 2:129.

5. John Brereton, *A Briefe and true Relation of the Discoverie of the North part of Virginia* (London, 1602), pp. 4–5, 12, 17.

6. David Cressy, *Coming Over: Migration and Communication between England and New England in the Seventeenth Century* (New York: Cambridge University Press, 1987), p. 8.

7. Christopher Levett, "Levett's Voyage, A.D. 1623," *Collections of the Massachusetts Historical Society*, vol. 8 (Boston, 1843), pp. 159–190, quotation on p. 190.

8. "Francis Higginson to His Friends in England," July 24, 1629, in Everett Emerson, ed., *Letters from New England: The Massachusetts Bay Colony, 1629–1638* (Amherst: University of Massachusetts Press, 1976), pp. 30–32.

9. William Bradford, *Of Plymouth Plantation*, ed. Samuel Eliot Morison (New York: Alfred A. Knopf, 1979), p. 24.

10. Virginia DeJohn Anderson, *New England's Generation: The Great Migration and the Formation of Society and Culture in the Seventeenth Century* (New York: Cambridge University Press, 1991), pp. 18–24, 224; Cressy, *Coming Over*, p. 66.

11. Daniel Vickers, *Farmers and Fishermen: Two Centuries of Work in Essex County, Massachusetts, 1630–1850* (Chapel Hill: University of North Carolina Press, 1994), pp. 56–57.

12. Bradford, *Of Plymouth Plantation*, p. 25.

13. William Cronon, *Changes in the Land: Indians, Colonists, and the Ecology of New England* (New York: Hill and Wang, 1983), esp. ch. 3.

14. Higginson, in *Letters from New England*, p. 30.

15. John Winthrop, "A Modell of Christian Charity," in Perry Miller and Thomas K. Johnson, eds., *The Puritans*, 2 vols. (New York: Harper & Row, 1938, 1963), 1:197.

16. David Grayson Allen, *In English Ways: The Movement of Societies and the Transferral of English Local Law and Custom to Massachusetts Bay in the Seventeenth Century* (Chapel Hill: University of North Carolina Press, 1981), pp. 38–54; Philip Greven, *Four Generations: Population, Land, and Family in Colonial Andover, Massachusetts* (Ithaca, N.Y.: Cornell University Press, 1970), pp. 42–44.

17. Bradford, *Of Plymouth Plantation*, p. 120.

18. John Frederick Martin, *Profits in the Wilderness: Entrepreneurs and the Founding of New England Towns in the Seventeenth Century* (Chapel Hill: University of North Carolina Press, 1991), esp. chs. 1–3.

19. John Winthrop, in *Winthrop's Journal: "History of New England,"* ed. James K. Hosmer, 2 vols. (New York: Charles Scribner's Sons, 1908), 1:120, 152, 112.

20. Edward Johnson, *Johnson's Wonder-Working Providence, 1628–1651*, ed. J. Franklin Jameson (New York: Charles Scribner's Sons, 1910), p. 210.

21. *Records of the Governor and Company of the Massachusetts Bay in New England*, ed. Nathaniel B. Shurtleff, 6 vols. (New York: AMS Press, 1968 [rpt. of 1854 Boston ed.]), 3:243–244.

22. Johnson, *Wonder-Working Providence*, p. 209.

23. See E. N. Hartley, *Ironworks on the Saugus* (Norman: University of Oklahoma Press, 1957); and Stephen Innes, *Creating the Commonwealth: The Economic Culture of Puritan New England* (New York: W. W. Norton, 1995), ch. 6.

24. Vickers, *Farmers and Fishermen*, p. 154.

25. Richard Vines to John Winthrop, July 19, 1647, in *Winthrop Papers*, 5:172.

26. Edmund Andros, "Description of New England" (1690), Colonial Office Papers, Public Record Office, London, class 5, 855:90.

27. John J. McCusker and Russell R. Menard, *The Economy of British America, 1607–1789* (Chapel Hill: University of North Carolina Press, 1983), pp. 108–109; James Shepherd and Samuel H. Williamson, "The Coastal Trade of the British North American Colonies," *Journal of Economic History* 32 (1972): 783–810, esp. pp. 800–801, 803, 808–809.

28. Edward Randolph, "Report to the Committee for Trade and Plantations," October 12, 1676, in Robert Toppan, ed., *Edward Randolph: Including His Letters and Official Papers from the New England, Middle, and Southern Colonies in America*, 7 vols. (Boston, 1898), 2:249.

29. John Josselyn, *An Account of Two Voyages to New England* (London, 1674), p. 162.

30. Carl Bridenbaugh, *Cities in the Wilderness: Urban Life in America, 1625–1742* (New York: Capricorn Books, 1964 [1938]), pp. 171–172, 251–253.

31. Edward Randolph to the Earl of Coventry, June 17, 1676, and "Report to the Committee for Trade and Plantations," in Toppan, *Edward Randolph*, 2:205, 249.

32. Bernard Bailyn, *The New England Merchants in the Seventeenth Century* (Cambridge, Mass.: Harvard University Press, 1979 [1955]), ch. 7.

33. Charles M. Andrews, *The Colonial Period of American History*, 4 vols. (New Haven: Yale University Press, 1964 [1934–1938]), 4:61–66.

34. Thomas Bartlet Account Book, 1679–1758, and Farm Accounts, Marblehead, Mass., 1703–1723 (unidentified), Account Books Collection, octavo vol. 1; both at the American Antiquarian Society, Worcester, Mass.

35. Robert Gibbs Business Records, 1669–1708, octavo vol. 6, American Antiquarian Society; Farm Accounts, Marblehead, Mass.

36. Laurel Thacher Ulrich, *Goodwives: Image and Reality in the Lives of Women in Northern New England, 1650–1750* (New York: Oxford University Press, 1983), pp. 17, 69.

37. Jonathan Trumbull Record Book, 1737–1738, Connecticut Historical Society, Hartford; Carole Shammas, "Consumer Behavior in Colonial America," *Social Science History* 6 (1982): 67–86; Gloria L. Main and Jackson T. Main,

"Economic Growth and the Standard of Living in Southern New England, 1640–1774," *Journal of Economic History* 48 (1988): 27–46.

38. James Henretta, *The Evolution of American Society, 1700–1815* (Lexington, Mass.: D. C. Heath, 1973), p. 15; Bruce Daniels, "Economic Development in Colonial and Revolutionary Connecticut: An Overview," *William and Mary Quarterly* 37 (1980): 429–450, esp. p. 432.

39. McCusker and Menard, *Economy of British America*, p. 61; Alice Hanson Jones, *Wealth of a Nation to Be: The American Colonies on the Eve of the Revolution* (New York: Columbia University Press, 1980), pp. 54, 56.

40. Jones, *Wealth of a Nation to Be*, p. 68.

41. Benning Wentworth, "His Majesty's Governor of New Hampshire in New England to the Respective Queries of the Right Honorable the Lords Commissioners for Trade and Plantations," 1754 mss., Huntington Library, San Marino, Calif.

42. Daniels, "Economic Development in Connecticut," p. 432; Marc Egnal, "The Economic Development of the Thirteen Continental Colonies, 1720–1775," *William and Mary Quarterly* 32 (1975): 191–222, esp. p. 205.

43. "Invoice of sundry merchandize shipped by Nicholas Brown & Company on b[o]ard the Brig *George* to Surinam," July 16, 1768, Brown Family Papers, John Carter Brown Library, Providence, R.I.

44. [Anonymous], *Reflections on the Importation of Bar-Iron, from Our Own Colonies of North America* (London, 1757), p. 10.

45. James Otis, *The Rights of the British Colonies Asserted and Proved* (Boston, 1764), in Bernard Bailyn, ed., *Pamphlets of the American Revolution* (Cambridge, Mass.: Harvard University Press, 1960), p. 462.

46. [Anonymous], *A Comparison between the British Sugar Colonies and New England* (London, 1732), pp. 8–9.

2 THE INVENTION OF AMERICAN CAPITALISM

1. "Capitalist" is a word I use with reluctance, fully cognizant of the "whiff of brimstone" (Fernand Braudel, *The Wheels of Commerce* [New York: Harper & Row, 1962], p. 238) that still attaches to it.

2. See Stanley L. Engerman and Kenneth L. Sokoloff, "Factor Endowments, Institutions and Differential Paths of Growth among New World Economies: A View from Economic Historians of the U.S.," NBER Historical Working Paper 66 (Dec. 1994); Joyce Appleby, "The Popular Sources of American

Capitalism," *Studies in American Political Development* 9, no. 2 (Fall 1995): 457; and Frederick Krantz and Paul M. Hohenberg, eds., *Failed Transitions to Modern Industrial Society: Renaissance Italy and Seventeenth Century Holland* (Montreal: Interuniversity Centre for European Studies, 1975).

3. Edmund Burke, *On Conciliation*, vol. 1, quoted in Gerald W. Chapman, *Edmund Burke: The Practical Imagination* (Cambridge, Mass.: Harvard University Press, 1967), p. 25.

4. Robert Turgot and Jacques Necker, leading French economists, thought fiscal restraint and bureaucratic reforms would suffice to avert a constitutional crisis over new taxes. The expenses of the American war undermined that strategy. See François R. Velde and David R. Weir, "The Financial Market and Government Debt Policy in France, 1746–1793," *Journal of Economic History* 52 (Mar. 1992): 1–39.

5. Charles Calomiris, "Institutional Failure, Monetary Scarcity, and the Depreciation of the Continental," *Journal of Economic History* 48 (Mar. 1988): 58.

6. Ibid., p. 54.

7. Edwin J. Perkins, *American Public Finance and Financial Services, 1700–1815* (Columbus: Ohio State University Press, 1994), p. 173.

8. Ibid., p. 176.

9. Jonathan Chu, "Debt and Taxes: Public Finance and Private Economic Behavior in Post-Revolutionary Massachusetts," in Conrad E. Wright and Kathryn Beals, eds., *Entrepreneurs: The Boston Business Community, 1700–1850* (Boston: Massachusetts Historical Society, 1997), pp. 121–150, quotation on p. 141.

10. Perkins, *American Public Finance*, p. 184.

11. When in 1790 the U.S. Treasury assumed the war debts of the states, Massachusetts, despite all its urgency, was found "with the greatest debt of all." Claude G. Bowers, *Jefferson and Hamilton* (Cambridge, Mass.: Riverside Press, 1925), p. 59.

12. In James Madison's *Notes of Debates in the Federal Convention of 1787* (New York: Norton, 1969), the specter of Shays's Rebellion was raised at five points in the Constitutional debates; see pp. 131, 144, 202, 321, 475.

13. I am (mis?)appropriating this phrase from Douglass C. North, *Institutions, Institutional Change and Economic Development* (New York: Cambridge University Press, 1990).

14. Jeremy Atack and Peter Passell, *A New Economic View of American History*, 2d ed. (New York: W. W. Norton, 1994), p. 214.

15. Daniel Scott Smith, "Population, Family and Society in Hingham, Massachusetts, 1635–1880," Ph.D. diss., University of California, Berkeley, 1973. After twenty-five years, this dissertation remains the *ur*-text for the demographic history of rural Massachusetts.

16. Maris A. Vinovskis, *Fertility in Massachusetts from the Revolution to the Civil War* (New York: Academic Press, 1981), p. 121.

17. Jens Christiansen and Peter Philips, "The Transition from Outwork to Factory Production in the Boot and Shoe Industry, 1830 to 1880" in Sanford M. Jacoby, ed., *Masters to Managers* (New York: Columbia University Press, 1991), pp. 21–42, Table 1-1.

18. Lee A. Craig, *To Sow One Acre More: Childbearing and Farm Productivity in the Antebellum North* (Baltimore: Johns Hopkins University Press, 1993).

19. Ibid., p. 92.

20. William B. Weeden, *Economic and Social History of New England, 1620–1789* (Boston: Houghton Mifflin, 1894), p. 116.

21. Gov. John Winthrop in John Kendall Hosmer, ed., *[John] Winthrop's Journal: History of New England, 1630–1649* (New York: Scribners, 1908), vol. 2, p. 20.

22. Joseph S. Wood, *The New England Village* (Baltimore: Johns Hopkins University Press, 1997), p. 4.

23. Over one-quarter of the value of Massachusetts' exports in 1787 was the product of its farms and woodlands.

24. Alice Hanson Jones, *Wealth of a Nation to Be: The American Colonies on the Eve of the Revolution* (New York: Columbia University Press, 1980), p. 141.

25. The surviving manuscript of Abner Sanger's journal is in the Library of Congress. It has been edited by Lois K. Stabler and published as *"Very Poor and of a Lo Make": The Diary of Abner Sanger* (Portsmouth, N.H.: The Historical Society of Cheshire County, 1986).

26. In Worcester County, where because of King Philip's War white settlement had been delayed more than 80 years, such convergence did not occur until 1822.

27. John Ritchie Garrison, "Surviving Strategies: The Commercialization of Life in Rural Massachusetts, 1790–1860," Ph.D. diss., University of Pennsylvania, 1985.

28. Sarah F. McMahon, "A Comfortable Subsistence: The Changing Composition of Diet in Rural New England, 1620–1840," *William and Mary Quarterly*, 3d ser., 42, no. 1 (1985).

29. Christopher Clark, *The Roots of Rural Capitalism: Western Massachusetts, 1780–1860* (Ithaca, N.Y.: Cornell University Press, 1990), esp. p. 85.

30. Thomas C. Hubka, *Big House, Little House, Back House, Barn: The Connected Farm Buildings of New England* (Hanover, N.H.: University Press of New England, 1984), p. 180.

31. Quoted in Paul E. Waggoner, *Fertile Farms among the Stones* (New Haven: Connecticut Academy of Arts and Sciences, 1999).

32. Harold Fisher Wilson, *The Hill Country of New England: Its Social and Economic History* (New York: AMS Press, 1967), p. 78.

33. This discussion of merino sheep is based on Robert R. Livingston, "Essay on Sheep" (New York, 1809), in the Houghton Library, Harvard University. A copy is said to be in Jefferson's library at Monticello. Livingston warns that the animals require painstaking care. If a lamb dies, an orphaned lamb is wrapped in the skin of the dead one and presented to the bereft ewe, in the hope that it will adopt the otherwise doomed lamb. Pregnant ewes must be sheltered in winter for five months, and in deep winter a path must be beaten in the snow for them to get to the evergreen bushes. In summer they must be provided with shade. And always they must be fed on "the most succulent food." Livingston was president of the Society for the Promotion of Useful Arts and a member of the American Philosophical Society.

34. Wilson, *Hill Country*, p. 91.

35. Ibid., pp. 93, 76.

36. "Prior to 1860, the average expense per year to keep a sheep in the East was from $1.00 to $2.00 a head, in contrast to $1.00 down to $0.25 a head in the West." Wilson, *Hill Country*, p. 83.

37. Samuel Blodget, *Economica: A Statistical Manual for the U.S. of A.* (New York: Augustus M. Kelley, 1964 [1806]), p. 2n.

38. Judith A. McGaw, ed., *Early American Technology: Making and Doing Things from the Colonial Era to 1850* (Chapel Hill: University of North Carolina Press, 1994), p. 6.

39. J. D. Van Slyck, *New England Manufacturers and Manufactories*, 2 vols. (Boston: Van Slyck and Co., 1879); and Louis Kaplan, ed., *A Bibliography of American Autobiographies* (Madison: University of Wisconsin Press, 1961). The

Van Slyck work was analyzed in part by David Galenson in "On the Age at Leaving Home in the Early Nineteenth Century: Evidence from the Lives of New England Manufacturers," NBER Working Paper 1706 (Cambridge, Mass., Sept. 1985). The Kaplan collection was analyzed by Joyce Appleby in "The Popular Sources of American Capitalism," *Studies in American Political Development* 9 (Fall 1995).

40. Appleby, "Popular Sources," p. 449.

41. Ibid., pp. 437–457.

42. Paul E. Johnson, "The Modernization of Mayo Greenleaf Patch: Land, Family and Marginality in New England, 1766–1818," *New England Quarterly* 55 (Dec. 1982), pp. 488–516.

43. Appleby, "Popular Sources," p. 448.

44. Edward S. Cooke Jr., *Making Furniture in Preindustrial America: The Social Economy of Newtown and Woodbury, Connecticut* (Baltimore: Johns Hopkins University Press, 1996).

45. Ibid., p. 197.

46. Ibid., Table 12, p. 79.

47. Pennsylvania's historians deserve an acknowledgment of their claim that the American industrial revolution began in Philadelphia, not New England. But statements like "the primary industry . . . was agriculture" do not seem to advance their argument. See Mary M. Schweitzer, *Custom and Contract: Household, Government and the Economy in Colonial Pennsylvania* (New York: Columbia University Press, 1987), p. 63.

48. Rob Martello, "Paul Revere's Last Ride: The Road to Rolling Copper," Massachusetts Historical Society, Boston, 1998. We learn in this paper the crucial role played by the several state governments, the U.S. Navy, and the federal government in subsidizing the development of an important and entirely new industry. The intimate relationship between military contracting and the growth of private industry in early New England is discussed at length in Chapter 6.

49. Adapted from Jeremy Atack and Peter Passell, *A New Economic View of American History* (New York: Norton, 1994), Table 7.2, p. 192.

50. The phrase, taken out of context, is from Jane Jacobs, "Why the TVA Failed," *New York Review of Books*, May 10, 1984, p. 45.

51. S. A. Marglin, "What Do Bosses Do? The Origins and Functions of Hi-

erarchy in Capitalist Production," *Review of Radical Political Economics* 6 (1974): 33–66.

52. Kenneth L. Sokoloff, "Productivity Growth in Manufacturing during Early Industrialization: Evidence from the American Northeast, 1820–1860," in Stanley L. Engerman and Robert E. Gallman, eds., *Long-Term Factors in American Economic Growth* (Chicago: NBER and University of Chicago Press, 1986), pp. 679–736, esp. pp. 724–725. The industries are boots and shoes, coaches and carriages, cotton textiles, furniture, glass, hats, iron, liquors, flour, paper, tanning, tobacco, and woolens.

53. In an interesting empirical test, William Lazonick and Tom Brush have examined the payroll records of the weaving room of Lawrence Mill No. 2. Cloth output per weaver hour rose on a linear trend from less than six yards in 1834 to just under 16 in 1855. Over the same period, the nominal piece rate wage in the weaving room fell from 6.5 cents a yard to less than 3.5 cents. See their "The 'Horndal' Effect in Early U.S. Manufacturing," *Explorations in Economic History* 22 (1985): 53–96. Their study lies properly within the time frame of the next essay, but it is relevant to the issues raised here. See also Gregory Clark, "Factory Discipline," *Journal of Economic History* 54 (Mar. 1994): 128–163, esp. 141–144.

54. Thomas Dublin, "Women and Outwork in a Nineteenth Century New England Town: Fitzwilliam, New Hampshire, 1830–1850," in Stephen Hahn and Jonathan Prude, eds., *The Countryside in the Age of Capitalist Transformation* (Chapel Hill: University of North Carolina Press, 1985), p. 52.

55. Robert G. LeBlanc, "Location of Manufacturing in New England in the Nineteenth Century," *Geography Publications at Dartmouth* 7 (1969): 60–66.

56. See Christopher Clark, "The Truck System in Nineteenth Century New England: An Interpretation," in Rosemary E. Ommer, ed., *Merchant Credit and Labour Strategies in Historical Perspective* (Fredericton, New Brunswick: Acadiensis Press, 1990), pp. 318–332.

57. Dublin, "Women and Outwork," pp. 53–54.

58. Frances W. Gregory, *Nathan Appleton: Merchant and Entrepreneur, 1779–1861* (Charlottesville: University Press of Virginia, 1975), p. 141.

59. Robert F. Dalzell Jr., *Enterprising Elite: The Boston Associates and the World They Made* (Cambridge, Mass.: Harvard University Press, 1987), p. 6.

60. Gregory, *Nathan Appleton*, p. 143.

61. Dalzell, *Enterprising Elite*, p. 17.

62. Ibid., pp. 79–81.

63. Robert B. Zevin, "The Growth of Cotton Textile Production after 1815," in Robert W. Fogel and Stanley L. Engerman, eds., *The Reinterpretation of American Economic History* (New York: Harper & Row, 1971), p. 141.

64. Ibid., p. 143.

65. Pauline Maier, "The Revolutionary Origins of the American Corporation," *William and Mary Quarterly* 3d ser., vol. 50 (Jan. 1993): 83.

66. Naomi R. Lamoreaux, *Insider Lending: Banks, Personal Connections, and Economic Development in Industrial New England* (New York: Cambridge University Press and NBER, 1994), p. 19.

67. Ibid., pp. 19–20.

68. Wages in the weaving rooms were paid by the piece; wages of other operatives appear to have been paid by the day. Day wages averaged 54.4 cents between May 1825 and November 1831. At about 4.5 cents an hour, the average workday was over 12 hours long. The gender mix is not given in these data, but is relevant. See Robert G. Layer, "Earnings of Cotton Mill Operatives, 1825–1914," Committee on Research in Economic History (Cambridge, Mass.: Harvard University Press, 1955). According to a graph made available to me by William Lazonick, weavers on piece rate averaged between 4.2 and 4.8 cents an hour during the 1830s.

69. Robert J. Steinfeld, *The Invention of Free Labor* (Chapel Hill: University of North Carolina Press, 1991).

70. Zevin, "The Growth of Cotton Textile Production," Table 1 and p. 123.

71. LeBlanc, "Location of Manufacturing in New England," pp. 48–50.

72. Mark Bils, "Tariff Protection and Production in the Early U.S. Textile Industry," *Journal of Economic History* 44 (Dec. 1984): 1045.

73. C. Knick Harley, "International Competitiveness of the Antebellum Cotton Textile Industry," *Journal of Economic History* 52 (Sept. 1992): 560.

74. Timothy Leunig, "The Myth of the Corporate Economy: Factor Costs, Industrial Structure, and Technological Choice in the Lancashire and New England Cotton Textile Industries, 1900–1913," *Journal of Economic History* 58 (June 1998): 530, 531. Emphasis mine.

75. Henry J. Bruton, "A Reconsideration of Import Substitution," *Journal of Economic Literature* 36 (June 1998): 903.

76. Paul A. David, "Learning-by-Doing and Tariff Protection: A Reconsideration of the Case of the Antebellum U.S. Cotton Textile Industry," *Journal of Economic History* 30 (Sept. 1970): 593–595.

77. Leonard Jarvis, Comptroller General of the Commonwealth, "General Account of the Exports from the Commonwealth of Massachusetts for the United States of America, Nova Scotia, West Indies, Europe, Africa and the East Indies from January 1st, 1787 to December 31st following, inclusive," *Massachusetts Magazine* (Boston, 1789), pp. 167–169, in the collections of the Houghton Library, Harvard University. (Pounds sterling converted to dollars at 1:5.)

78. Samuel Eliot Morison, *The Maritime History of Massachusetts, 1783–1860* (Boston: Houghton Mifflin, 1923), p. 41.

79. Ibid., p. 80.

80. Ibid., p. 214.

81. Daniel Vickers, *Farmers and Fishermen* (Chapel Hill: University of North Carolina Press, 1994), p. 275.

82. Morison, *Maritime History*, p. 217.

83. Lance E. Davis, Robert E. Gallman, and Karin Gleiter, *In Pursuit of Leviathan: Technology, Institutions, Productivity, and Profits in American Whaling, 1816–1906* (Chicago: University of Chicago Press, 1997), p. 258.

84. Morison, *Maritime History*, p. 319, n. 1; Charles Enderby, "Proposal for Re-establishing the British Southern Whale Fishery," cited in Davis, Gallman, and Gleiter, *In Pursuit of Leviathan*, p. 427, n. 7.

85. Davis, Gallman, and Gleiter, *In Pursuit of Leviathan*, p. 185.

86. Layer, "Earnings of Cotton Mill Operatives," Table 3, p. 18.

87. One of the latest estimates of per capita output growth is 0.9 percent per annum between 1800 and 1840. See Paul A. David, "Real Income and Economic Welfare Growth in the Early Republic; or, Another Try at Getting the American Story Straight," prepared for the Huntington Conference on the Economy of Early British America: The Domestic Economy, Pasadena, Calif., October 1995.

88. Winifred B. Rothenberg, *From Market-Places to a Market Economy: The Transformation of Rural Massachusetts, 1750–1850* (Chicago: University of Chicago Press, 1992).

89. Sokoloff, "Productivity Growth in Manufacturing," p. 725.

3 THE INDUSTRIALIZATION OF NEW ENGLAND, 1830–1880

I thank David Hellmuth for research assistance and Steven Sass for comments.

1. Peter Temin, "Is It Kosher to Talk about Culture?" *Journal of Economic History* 57 (June 1997): 262–287.

2. Kenneth L. Sokoloff, "Inventive Activity in Early Industrial America: Evidence from Patent Records, 1790–1846," *Journal of Economic History* 48 (Dec. 1988): 813–850.

3. Great Britain, "Report of the Committee on the Machinery of the United States," *Parliamentary Papers* 50 (1854–1855): 539–634, at 547.

4. E. Rothbarth, "Causes of the Superior Efficiency of U.S.A. Industry as Compared with British Industry," *Economic Journal* 56 (1946): 383–390.

5. H. J. Habakkuk, *American and British Technology in the Nineteenth Century* (Cambridge: Cambridge University Press, 1962).

6. Peter Temin, "Labor Scarcity and the Problem of American Industrial Efficiency in the 1850's," *Journal of Economic History* 26 (Sept. 1966): 277–298.

7. C. Knick Harley, "International Competitiveness of the Antebellum American Cotton Textile Industry," *Journal of Economic History* 52 (Sept. 1992): 559–584.

8. Peter Temin, "Product Quality and Vertical Integration in the Early Cotton Textile Industry," *Journal of Economic History* 48 (Dec. 1988): 891–907.

9. Peter Temin, "Notes on Labor Scarcity in America," *Journal of Interdisciplinary History* 1 (Winter 1971): 251–264.

10. Claudia Goldin and Kenneth Sokoloff, "Women, Children, and Industrialization in the Early Republic: Evidence from the Manufacturing Census," *Journal of Economic History* 42 (Dec. 1982): 741–774.

11. U.S. Census, Eighth Census, *Manufactures of the United States in 1860* (Washington, D.C.: Government Printing Office, 1865), pp. 686, 742.

12. Peter Temin, "Steam and Waterpower in the Early Nineteenth Century," *Journal of Economic History* 26 (June 1966): 187–205.

13. Great Britain, "Report of the Committee on the Machinery of the United States," p. 631.

14. Joseph W. Roe, *English and American Tool Builders* (New Haven: Yale University Press, 1916).

15. Merritt Roe Smith, *Harpers Ferry Armory and the New Technology* (Ithaca, N.Y.: Cornell University Press, 1977).

16. William Hosley, *Colt: The Making of an American Legend* (Amherst: University of Massachusetts Press, 1996).

17. Roe, *English and American Tool Builders.*

18. Philip Scranton, *Endless Novelty: Specialty Production and American Industrialization, 1865–1925* (Princeton, N.J.: Princeton University Press, 1997).

19. David A. Hounshell, *From the American System to Mass Production, 1800–1932* (Baltimore: Johns Hopkins University Press, 1984).

20. Charles Fitch, "Report on the Manufactures of Interchangeable Parts," U.S. Census, 1883, *Manufactures*, pp. 611–701, at p. 618.

21. U.S. Census, Eighth Census, *Manufactures of the United States in 1860*, pp. 677–686, 733–742; U.S. Census, Tenth Census, *Manufactures of the United States in the Tenth Census* (Washington, D.C.: Government Printing Office, 1883), pp. 9–14.

22. Robert B. Zevin, "The Growth of Cotton Textile Production after 1815," in Robert W. Fogel and Stanley L. Engerman, eds., *The Reinterpretation of American Economic History* (New York: Harper & Row, 1971), pp. 122–147.

23. George S. Gibb, *The Saco-Lowell Shops: Textile Machinery Building in New England, 1813–1949* (Cambridge, Mass.: Harvard University Press, 1950), pp. 98, 243.

24. Mary H. Blewett, *Men, Women, and Work: Class, Gender, and Protest in the New England Shoe Industry, 1780–1910* (Urbana: University of Illinois Press, 1988), pp. 44–45, 97.

25. U.S. Census, Eighth Census, *Manufactures of the United States in 1860*, pp. 733–735; U.S. Census, Tenth Census, *Manufactures of the United States in the Tenth Census*, pp. 9–10; Edgar M. Hoover Jr., *Location Theory and the Shoe and Leather Industries* (Cambridge, Mass.: Harvard University Press, 1937), pp. 264–269.

26. Lance E. Davis, Robert E. Gallman, and Karin Gleiter, *In Pursuit of Leviathan: Technology, Institutions, Productivity, and Profits in American Whaling, 1816–1906* (Chicago: University of Chicago Press, 1997).

27. S. N. Broadberry, *The Productivity Race: British Manufacturing in International Perspective, 1850–1990* (Cambridge: Cambridge University Press, 1997), p. 106.

28. Richard B. DuBoff, "The Telegraph and the Structure of Markets in the United States, 1845–1890," in Paul Uselding, ed., *Research in Economic History* (Greenwich, Conn.: JAI Press, 1983), 8:263.

29. Michael Chevalier, *Society, Manners and Politics in the United States* (Boston: Weeks, Jordan and Co., 1839), p. 84.

30. Henry David Thoreau, *Walden and Other Writings* (New York: Random House, 1950), p. 110.

31. Albert Fishlow, *American Railroads and the Transformation of the Ante-Bellum Economy* (Cambridge, Mass.: Harvard University Press, 1966), pp. 240–241.

32. Basil Lubbock, *The China Clippers* (Glasgow: James Brown and Son, 1922), pp. 69–76.

33. National Geographic Society, *Men, Ships, and the Sea* (Washington, D.C.: National Geographic Society, 1962).

34. Peter Temin, "Steam and Waterpower in the Early Nineteenth Century."

35. Thomas Dublin, *Transforming Women's Work* (Ithaca, N.Y.: Cornell University Press, 1994), p. 155; Arthur L. Eno Jr., ed., *Cotton Was King: A History of Lowell, Massachusetts* (Lowell: Lowell Historical Society, 1976), p. 255.

36. U.S. Census, Eighth Census, *Manufactures of the United States in 1860*, pp. 231–257; U.S. Census, Tenth Census, *Manufactures of the United States in the Tenth Census*, pp. 131–134, 255–265.

37. Peter R. Knights, *The Plain People of Boston, 1830–1860* (New York: Oxford University Press), pp. 11–13.

38. Walter M. Whitehill, *Boston: A Topographical History* (Cambridge, Mass.: Harvard University Press, 1959).

39. Chevalier, *Society, Manners and Politics*, p. 143.

40. John Coolidge, *Mill and Mansion: Architecture and Society in Lowell, Massachusetts, 1820–1865* (New York: Columbia University Press, 1942).

41. Nancy Zaroulis, "Daughters of Freemen: The Female Operatives and the Beginning of the Labor Movement," in Eno, *Cotton Was King*, p. 126.

42. Anthony Trollope, *North America* (New York: Knopf, 1951 [1862]), p. 247.

43. Dublin, *Transforming Women's Work*, p. 68.

44. Wendy Gamber, *The Female Economy: Millinery and Dressmaking Trades, 1860–1930* (Urbana: University of Illinois Press, 1997).

45. Dublin, *Transforming Women's Work*, pp. 77–79.

46. Ibid., p. 99.

47. Barbara Finkelstein, *Governing the Young: Teacher Behavior in Popular Primary Schools in Nineteenth Century United States* (New York: Falmer Press, 1989).

48. Barbara Finkelstein, "Dollars and Dreams: Classrooms as Fictitious Message Systems, 1790–1930," *History of Education Quarterly* 31 (Winter 1991): 463–487.

49. Horace Mann, *Life and Works* (Boston: Lee and Shepard, 1891), 3: 96–97.

50. Brian C. Mitchell, *The Paddy Camps: The Irish of Lowell, 1821–61* (Urbana: University of Illinois Press, 1988), p. 92; Robert F. Dalzell Jr., *Enterprising Elite: The Boston Associates and the World They Made* (Cambridge, Mass.: Harvard University Press, 1987), p. 68.

51. Paul C. Faler, *Mechanics and Manufacturers in the Early Industrial Revolution, Lynn, Massachusetts, 1780–1860* (Albany: State University of New York Press, 1981), p. 147.

52. Carl F. Kaestle and Maris A. Vinovskis, *Education and Social Change in Nineteenth-Century Massachusetts* (Cambridge: Cambridge University Press, 1980), p. 285.

53. Dublin, *Transforming Women's Work*, p. 218.

54. U.S. Census, Eighth Census, *Manufactures of the United States in 1860*, pp. 231–257.

55. Philip R. Coelho and James F. Shepherd, "Regional Differences in Real Wages: The United States, 1851–1880," *Explorations in Economic History* 13 (Apr. 1976): 203–230.

56. George S. Gibb, *The Saco-Lowell Shops: Textile Machinery Building in New England, 1813–1949* (Cambridge, Mass.: Harvard University Press, 1950), p. 217.

57. Charles Fitch, "Report on the Manufactures of Interchangeable Parts," p. 650.

58. Richard A. Easterlin, "Interregional Differences in Per Capita Income, Population, and Total Income, 1840–1950," in William N. Parker, ed., *Trends in the American Economy in the Nineteenth Century* (Princeton, N.J.: Princeton University Press, 1960), pp. 73–140.

59. Lance E. Davis, "Stock Ownership in the Early New England Textile Industry," *Business History Review* 32 (Summer 1958): 204–222.

60. Lance E. Davis, "Sources of Industrial Finance: The American Textile Industry—A Case Study," in *Purdue Faculty Papers in Economic History, 1956–66* (Homewood, Ill.: Richard D. Irwin, 1967), pp. 625–642.

61. Lance E. Davis, "The New England Textile Mills and the Capital Mar-

kets: A Study of Industrial Borrowing, 1840–60," *Journal of Economic History* 20 (Mar. 1960): 1–30.

62. Stephen Salsbury, *The State, the Investor, and the Railroad: The Boston & Albany, 1825–1867* (Cambridge, Mass.: Harvard University Press, 1967).

63. Arthur M. Johnson and Barry E. Supple, *Boston Capitalists and Western Railroads* (Cambridge, Mass.: Harvard University Press, 1967), p. 81.

64. Ibid., p. 83.

65. Robert W. Fogel, *The Union Pacific: A Case in Premature Enterprise* (Baltimore: Johns Hopkins University Press, 1960).

66. Johnson and Supple, *Boston Capitalists and Western Railroads*.

67. Dalzell, *Enterprising Elite*, p. 95.

68. Naomi R. Lamoreaux, *Insider Lending: Banks, Personal Connections and Economic Development in Industrial New England* (Cambridge: Cambridge University Press, 1994), p. 65.

69. Ibid.

70. Peter Temin, *The Jacksonian Economy* (New York: W. W. Norton, 1969).

71. Robert Dugan, "The Outsider's View: Visitors to the Industrial Showcase," in Eno, *Cotton Was King*, p. 249.

4 THE CHALLENGES OF ECONOMIC MATURITY

I am indebted to Louis Cain, Dora Costa, Price Fishback, Claudia Goldin, Morton Keller, Naomi Lamoreaux, Marcus McCorison, Mary Rosenbloom, Steven Sass, Kenneth Snowden, Tom Weiss, Eugene White, Gavin Wright, and participants in the conference on the economic history of New England (Boston Federal Reserve Bank, October 2, 1998) for their advice and comments. I am especially grateful to Peter Temin for his many helpful suggestions.

1. Prominent among these studies are Seymour E. Harris, *The Economics of New England: A Case Study of an Older Area* (Cambridge, Mass.: Harvard University Press, 1952); Oscar Handlin, "The Prophets of Gloom," *Atlantic* 185 (Apr. 1950): 49–51; National Planning Association, *The Economic State of New England: Report of the Committee of New England of the National Planning Council* (New Haven: Yale University Press, 1954).

2. It is worth noting that even in the 1950s pessimism was not unanimous. In "The Recovery of New England," *Atlantic* 185 (Apr. 1950): 51–53, for example, Howard Mumford Jones argued that it was New England's prominence in

the 1870s that had been anomalous and that the subsequent period had been one of "readjustment, as New England slowly assumes its more modest, but secure, place in the economy of a continental nation." Even more pessimistic writers, such as Harris in his *Economics of New England,* p. 8, conceded that New England's decline had so far been only in relative terms—but they argued that unless action was taken to reverse this course, relative decline would eventually become absolute decline.

3. It is interesting to contrast New England's experience in this period with that of the postbellum southern United States. Gavin Wright, in his *Old South, New South: Revolution in the Southern Economy since the Civil War* (New York: Basic Books, 1986), has argued that one of the chief reasons for the persistence of low incomes in the South was the isolation of the region's labor and capital markets from the rest of the country.

4. The source of these sectoral breakdowns is Simon Kuznets and Dorothy Swaine Thomas, eds., *Population Redistribution and Economic Growth: United States, 1870–1950,* vol. 1: Everett S. Lee et al., *Methodological Considerations and Reference Tables* (Philadelphia: American Philosophical Society, 1957), pp. 623–631. I have included construction workers in the manufacturing total.

5. John S. Heckman, "The Product Cycle and New England Textiles," *Quarterly Journal of Economics* 94 (June 1980): 704.

6. Kuznets and Thomas, *Population Redistribution,* 1:623–631.

7. Alfred D. Chandler Jr., *Scale and Scope: The Dynamics of Industrial Capitalism* (Cambridge, Mass.: Harvard University Press, 1990), chs. 3–6. Conditions in the late nineteenth century encouraged the rapid growth of vertically integrated firms, which combined scale- and capital-intensive production techniques with mass marketing—and control over key inputs to the production process—to serve national and international markets.

8. Paul A. David, "Understanding the Economics of QWERTY: The Necessity of History," in William N. Parker, ed., *Economic History and the Modern Economist* (Oxford: Basil Blackwell, 1986); and Paul Krugman, *Geography and Trade* (Cambridge, Mass.: MIT Press, 1991).

9. Heckman, "Product Cycle," pp. 708–709.

10. Ibid., pp. 711–713.

11. Joshua L Rosenbloom, "Was There a National Labor Market at the End of the Nineteenth Century? New Evidence on Earnings in Manufacturing," *Journal of Economic History* 56 (Sept. 1996): 626–655.

12. Alice Galenson, *The Migration of the Cotton Textile Industry from New England to the South, 1880–1930* (New York: Garland Publishing, 1985), p. 139.

13. Gavin Wright, "Cheap Labor and Southern Textiles, 1880–1930," *Quarterly Journal of Economics* 95 (Nov. 1981): 605.

14. Lawrence F. Gross, *The Course of Industrial Decline: The Boott Cotton Mills of Lowell, Massachusetts, 1835–1955* (Baltimore: Johns Hopkins University Press, 1993), pp. 44–46.

15. Galenson, *Migration*, pp. 62–94; Wright, "Cheap Labor."

16. This process is clearly reflected in the shifting distribution of counts (threads per inch) produced in New England and the South. In 1889, 94 percent of southern output by weight was in yarns with counts of 20 or below. In comparison, at this time, just 36.2 percent of New England's output was in these low counts. By 1919, 41 percent of southern output was in counts numbering 21 or higher, compared to 70 percent for New England. See Galenson, *Migration*, p. 6.

17. Gross, *Course of Industrial Decline*, pp. 102–117.

18. Wright, "Cheap Labor."

19. Between 1849 and 1879, Massachusetts' share of total value of shoes produced in the country increased from nearly 44.7 percent to 57.8 percent. See Edgar M. Hoover Jr., *Location Theory and the Shoe and Leather Industries* (Cambridge, Mass.: Harvard University Press, 1937), pp. 168–174, 209.

20. Nathan Rosenberg, *Perspectives on Technology* (Cambridge: Cambridge University Press, 1976), pp. 15–17.

21. Ibid.; David A. Hounshell, *From the American System to Mass Production, 1800–1932: The Development of Manufacturing Technologies in the United States* (Baltimore: Johns Hopkins University Press, 1984).

22. Hounshell, *From the American System*, p. 81.

23. Leonard S. Reich, *The Making of American Industrial Research: Science and Business at GE and Bell, 1876–1926* (Cambridge: Cambridge University Press, 1985), pp. 42–45.

24. Ibid., pp. 48–66.

25. Charles W. Cheap, *Family Firm to Modern Multinational: Norton Company, a New England Enterprise* (Cambridge, Mass.: Harvard University Press, 1985), pp. 74–81.

26. Roger L. Geiger, *To Advance Knowledge: The Growth of American Research Universities, 1900–1940* (New York and Oxford: Oxford University Press, 1986),

p. 2; Claudia Goldin and Lawrence F. Katz, "The Shaping of Higher Education: The Formative Years in the United States, 1890 to 1940," paper presented at the National Bureau of Economic Research, Development of the American Economy, Summer Institute, Cambridge, Mass., 1998 (photocopy).

27. Interestingly, the high concentration of privately funded universities in New England appears to have discouraged public sponsorship of higher education. See Goldin and Katz, "Shaping of Higher Education," pp. 23–24, fig. 7.

28. Geiger, *To Advance Knowledge*, pp. 177–181; Chrisophe Lecuyer, "Academic Science and Technology in the Service of Industry: MIT Creates a 'Permeable' Engineering School," *American Economic Review* 88 (May 1998): 28–33.

29. Lecuyer, "Academic Science," pp. 30–31.

30. Joshua L. Rosenbloom, "The Extent of the Labor Market in the United States, 1870–1914," *Social Science History* 22 (Fall 1998): 287–318.

31. Seymour Louis Wolfbein, *The Decline of a Cotton Textile City: A Study of New Bedford* (New York: Columbia University Press, 1944).

32. E. P. Hutchinson, *Immigrants and Their Children, 1850–1950* (New York: John Wiley & Sons, 1956), p. 27.

33. David Ward, *Cities and Immigrants* (New York: Oxford University Press, 1971), pp. 51–83.

34. Hutchinson, *Immigrants*, p. 27.

35. David Roth, *Connecticut: A Bicentennial History* (New York and Nashville: W. W. Norton and American Association for State and Local History, 1979), pp. 158–162; Richard D. Brown, *Massachusetts: A Bicentennial History* (New York and Nashville: W. W. Norton and American Association for State and Local History, 1978), pp. 203–204.

36. There is no direct information about migration in this period, but a number of inferences can be made on the basis of decennial census data collected by the federal government. Two complementary approaches have been employed by scholars interested in this topic. The first relies on rates of net migration. For the native born this reflects the difference between the actual population living in a state or region, and the population that would be predicted by applying the national average rate of natural increase (adjusted for the demographic composition of the state or region) to the population at the previous census. For the foreign born, net migration is simply the change in the number of foreign born living in the state or region. The second approach utilizes data on state-of-birth collected by the census. By comparing this information with current state-of-

residence, it is possible to track lifetime migration streams. For further details on both methods, see the discussion in Simon Kuznets and Dorothy Swaine Thomas, *Population Redistribution and Economic Growth: United States, 1870–1950*, vol. 2: Simon Kuznets, Ann Ratner Miller, and Richard A. Easterlin, *Analyses of Economic Change* (Philadelphia: American Philosophical Society, 1964), chs. 3, 5.

37. Ibid., pp. 33, 65, 118–119.

38. Sam B. Warner, *Streetcar Suburbs: The Process of Growth in Boston, 1870–1900* (Cambridge, Mass.: Harvard University Press and MIT Press, 1962); Charles N. Glaab and A. Theodore Brown, *A History of Urban America* (New York: Macmillan, 1967), p. 164.

39. Edward Meeker, "The Improving Health of the United States, 1850–1915," *Explorations in Economic History* 9 (Summer 1972): 354.

40. Ibid., p. 354; see also Louis P. Cain and Elyce J. Rotella, "Urbanization, Sanitation, and Mortality in the Progressive Era, 1899–1929," paper presented at the International Economic History Congress, Leuven, Belgium, 1990 (photocopy).

41. Warner, *Streetcar Suburbs*.

42. Kenneth T. Jackson, *Crabgrass Frontier: The Suburbanization of the United States* (New York: Oxford University Press, 1985).

43. Rosenbloom, "Extent of the Labor Market"; Tamara K. Hareven, *Family Time and Industrial Time: The Relationship between the Family and Work in a New England Industrial Community* (Cambridge: Cambridge University Press, 1982), ch. 5.

44. Roy Rosenzweig, *Eight Hours for What We Will: Worker and Leisure in an Industrial City, 1870–1920* (Cambridge: Cambridge University Press, 1983), pp. 27–32.

45. Quoted in Robert Babcock et al., "Work and Workers in the Industrial Age, 1865–1930," in Richard W. Judd, Edwin A. Churchill, and Joel W. Eastman, eds., *Maine: The Pine Tree State from Prehistory to the Present* (Orono: University of Maine Press, 1995), p. 449.

46. Rosenzweig, *Eight Hours*, pp. 171–190.

47. Between 1869 and 1899 average employment per establishment nationwide increased in every industrial category except printing and publishing. In textiles, where factory methods were already dominant, average employment rose from 50.6 workers per plant in 1869 to 123.5 in 1899. Paper and paper

products, another factory product, saw average plant size increase from 24.8 workers to 52.2 in the same period. Leather and leather products, which remained a primarily craft industry in 1869, had an average of just 5.6 workers per establishment in 1869. By 1899, the average establishment had increased nearly sixfold to 32 workers. See Jeremy Atack and Peter Passell, *A New Economic View of American History*, 2nd ed. (New York: W. W. Norton, 1994), pp. 474–477.

48. Herbert Gutman, *Work, Culture and Society in Industrializing America* (New York: Vintage Books, 1977), ch. 1; Alexander Keyssar, *Out of Work: The First Century of Unemployment in Massachusetts* (Cambridge: Cambridge University Press, 1986), p. 43.

49. Ibid., pp. 10–12.

50. David Montgomery, "Strikes in Nineteenth-Century America," *Social Science History* 4 (Spring 1980): 81–104.

51. Keyssar, *Out of Work*, p. 179.

52. Ibid., p. 181.

53. Ibid., pp. 2–3.

54. Ibid., pp. 50–58.

55. Ibid., ch. 4.

56. Quoted in ibid., p. 63.

57. Ibid., chs. 6, 8.

58. As Alexander Keyssar perceptively notes, one indication of this intellectual shift is provided by the changing terminology used to describe variations in aggregate economic activity. Rather than describing downturns as "panics" or "crises," terms that suggest an episodic and idiosyncratic character, economists began to refer to them as "business cycles," acknowledging that fluctuations in economic activity had certain regular and recurrent features. In addition, during the early twentieth century a number of important empirical studies of unemployment were published. Especially influential was William Beveridge's *Unemployment: A Problem of Industry*, published in 1909. See ibid., pp. 263–266.

59. Ibid., pp. 272–282.

60. Summer H. Slichter, "The Current Labor Policies of American Industries," *Quarterly Journal of Economics* 43 (May 1929): 393–435; Laura J. Owen, "Worker Turnover in the 1920s: What Labor-Supply Arguments Don't Tell Us," *Journal of Economic History* 55 (Dec. 1995): 822–841.

61. Gross, *Course of Industrial Decline*, pp. 69–70.

62. Moral hazard refers to the problem of an individual, once insured, failing

to take adequate steps to prevent the occurrence of events against which he or she is insured. Adverse selection refers to the fact that among observably equivalent individuals, those at the greatest risk of suffering a loss are most likely to seek insurance.

63. Price V. Fishback and Shawn Everett Kantor, "How Minnesota Adopted Workers' Compensation," *Independent Review* 2 (Spring 1998): 557–578.

64. Stanley Lebergott, *Pursuing Happiness: American Consumers in the Twentieth Century* (Princeton, N.J.: Princeton University Press, 1993), pp. 99–102.

65. Ibid., pp. 104–106.

66. Ibid., pp. 112–117.

67. Roth, *Connecticut*, p. 179.

68. Ibid.

69. Claudia Goldin, "How America Graduated from High School: 1910 to 1960," National Bureau of Economic Research, working paper 4762 (June 1998), p. 17.

70. Claudia Goldin, "America's Graduation from High School: The Evolution and Spread of Secondary Schooling in the Twentieth Century," *Journal of Economic History* 58 (June 1998): 352.

71. Ibid., p. 361.

72. See the discussion in Temin's essay. In 1850 there were 15.1 bank offices and 4.4 million dollars in deposits per 100,000 population in New England. In the next most densely banked region, the Middle Atlantic, there were just 5.4 bank offices and 2.2 million dollars in deposits per 100,000 population. By 1900, the gap between New England and the Middle Atlantic region had narrowed substantially, but bank deposits per person in the region still were more than double those for the nation as a whole. See Raymond W. Goldsmith, *Financial Intermediaries in the American Economy since 1900*, NBER Studies in Capital Formation and Financing (Princeton, N.J.: Princeton University Press, 1958), pp. 110–111.

73. Lance E. Davis, "The Investment Market, 1870–1914: The Evolution of a National Market," *Journal of Economic History* 25 (Sept. 1965): 355–399; John A. James, *Money and Capital Markets in Postbellum America* (Princeton, N.J.: Princeton University Press, 1978); Howard Bodenhorn, "A More Perfect Union: Regional Interest Rates in the United States, 1880–1960," in Michael D. Bordo and Richard Sylla, eds., *Anglo-American Financial Systems: Institutions and*

Markets in the Twentieth Century (Burr Ridge, Ill.: Irwin Professional Publishing, 1995).

74. Penelope C. Hartland, *Balance of Interregional Payment of New England* (Providence, R.I.: Brown University Press, 1950).

75. Vincent P. Carosso, *Investment Banking in America: A History* (Cambridge, Mass.: Harvard University Press, 1970), p. 29.

76. Ibid., p. 30.

77. Alfred D. Chandler Jr., *The Visible Hand: The Managerial Revolution in American Business* (Cambridge, Mass.: Harvard University Press, 1977), chs. 9–10.

78. Carosso, *Investment Banking*, pp. 48–49.

79. Kenneth A. Snowden, "The Evolution of Interregional Mortgage Lending Channels, 1870–1940: The Life Insurance-Mortgage Company Connection," in Naomi Lamoreaux and Daniel M. G. Raff, eds., *Coordination and Information: Historical Perspectives on the Organization of Enterprise* (Chicago: University of Chicago Press, 1995), pp. 230–241.

80. Because bank assets are less liquid than their liabilities, banks may be unable to meet the immediate demands of their depositors, even though they remain solvent (that is, their assets are greater than their liabilities). Under such circumstances, uncertainty on the part of depositors can lead them to attempt to cash in, leading to precisely the problem that they had initially feared. Adding to the instability in this situation is the fact that those depositors who are the first to withdraw their funds are the most likely to do so before convertibility is suspended. In this situation, even a depositor who is not concerned about the bank's solvency will have an incentive to liquidate personal assets if he or she fears that other depositors are going to do so as well.

81. Charles W. Calomoris and Gary Gorton, "The Origins of Banking Panics: Models, Facts, and Bank Regulation," in R. Glenn Hubbard, ed., *Financial Markets and Financial Crises* (Chicago: University of Chicago Press, 1991), pp. 113–114.

82. Robert A. Degen, *The American Monetary System: A Concise Survey of Its Evolution since 1896* (Lexington, Mass.: Lexington Books, 1987), p. 18.

83. Benjamin J. Klebaner, *American Commercial Banking: A History* (Boston: Twayne Publishers, 1990), pp. 92–98.

84. Degen, *American Monetary System*, pp. 16–17; Eugene White, *The Regula-*

tion and Reform of the American Banking System, 1900–1920 (Princeton, N.J.: Princeton University Press, 1983), pp. 95–107.

85. The relationship between the Depression and the stock market crash is a matter of some controversy. But most economic historians agree that the crash was a consequence, not a cause, of the Depression. Recent events have shown that it is possible for stock prices to fall sharply without causing a major economic disruption, and there is little evidence to suggest that the decline in stock prices that occurred in the fall of 1929 can account for more than a small fraction of the decline in aggregate demand that occurred during the Depression. See Peter Temin, *Did Monetary Forces Cause the Great Depression?* (New York: W. W. Norton, 1976), pp. 62–83; and Peter Temin, *Lessons from the Great Depression* (Cambridge, Mass.: MIT Press, 1989), pp. 43–45. The major recent proponent of a causal link between the crash and the Depression is Christina Romer. See her paper "The Great Depression and the Onset of the Great Depression," *Quarterly Journal of Economics* 105 (Aug. 1990): 597–624.

86. Temin, *Lessons*, ch. 1; Barry Eichengreen, *Golden Fetters: The Gold Standard and the Great Depression, 1919–1939* (New York: Oxford University Press, 1992), ch. 8.

87. Temin, *Lessons*, ch. 2.

88. Joshua L. Rosenbloom and William A. Sundstrom, "The Sources of Regional Variation in the Severity of the Great Depression: Evidence from U.S. Manufacturing, 1919–1937," National Bureau of Economic Research, working paper 6288 (Nov. 1997).

89. John J. Wallis, "Employment in the Great Depression: New Data and Hypotheses," *Explorations in Economic History* 26 (Jan. 1989): 45–72.

90. From 1930 through 1933 there were over 5,000 commercial bank suspensions nationwide. Deposits at these banks totaled $6.8 billion. In New England only 136 banks, with deposits of $92 million, were involved in either temporary or permanent suspensions. See Board of Governors, Federal Reserve System, *Banking and Monetary Statistics* (Washington, D.C.: U.S. Government Printing Office, 1943), pp. 284–285.

91. Charles H. Trout, *Boston, the Great Depression and the New Deal* (New York: Oxford University Press, 1977), p. 177.

92. Ibid., pp. 75–100.

93. Government's share of GNP did increase during the 1930s, but this was a continuation of a longer-standing trend. Between 1902 and 1922, government

expenditures as a share of GNP had approximately doubled (rising from 7.7 percent to 12.5 percent). From 1922 to 1940 it again almost doubled (rising to 20.4 percent). See John Joseph Wallis and Wallace E. Oates, "The Impact of the New Deal on American Federalism," in Michael D. Bordo, Claudia Goldin, and Eugene White, eds., *The Defining Moment: The Great Depression and the American Economy in the Twentieth Century* (Chicago: University of Chicago Press, 1998), pp. 157–158.

94. Ibid., pp. 157–158, 162–166.

95. Trout, *Boston*, pp. 147–170.

96. The highest expenditures were in the mountain states, which averaged $716 per capita from 1933 to 1939. In comparison, Vermont received $390 per capita, and Connecticut just $237. See Atack and Passell, *New Economic View*, p. 643.

97. Gavin Wright, "The Political Economy of New Deal Spending: An Econometric Analysis," *Review of Economics and Statistics* 56 (Feb. 1974): 30–38; John Wallis, "The Political Economy of New Deal Fiscal Federalism," *Economic Inquiry* 29 (July 1991): 510–524.

5 THE TRANSITION FROM A MILL-BASED TO A KNOWLEDGE-BASED ECONOMY

We thank Peter Temin for sage advice and comments, and Mizue Morita, Phuc Tran, and Eraina Ortega for excellent research assistance.

1. U.S. Bureau of Labor Statistics, Internet site, www.bls.gov.

2. Robert W. Eisenmenger, *The Dynamics of Growth in New England's Economy, 1870–1964* (Middletown, Conn.: Wesleyan University Press, 1967), p. 10.

3. Council of Economic Advisers, Committee on the New England Economy, *The New England Economy* (Washington, D.C.: Government Printing Office, 1951).

4. U.S. Bureau of Labor Statistics, Internet site, www.bls.gov.

5. Arthur B. Bright Jr. and George H. Ellis, *The Economic State of New England*, report of the Committee of New England of the National Planning Association, p. 283, published by arrangement with the New England Council (New Haven: Yale University Press, 1954).

6. U.S. Bureau of Economic Analysis, SPI CD-ROM.

7. The discussion of the role of defense spending, particularly the sections

on Pratt and Whitney and the contribution of MIT, draws heavily on Ann Markusen, Peter Hall, Scott Campbell, and Sabina Deitrick, *The Rise of the Gunbelt: The Military Remapping of Industrial America* (New York: Oxford University Press, 1991) and Susan Rosegrant and David R. Lampe, *Route 128: Lessons from Boston's High-Tech Community* (New York: Basic Books, 1992).

8. These data are from a tabulation that one of the authors was given in either 1984 or 1985. With the passage of time, the author does not recall who produced the table, although it was probably an economist then working for the Commonwealth of Massachusetts.

9. Lynn E. Browne, "Can High Tech Save the Great Lakes States?" Federal Reserve Bank of Boston, *New England Economic Review* (Nov./Dec. 1983): 19–33.

10. According to the standard industrial classification that was used during most of the period covered by this paper, miscellaneous services and "finance, insurance, and real estate" were two major industries within the service-producing sector. Other service-producing industries were wholesale and retail trade and transportation and public utilities. Of these industries, miscellaneous services grew most rapidly and by the end of the period was much larger than the other service-producing industries. Business services were part of the services industry and grew very rapidly during the 1980s and 1990s. Elements of finance, insurance, and real estate also grew quite quickly and, as described in the text, seem to have played an important role in shaping the region's economic fortunes.

11. Extensive efforts were under way in the late 1990s to make the many old COBOL programs still being used for business applications capable of operating after the turn of the century.

12. U.S. Bureau of Labor Statistics, Internet site, www.bls.gov.

13. Massachusetts Technology Collaborative, *Index of the Massachusetts Innovation Economy* (Westborough: Massachusetts Technology Collaborative, 1997), p. 8.

14. Steven Sass, "The U.S. Professional Sector," *New England Economic Review* (Jan./Feb. 1990).

15. The new scramble for academic achievement sparked a competition for talented students that led to an agreement, among elite institutions, to limit scholarship grants to "need" as determined by a reasonably uniform methodology.

16. New England Board of Higher Education, *Connection Facts, 1998*

(Boston: New England Board of Higher Education, 1998), pp. 168–177, 180–182.

17. Ibid., pp. 153–154; Francis S. Doody, *The Immediate Impact of Higher Education in New England*, Bureau of Business Research, Education Studies, n.s., no. 1 (Boston: Boston University, 1961), p. 45; Penelope Hartland, *Balance of Interregional Payments of New England* (Providence, R.I.: Brown University Press, 1950), p. 6.

18. New England Board of Higher Education, *Connection Facts, 1998*, pp. 149–162.

19. American Council on Education, *Fact Book on Higher Education 1984–1985* (American Council on Education and Macmillan Publishing Company, 1984), pp. 153–160.

20. Bright and Ellis, *Economic State of New England.*

21. U.S. Department of Education, National Center for Education Statistics, *Digest of Educational Statistics* (Washington, D.C.: U.S. Department of Health, Education, and Welfare, Office of Education, 1997).

22. Steven Sass, *The Pragmatic Imagination: A History of the Wharton School, 1881–1981* (Philadelphia: University of Pennsylvania Press, 1982).

23. Richard B. Freeman, "Implications of the Changing U.S. Labor Market for Higher Education," National Bureau of Economic Research, working paper 697 (June 1981), p. 29.

24. U.S. Bureau of Economic Analysis, State Personal Income Database, SA05, SA25.

25. U.S. Bureau of the Census, March Current Population Survey, Tables P28 and P28a, obtained on the Internet from www.census.gov. While the U.S. education wage premium did not rise over the course of the 1990s, the educational attainment of the New England workforce vis-à-vis the nation did increase. The stability of average earnings relative to the nation over the decade implies a decline in earnings, vis-à-vis the nation, for New England workers at a given educational level.

26. This discussion follows the symposium on urban agglomeration appearing in *Journal of Economic Perspectives* (Spring 1998) and consisting of the following articles: John M. Quigley, "Urban Diversity and Economic Growth," pp. 127–174; Edward Glaeser, "Are Cities Dying?" pp. 139–160; and Paul Krugman, "Space: The Final Frontier," pp. 161–174.

27. Adam B. Jaffe, Manuel Trajtenberg, and Rebecca Henderson, "Geo-

graphic Localization of Knowledge Spillovers as Evidenced by Patent Citations," *Quarterly Journal of Economics* 108, no. 3 (1993): 577–598.

28. James E. Rauch, "Productivity Gains from Geographic Concentration of Human Capital: Evidence from the Cities," *Journal of Urban Economics* 34, no. 3 (1993): 380–400.

29. Edward Glaeser and David Mare, "Cities and Skills," Hoover Institution working paper E-94–11, Stanford, Calif., 1994.

30. Edward Glaeser, "Are Cities Dying?"

31. AnnaLee Saxenian, *Regional Advantage: Culture and Competition in Silicon Valley and Route 128* (Cambridge, Mass.: Harvard University Press, 1994).

32. Bright and Ellis, *Economic State of New England.*

33. *County and City Data Book, 1994,* Table C, pp. 700–702, 747–750, 699–700.

SLAVERY AND POPULATION GROWTH IN COLONIAL NEW ENGLAND

1. Alice Hanson Jones, *American Colonial Wealth: Documents and Methods* (New York: Arno Press, 1977).

2. Barbara L. Solow, ed., *Slavery and the Rise of the Atlantic Systems* (Cambridge: Cambridge University Press, 1991).

3. Mary Dobson, *Contours of Death and Disease in Early Modern England* (New York: Cambridge University Press, 1997).

4. Mary J. Dobson, "From Old England to New England: Changing Patterns of Mortality," research paper, School of Geography, University of Oxford, 1987.

NEW ENGLAND INDUSTRY AND THE FEDERAL GOVERNMENT

Adapted from *A History of the United States* by Merritt Roe Smith, Alexander Keyssar, Pauline Maier, and Daniel Kevles. Copyright © 2001 by Merritt Roe Smith, Pauline Maier, Daniel Kevles, and Alexander Keyssar. Reprinted by permission of W. W. Norton and Company, Inc.

1. Carter Goodrich, *The Government and the Economy, 1783–1861* (Indianapolis: Bobbs-Merrill, 1967).

2. See Nathan Rosenberg, "Technological Change in the Machine Tool Industry, 1840–1910," *Journal of Economic History* 23 (Dec. 1963); David A. Hounshell, *From the American System to Mass Production: The Development of*

Manufacturing Technology in the United States (Baltimore: Johns Hopkins University Press, 1984).

3. For a full account of the contract system and its implications, see Merritt Roe Smith, "The Military Roots of Mass Production," Richmond Lecture, Williams College, Williamstown, Mass., Sept. 20, 1995.

4. The one exception was Thomas Blanchard, who carefully protected his patent rights to various gunstocking machines that he developed during the late 1810s and early 1820s.

5. See Smith, "Military Roots," pp. 22–23.

6. "Report of the Committee on the Machinery of the United States of America," *British Sessional Papers* 50 (1855): 21.

7. Quoted by Colleen A. Dunlavy, *Politics and Industrialization* (Princeton, N.J.: Princeton University Press, 1994), p. 63. See also Forrest G. Hill, *Roads, Rails, and Waterways: The Army Engineers and Early Transportation* (Norman: University of Oklahoma Press, 1957).

8. Hill, *Roads, Rails, and Waterways*, pp. 209–210.

Contributors

BERNARD BAILYN is the Adams University Professor, emeritus, at Harvard University and the director of Harvard's International Seminar on Atlantic History. Among his books are *The Ideological Origins of the American Revolution* (1967), *Voyagers to the West* (1986), *The Peopling of British North America* (1986), and *Faces of Revolution* (1990).

LYNN ELAINE BROWNE is senior vice president and director of research at the Federal Reserve Bank of Boston. Previously, she was the Bank's primary regional economist and wrote extensively on the New England economy. She received her doctorate in economics from the Massachusetts Institute of Technology.

PAUL KRUGMAN is the Ford International Professor of Economics at MIT. He is the author or editor of 16 books and more than 200 papers in professional journals and edited volumes. In recognition of that work, in 1991 the American Economic Association awarded him its John Bates Clark medal, a prize given every two years to "that economist under forty who is adjudged to have made a significant contribution to economic knowledge." His latest book is *Pop Internationalism* (1996).

MARGARET ELLEN NEWELL is associate professor of history at The Ohio State University. She is the author of *From Dependency to Independence: Economic Revolution in Colonial New England* (1998) and currently is writing a book on Native American slavery in seventeenth- and eighteenth-century New England.

JOSHUA L. ROSENBLOOM is associate professor of economics at the University of Kansas and a research associate of the National Bureau of Economic Research. Among his recent publications are "The Extent of the Labor Market in the United States, 1870–1914," *Social Science History* 22 (1998), and "Strikebreaking and the Labor Market in the United States, 1881–1894," *Journal of Economic History* 58 (1998).

WINIFRED BARR ROTHENBERG is associate professor of economics at Tufts University. She is the author of *From Market-Places to a Market Economy: The Transformation of Rural Massachusetts, 1750–1850* (1992) and articles in the *Journal of Economic History.*

STEVEN SASS is an economist at the Federal Reserve Bank of Boston and director of its economic history museum project. He is the author of *The Promise of Private Pensions* (1997) and *The Pragmatic Imagination* (1982), and former editor of the Bank's economics magazine, *Regional Review.*

MERRITT ROE SMITH is the Cutten Professor of the History of Technology at MIT. His work includes *Harpers Ferry Armory and the New Technology* (1977) and, most recently, the edited volumes *Does Technology Drive History?* (1994, with Leo Marx) and *Major Problems in the History of American Technology* (1998, with Greg Clancey).

PETER TEMIN is the Elisha Gray II Professor of Economics at MIT. He is the author of *The Jacksonian Economy* (1969) and *Lessons from the Great Depression* (1989), and editor of *Inside the Business Enterprise* (1991) and *Elites, Minorities, and Economic Growth* (1999).

Index